About the Authors

Mary Ball is Senior Psychologist and Director of Education Services with the Dyslexia Association of Ireland. Before training as a psychologist she worked for many years as a teacher abroad and in Ireland, and later as school principal and lecturer.

Anne Hughes is a former Director of the Dyslexia Association of Ireland. The parent of an adult son with dyslexia and ADHD she has a particular interest in dyslexia in adulthood. She is co-author of a number of Dyslexia Association publications.

Wyn McCormack is a guidance counsellor and resource teacher. She is the author of the book *Lost for Words, a practical guide to dyslexia at second level*, first published in 1998. It is now in its 3rd edition. She lectures to parents, teachers and students on dyslexia. She is the parent of sons who have dyslexia.

Dyslexia
An Irish Perspective

MARY BALL

ANNE HUGHES

WYN McCORMACK

First published 2006 by
Blackhall Publishing,
33 Carysfort Ave, Blackrock, Co. Dublin.
Reprinted 2007, 2010

© Ball, Hughes and McCormack 2006, 2011

Revised 2011 and published by the Dyslexia Association of Ireland.
Printed in Ireland by Brunswick Press, Dublin 12.
Typeset by Artwerk Ltd., Dublin

ISBN: 978-0-9568491-0-6

TABLE OF CONTENTS

ACKNOWLEDGEMENTS

The authors would like to thank the Dyslexia Association of Ireland for support and encouragement in the writing of this book. They would also like to pay tribute to all the people with dyslexia whom they have met and worked with over the years. Particular mention should be made of Robin, Simon and Daragh, without whom two of the authors would never have become involved. Many thanks are due to Rosie Bissett for her meticulous editing and insightful comments.

FOREWORD

Somerset Maugham (I think) wrote a short story about a sexton in a small parish church who was extremely good at his job. The job was humble, the pay modest, but he was driven by a strong sense of commitment to his work, a sense that he was an important part of his local community. He took great pride in ensuring that the church was always clean, that the flowers were fresh, and that the boiler was always properly stoked. As a consequence, the church was always a warm and welcoming place.

All was well until a new curate was appointed to the parish. In his very first interview with the sexton, he discovered that his faithful servant of the church could neither read nor write. Thinking himself to be a highly progressive sort, the curate explained to the sexton that it would be impossible for him to undertake the new range of tasks he had in mind, such as maintaining the register of births and marriages, because of this defect. In vain the sexton protested that there was nothing that had prevented him from carrying out his duties to the highest possible standard. No, the curate insisted, he was sorry, but there would have to be a parting of the ways. A new sexton, with all the skills necessary, would have to be appointed. And, in the wink of an eye, the sexton found himself out of a job.

Normally he took the long walk home in his stride. This evening though, he felt a weariness in his step, and his journey through the town's main street seemed awfully long. Seeking comfort in a pipe of tobacco, he was even more upset to discover that his tobacco pouch was empty – and that there was nowhere, all along the length of the main street, where he could buy an ounce of tobacco to replenish it.

Sitting at home that night, he had an idea. Although he now had no job, he had accumulated some modest savings – enough, he discovered, to rent a small vacant store on the main street. Soon he had opened the town's first dedicated tobacconist shop, and with the skills he had applied to his previous job, he had made it into a warm and welcoming haven.

Within two years, he had seven shops, one in each of the towns and villages nearby. His thriving business soon caught the eye of a larger corporation, whose general manager was very impressed with the intimacy of these shops and the standards of quality and service their proprietor had insisted on. Seeking him out, the business magnate made the former sexton a handsome offer for the shops, more than enough to guarantee a happy and comfortable retirement.

Once the offer was accepted, the moment came for the handing over of a large cheque and the signing of the contract. It was then that the businessman discovered that the former sexton could neither read nor write.

'Good Lord,' said the businessman. 'With your talent and business acumen, heaven only knows what you would be if only you could read and write'.

The former sexton could only smile wryly. If he could read and write, he would still be a humble sexton.

Or maybe it could be put another way. If he hadn't been discriminated against in the first place, he might never have discovered his true calling. The discovery that he was unable to read and write led to assumptions being made about him that simply weren't true. I don't know if that sexton had dyslexia, but I do know that dyslexia is not, in itself, a barrier to achievement that cannot be overcome. The insurmountable barriers are all created by assumptions and attitudes.

I don't have dyslexia, though I have friends who do. Through other circumstances, I have some experience of what it feels like to be treated as a second-class citizen, and I know some of my friends have felt stigmatised by their dyslexia. But they are talented, intelligent, social and creative people, who know that life places hurdles in everyone's way. The tragedy is when the hurdles are built up higher by ignorance, misunderstanding and sometimes sheer intolerance. And it happens.

The result is that for a great many individuals and families, the circumstances surrounding dyslexia amount to a sense of stigmatisation. The purpose of this book, at least in part, is to end the stigma, and place dyslexia in its proper perspective.

On average, at least ten members of Dail Eireann have dyslexia. Of all the people who have served in Government over the last fifteen years or so, at least two or three have had dyslexia. Dyslexia exists in the upper reaches of the civil service, in the boardrooms of our major corporations, among leading sportspeople, musicians and artists. All had, and have, a disability. Some got the appropriate level of assessment and support. Others did not.

There are keys to overcoming any disability, in tearing down the barriers. The first is early assessment. The second is suitable and appropriate support. And the third is openness. There is no reason whatever why dyslexia should be a subject people are afraid to discuss, because the more we know, the less reason there is for misunderstanding and fear.

I hope this book helps to put the subject of dyslexia on the agenda. As well as being a practical guide, it helps to dispel the myths and create a proper sense of dyslexia as one more of life's hurdles – and a hurdle that can be overcome.

Fergus Finlay
CEO, Barnardos

INTRODUCTION

Dyslexia was not a major problem two hundred years ago. True, it did exist but as few people needed to read and write fluently and accurately at that time, it did not bother a great number of people. Dyslexia will not be a major problem in two hundred years' time. We can confidently predict that by then all written communication will be handled effortlessly by technology. There will be no need to read words from a page, no need to remember complex spelling and grammatical rules, no need to worry about learning other languages.

The technology necessary to achieve this happy state of affairs is being developed. Until it becomes widely available however, countless numbers of children and adults will continue to be seriously disadvantaged by a specific learning difficulty which affects their school, work and social life from cradle to grave.

While dyslexia has been described, if not actually identified, for hundreds of years, it was not widely recognised until the middle of the last century. This led some commentators to suggest that dyslexia had just been invented and was not an actual and very stressful condition. This view caused a great deal of pain to people with dyslexia and allowed many of those who ought to have known better not to take dyslexia seriously.

Fortunately, scientific research has provided evidence that dyslexia is a neurological condition that most certainly affects the lives of many people. Educationalists now agree that dyslexia is indeed a fact, and while there is still some argument about the prevalence of the difficulty, nobody seriously questions its existence. Research from English speaking countries indicates that 6% to 8% of the population is affected by dyslexia to some extent. Some professionals put the figure at 10%. This means that, in a class of thirty students, there could be three pupils with some degree of dyslexia. These statistics highlight the challenge dyslexia poses to our education system.

In Ireland, the Department of Education and Skills (DES) recognises that children with dyslexia have distinct educational needs. Support for children with specific learning disabilities has been in place since 1975. In the years of economic plenty some substantial developments took place. In recent years however, there has been a distinct slowdown in the pace of change.

Factors which have improved the lot of students in the education system include:

- *The Report of the Task Force on Dyslexia* published by the then Department of Education and Science in 2001. This was followed a year later by a similar Task Force Report in Northern Ireland. Both reports adopt the same comprehensive definition of dyslexia. The report published by the Irish Department of Education and Science described the existing provision and made 61 recommendations, some of which have been implemented.

- Recommendation One of the report was that information and advice should be readily available to teachers and parents/guardians of children with dyslexia through the development of printed and electronic material for distribution through the schools. This resulted in the publication in 2005 of the video/CD ROM/DVD *Understanding Dyslexia*. This excellent and comprehensive package has been distributed to all primary and post-primary schools. This resource is now available free online thanks to the Special Education Support Service (SESS) and the Department of Education and Skills. It can be accessed on the SESS website. It contains audio-visual content, a huge array of information on supporting and teaching children with dyslexia. There are sections for primary and post primary teachers including guidelines on managing dyslexia at both levels. There is also a guide for parents on dyslexia and practical, self-help section for students. The online version can be found on the SESS website: www.sess.ie/dyslexia-section/understanding-dyslexia-guide-schools

- *The Education Act 1998* made provision for equality of access to and participation in Irish schools for students. It states that schools should provide appropriate education for pupils, taking into account the child's abilities and needs.

- *The Education of Persons with Special Educational Needs Act 2004* proclaimed the right of children with special educational needs to be educated within mainstream schools. Special educational needs are defined in the Act as: 'A restriction in the capacity of the person to participate in and benefit from education on account of an enduring physical, sensory, mental health or learning disability, or any other condition which results in a person learning differently from a person without that condition. This definition means that children with dyslexia are covered under this Act and so have certain rights and entitlements which are set out in sections two to eighteen of the Act. Children with special educational needs should have an individual education plan (IEP). Parents have the right to be involved when the IEP is being drawn up.

■ The *Learning Support Guidelines* were published by the then Department of Education and Science in 2000. These Guidelines provide practical guidance to teachers and to parents on the provision of effective learning support to pupils with low achievement/learning difficulties. The Guidelines recommend that an individual profile and learning programme (IPLP) should be drawn up and parents should be involved in the planning of this document.

■ The *Post Primary Guidelines on Inclusion of Students with Special Educational Needs (SEN)* were published by the Department of Education and Skills in 2007. The guidelines set out advice for school management and teachers in relation to the education of students with SEN in post primary school. Specific guidance is given on planning at the whole-school level and for the individual student. Suggestions are made about school organisation, teaching methodologies and teaching approaches that reflect best practice.

■ The establishment of the National Educational Psychological Service (NEPS). NEPS is funded by the Department of Education and Skills and aims to offer a service to every primary and post-primary school in the country eventually. Psychologists are concerned with identifying educational needs and working closely with schools to ensure that these needs are met.

■ The establishment of the Special Education Support Service (SESS). This body promotes the acceptance of every pupil with special educational needs at primary and post-primary level. Its mission statement says: 'As a service that acknowledges and values difference, we work with schools to secure these principles and to provide high quality continuing professional development and support structures for teachers'.

■ The development of supports for students in the state examinations and at third-level colleges.

■ Increased awareness of the importance of tackling specific learning difficulties at the earliest possible time.

■ Greater emphasis on the understanding and support of pupils with specific reading difficulties in teacher training.

■ Students with dyslexia have benefited from the advances made in information and communications technology. These developments are, arguably, the way forward for all students but particularly for those who struggle to acquire literacy. Technology which converts voice to text and vice versa will largely eliminate the need to read, write and spell on an individual basis. Programmes designed to process information, making storage and retrieval of facts, formulae and complex data readily available will revolutionise education for students with dyslexia. Children will be able to concentrate their attention on the application of knowledge rather than on acquiring the tools to access that knowledge.

While there have been undoubted improvements in the approach to dealing with dyslexia within the education system, and there are hopes for further improvements when economic circumstances allow, there is much that remains to be done. It would not be wise to assume that children with dyslexia have all their needs met within the official education system. There are grounds for concern by parents and teachers that gaps and anomalies remain. Some of these are:

■ Absence of a continuum of provision. Support within the school system is provided, for the most part, to those students who experience the most severe difficulties. In theory, schools may allocate learning support where they see the need. In reality, time and resources are limited, so only those with the lowest reading and spelling attainments are targeted. This means that there are many children with dyslexia who are not achieving their full learning potential, but who are not perceived as in need of learning support. Because the difficulties experienced by students range from mild to severe, support should be available at a variety of levels, appropriate to the individual learning needs. This was a guiding principle of the work of the Task Force on Dyslexia which stated that:

> A continuum of support and services should be available to students with learning difficulties arising from dyslexia matched to the severity and persistence of their learning

difficulties. ..... Programme planning and provision for students with learning difficulties arising from dyslexia should focus on individual learning needs.

Unfortunately, this is not yet the case. Indeed the increasing numbers of students identified with dyslexia has led to its being classified by the Department of Education and Skills as a **high incidence** disability and students in this classification do not qualify for individual resource teaching at primary level, whatever the degree of their difficulty. The adoption of a general allocation model of support for children with difficulties such as dyslexia is presented as a means to providing a continuum of support, but in reality it appears to spread available resources to an unacceptable extent.

■ Delays in the identification of dyslexic difficulties. While improvements have taken place in pre-service teacher training, many parents report an inability or an unwillingness in teachers to identify a dyslexic type difficulty.

■ Continuing difficulty in obtaining full psycho-educational assessment.

■ A trend towards minimising the importance of psycho-educational assessment. This has been influenced by the change in policy whereby children may receive learning support without having a full assessment.

■ The difficulties experienced by classroom and special needs teachers in preparing and implementing appropriate education plans for children with dyslexia.

■ The lack of knowledge about dyslexia which persists amongst many teachers, particularly at second level.

■ The small number of second level teachers who attend in-service courses on dyslexia.

■ Limitation of support for second level students with dyslexia.

■ The use of rigid criteria for the granting of Reasonable Accommodation in State Examinations (RACE) causes problems for students. No account is taken of the discrepancy between the overall ability of the student and their performance on standardised literacy tests. Students achieving above the l6th percentile on standardised literacy tests are considered to be in the average range and not eligible for accommodations. So, for example, a student whose general ability is at the 90th percentile, but whose spelling is at the 20th percentile will not be granted an exemption from spelling requirements.

- Presence of endorsements on certificates of students who do receive reasonable accommodation in state exams.

- The criteria for accessing the Disability Access Route to Education (DARE) at third level are even more problematic. The DARE criteria state that standard scores in two literacy areas should be at or below the l0th percentile. Again, no account is taken of the difference between a student's general ability and their reading, writing or spelling attainments.

There have been some positive developments in policy and administration within the Department of Education and Skills in recent years. However, as reduced budgets are now adversely affecting every aspect of service provision it is hard to be optimistic for the future. It is unfortunately true that good educational provision is expensive. It is also true that not providing adequate education proves even more costly in the long run. It is to be hoped that the long term good will prevail over the short-term need to balance budgets. Factors other than budgetary constraints also affect the level of provision for students with dyslexia: the outcome of court cases; developments in educational theory; changes of personnel in crucial areas of government; demands from employers; all play a part in determining the provision of services. Public, and particularly parental demand, is hugely significant too, but parents are not always conscious of the difficulties which exist.

It is easy to see the flaws in the physical structures of schools. Dilapidated school buildings, leaky pre-fabricated classrooms or inadequate toilet facilities are very obvious and parents and teachers rightly campaign for their replacement. It is not as easy to see where the systemic difficulties lie. Unless a parent encounters a specific difficulty, the absence of the relevant service may never become apparent. Sometimes the gap in provision is only evident in retrospect. Sins of omission are less easy to detect than those of commission.

Perhaps the single most frequent omission cited by parents is the Ffailure of school authorities to identify a dyslexic difficulty at an early stage. The reason for this is likely to be linked to the pre-service training which teachers receive. This does not always equip teachers to identify a dyslexic difficulty or to assess a child's learning needs adequately. The *Report of the Task Force on Dyslexia* strongly recommended in-service and in-career development courses for teachers, as well as more pre-service training in the area of dyslexia.

An *Evaluation of Literacy and Numeracy in Disadvantaged Schools* published in 2005 by the Inspectorate of the then Department of Education and Science noted:

> The vast majority of teachers interviewed indicated that their initial teacher training did not prepare them sufficiently for the challenge of their present teaching situation and that their training was not an effective preparation for teaching in a disadvantaged setting. The teachers referred to their day-to-day practice in the schools as being very removed from theory addressed in colleges.

In relation to in-school assessment of the learning needs of children the Inspectors reported:

> The provision of a coherent approach to the assessment and monitoring of children's progress was very weak and required significant development. The majority of teachers were rated as experiencing significant difficulty or requiring development in the area of organising assessment information about individual pupils.

The Inspectors also found that the group tests used did not give 'sufficient details of individual children's strengths and weaknesses'.

There is no reason to assume that these difficulties exist only in schools in disadvantaged areas. There appears to be a significant cause for parents of children with dyslexia to wonder if teachers are sufficiently informed to be able to detect the difficulty at an early stage and whether the test procedures available within schools are sensitive enough to pinpoint the problem and thorough enough to inform appropriate interventions.

It is interesting to note that parents surveyed by the Dyslexia Association of Ireland are not at all satisfied with provision for dyslexia in our educational system. A survey of 334 members in autumn 2010 found that 63% of respondents reported difficulty with awareness of dyslexia among primary teachers. 61% reported similar concerns about awareness at second level. 68% of respondents reported difficulty in securing psycho-educational assessment through their school. 62% reported difficulty in having the recommendations from psycho-educational assessment reports implemented. Surely a cause for concern.

It is widely recognised that the earlier a dyslexic difficulty is recognised and appropriate support given, the better the chance that the child will cope effectively with the school curriculum. Delays in identification leave time for a culture of failure to set in, for damage to self-esteem and a dislike for school and learning to be acquired. Children, whose difficulties are recognised and who get educational and emotional support, can usually achieve their potential. They can grow up as happy human beings, coping with school, with examinations and with college or further training. Third-level institutions report ever-increasing numbers of such students, at undergraduate and postgraduate level. They are to be found in all occupations, trades, professions and amongst the self-employed and entrepreneurs. They are productive citizens who achieve in their chosen career, despite their learning difficulties.

Given the importance of early and adequate diagnosis of dyslexia, it is worrying that despite the establishment of a national educational psychological service, parents and teachers still experience difficulties and delays in securing full psycho-educational assessment. There is a view in certain educational circles that parents request assessment too readily and the demand on scarce resources is not warranted. It is true that learning support may be available in schools without resort to full assessment. This gives much needed flexibility to schools and allows for the provision of learning support at an early stage. However, this does mean that there is a risk that the support provided to a child who has not been fully assessed may not be the most appropriate kind.

Psycho-educational assessment is a time-consuming and expensive procedure. It is also a very necessary procedure. Parents are sometimes told that securing an assessment is pointless as the child may not qualify for learning support, or the appropriate learning support may not be available. This is to misunderstand the purpose of an assessment. The focus must be on identifying the child's needs not just on establishing eligibility for learning support. Assessment may be necessary for the subtler details of a child's difficulty to be pinpointed or to distinguish between general and specific learning difficulty. Assessment is also vital in determining whether any other learning disability such as dyspraxia, ADHD or specific language impairment may be present. The importance to the child and to parents of precise knowledge of the nature and extent of any difficulty is incalculable.

Preparation of a detailed individual profile and learning programme (IPLP), advice to parents in terms of expectations and levels of support, referral for additional medical or professional investigation, referral to special reading schools and applications for exemption from the study of Irish and exam accommodations all rely heavily on the expertise of the psychologist and the information provided in a professional assessment report.

While the numbers of special educational needs teachers at primary level is substantial, resources are only now being put in place at second level. Indeed, the impression could well be gained that dyslexia is a problem of primary school children which vanishes with the transition to second level. Only those children, whose literacy attainments are at or below the 2nd percentile and whose ability is at the average level or above, are entitled to resource teaching at second level.

Supports for students with dyslexia at second level are, probably, even more necessary than at primary level because of the wide range of subjects and teachers to which the student is exposed. Completely new subjects, additional languages, a change of environment, frequent changes of classroom and timetables all create stress for the student with dyslexia. Not surprisingly, many students feel lost and unable to cope. A number will fail to make the transfer from primary to secondary schooling or will drop out prior to Junior Certificate. These are among the most vulnerable young people in society.

By mid-second level, state examinations loom for the student with dyslexia, bringing questions about which special accommodations to apply for and whether to avail of such arrangements because these will be noted on the examination certificate.

So, though many reports have been published, legislation passed and circulars issued, all is not rosy in the garden of dyslexia. Some weeds, snags and traps for the unwary still remain. Many children with dyslexia are never identified and do not receive the specialist help they desperately need. Many drop out of school at an early age because they cannot cope with reading and writing. Early school leaving carries great risks for the future. Research in Britain and America reveals that a disproportionate number of prisoners are school dropouts with specific reading difficulties. At best, young people with no formal qualifications and poor literacy skills will be at the end of the queue when it comes to job opportunities. This is a situation which is preventable. Students with dyslexia **can** learn but they need to be taught appropriately and supported adequately.

The purpose of this book is to show how this can be achieved. It aims to highlight the importance of recognising dyslexia and dealing with it.

The authors come from different disciplines and bring to the book their varied experience and training. Chapters 1, 2 and 6 come from the pen of a psychologist, carrying the expertise and technical knowledge of the professional in this area. The first two chapters consider the definitions of dyslexia, causal theories, formal assessment and interventions. Chapter 6 provides comprehensive information on child development as it relates to learning. Chapters 3, 7, 8, 9, 10 and 11, which deal with the formal educational aspects, are written by a serving second level teacher. They provide a practical and informative approach to tackling day-to-day issues in the classroom. The introduction and chapters 4, 5, 12, 13 and 14 are written by a former Director of the Dyslexia Association of Ireland and derive from experience gained from working for over twenty years with that organisation. These chapters deal with the child within the family and with dyslexia in adulthood. Two of the writers are parents of children with dyslexia.

The mix of practical knowledge, professional expertise and teaching experience will, it is hoped, offer information, understanding and advice to parents, teachers and adults about dyslexia, about the services which are available and how dyslexia can be set in context.

Naturally, some information may be more relevant to parents, some to teachers and some to students or adults with dyslexia. The authors have tried to indicate in chapter headings which section of the readership is being addressed but it is hoped that all the information is useful. Some topics have been covered by more than one writer. The material provided will, we hope, reflect the discipline from which the writer comes and may give the reader a broader perspective on the topic in question.

Information has been checked for accuracy at the time of going to print but changes take place rapidly. Parents and teachers are advised to keep up-to-date with circulars issued by the Department of Education and Skills and with developments in the field of dyslexia.

The positive message to people with dyslexia, their families and teachers is that dyslexia is a hurdle which can be overcome with appropriate understanding and support. Acquiring information about dyslexia, putting it in perspective and taking control of the learning situation can turn a potentially damaging disability into a manageable difficulty. It is hoped that this book will, for some, be the first step on the road to that achievement.

CHAPTER 1
DEFINING DYSLEXIA

This chapter will be of most use to parents, teachers and others who suspect that someone they know may have undiagnosed dyslexia or another specific learning difficulty. In it you will read about:

- Historical and current research on dyslexia;
- Defining/describing dyslexia;
- Main characteristics/indicators of dyslexia;
- Specific learning difficulties.

Dyslexia is classified as being a 'specific learning difficulty'. What is meant by this term? Learners are described as having a 'specific learning difficulty' when they have more than usual difficulty in processing certain or specific types of information e.g. (written) words, in the case of dyslexia; number, in the case of dyscalculia.

The word dyslexia comes from the Greek **dus/dys** meaning bad or difficult and **lexis** meaning word, vocabulary or language. Thus the term 'dyslexia' is used to describe 'a difficulty learning to read and write'.

Research on Dyslexia

Dyslexia was first written about in the mid-19th Century. Since then academic researchers and educators have continued to try to understand why some children learn to read relatively easily, or why some have exceptional difficulty. Can all reading delays be called 'dyslexia'? Are there different categories of reading difficulty? What is known now about the causes of reading delay or difficulty?

The earliest studies of dyslexia came from the medical world where the condition was thought to be acquired rather than developmental. In 1877 it was identified by a German physician, Adolf Kussmaul[1] when writing of patients who had acquired a loss of ability to read as a result of a brain injury they had sustained. Dr. Kussmaul's focus was on what was called acquired dyslexia, because his patient, an adult, had lost the ability to read and write. To describe what he observed he used the term 'word blindness'. Ten years later the word 'dyslexia' was used for the same medical condition. It was not until the end of that century that dyslexia as a developmental condition was considered in the literature. In 1895, a British ophthalmologist, James Hinshelwood[2], wrote an article in *The Lancet* on word blindness and visual memory. The following year a general practitioner in Sussex, William Pringle Morgan[3], wrote in the *British Medical Journal* of a fourteen year old boy who had great difficulty with reading and writing. The difference in the boy's case was that his difficulties did not occur as a result of some injury. Morgan concluded that his word blindness was congenital and was either inherited or acquired in the womb. By coincidence, his article was published just several weeks after a Medical Officer in Yorkshire, James Kerr[4], noted in his report that some pupils, who had no other learning difficulties appeared to have congenital word blindness. By this he meant that difficulties specific to reading and writing appeared to be genetic. Thus began the research into developmental dyslexia that is reckoned to affect as many at 8% of a population, to some degree.

Current Research

Current research may be said to be two-pronged:

- Identifying and understanding the causes of dyslexia;
- Analysing the content and methodologies that facilitate the child's learning.

These are complementary studies. Both the causes of the difficulty and the methods of teaching and learning which alleviate the difficulties need to be known. It is important to find out if the difficulties are transitory or permanent and what changes occur at different stages, particularly as a result of intervention. In other words, what makes a difference?

A very good example of the interconnectedness of cause and intervention can be drawn from the early history of research in America. The neurologist-psychiatrist Samuel T. Orton[5], working in New York in the 1920s and 1930s had been working on possible visual explanations of strephosymbolia. This means a twisting of symbols, which is how he characterised dyslexia. It led him to collaborate with psychologist-educator, Anna Gillingham, in the development of the first structured, sequential, multisensory programme of instruction for children with dyslexia. The Orton-Gillingham method has been the basis of successful teaching programmes for people with dyslexia since that time.

Much of the earlier knowledge of dyslexia was gleaned from observing reading and writing behaviours such as when the child could not easily recall the alphabet in sequence, did not like nursery rhymes or could never remember the rhyming word, often substituting a word with a similar meaning. When writing, the child could remember the correct letters in a word but could not recall the correct sequence. As neuroscience and research methods have developed, particularly with the advent of EEG and MRI scanning techniques, it is possible to gain more accurate information which helps in understanding the brain sites and processes that appear to be involved. One would expect that this knowledge, then, can be used to inform the way children with dyslexia are taught to read and write.

The search for programmes that actually change the way information is processed is very much in its early stages. Important questions which need to be answered include:

■ Does the programme actually change the structures and make the activity more easily accomplished?
■ Does improving specifically targeted processes bring about improvement in all the areas implicated in the activity?
■ Does intensive training bring about long-term changes?

In terms of dyslexia the questions to be asked are 'if a working memory programme is developed, will it improve reading and writing in the short term and in the long-term?' How can parents and teachers be sure that the programme lives up to what it claims to do? These questions are discussed further in Chapter 2, when discussing intervention.

Since reading and writing are relatively young skills on the scale of human evolution, being about 4,000 years old, it is theorised that the neurological structures involved originally developed for purposes other than for reading and writing. The research into processes underlying reading and writing is an important direction to take. Identifying dyslexia at the level of biology means that children's delay and persisting difficulties in reading and writing are recognised as real and part of who they are rather than as a result of temperament, irregular school attendance or other environmental factors.

Causal Theories

Dyslexia describes differences in the ways in which the individual processes written information. These differences make it more than usually difficult to learn to read, write and, sometimes, deal with numbers. On the other side, it is documented that people with dyslexia can be more advanced in the ways they see, understand and process non-verbal information and can be very creative and novel in problem-solving. Dyslexia describes a complex of processing activities and abilities which come into play when one needs to read and write, so theories of the causes of dyslexia have to try to account for the multiple areas of processing that appear to be interconnected or, perhaps, not sufficiently interconnected.

Since reading requires both visual and auditory analysis and since many children complain of visual difficulties, it is not surprising that some research needed to focus on reading and writing behaviours which seem to indicate disruption in the visual processing system. Dr. Samuel Orton hypothesised failure to establish appropriate cerebral organisation to match visual words with spoken forms. He didn't have the facility of neuroimaging to prove his hypothesis but his work on the difficulties in visual processing has continued to be a direction for research. One such proponent of a visual-motor cause of dyslexia is Professor John Stein[6] from Oxford. He theorises that dyslexia can be explained primarily in terms of differences in the visual magnocellular systems in the brain. Stein's research points to two pathways which simultaneously carry visual information. There are different types of cells in the retina of the eye which carry information to the brain. Ten per cent of these are large (magnocells), while the other ninety per cent are small (parvocells). Stein argues the case for impaired development of the magnocellular system leading to reduced visual motion sensitivity, poor visual sequential attention, slower visual search and lower sensitivity to flicker, some or all of which contribute to the discomfort and slow visual processing that is reported by people with dyslexia. He acknowledges that his theory is controversial but asserts that in the last ten years 90% of new research has found evidence of magnocellular deficit (Stein 2010).[7]

Another starting point for research are questions such as:

- How to account for the individual variations in profiles?
- How to explain the high incidence of co-existing conditions, many of which seem to share some common features with dyslexia?

Current research in this country is targeted at exploring the importance of executive functioning in a wide range of conditions and disabilities. Perhaps this research will find some answers where, at present, individual theories of dyslexia do not adequately account for the number of persons who will have dual diagnoses such as co-occurring dyslexia and dyscalculia, dyslexia and language disorder, or dyslexia and dyspraxia. Many children with dyslexia experience a range of other difficulties affecting motor co-ordination, mental calculation, concentration or personal organisation. In his report to the UK Secretary of State for Children, Schools and Families in 2009 Sir Jim Rose[8] acknowledges that these occur but that they 'are not of themselves markers of dyslexia'.

Any major causal theory of dyslexia must seek to provide some explanation of these variations. Theories that propose dyslexia as a predominantly visual disorder do not fully explain the variety of difficulties seen in the child with dyslexia. Stein, in keeping with this current thrust of research, seeks to find a comprehensive explanation of the causes of dyslexia. He includes in his consideration the possibility that poor phonology may result from impaired development of auditory magnocells, which make it difficult for the child to identify subtle changes in sound frequency and for impairment in other sensory motor magnocellular systems.

Another line of research into possible causes of dyslexia locates the main area of difficulty within the cerebellum, at the base of the brain and the 'autopilot' for timing and motor prediction for balance and skilled movement. Rod Nicolson and Angela Fawcett[9], the main proponents of this theory, suggest that the timing of sequences may be of paramount importance to how quickly or how effectively one acquires a skill, to the point that it can be accomplished automatically. Thus research on the basis of this theory seeks to explain why much of the difficulty in dyslexia relates to a difficulty becoming automatic at the required tasks.

The Phonological Deficit Hypothesis is the dominant theory in current research. Reading requires one to map the sounds of a language onto a symbolic, alphabetic visual code. For the past twenty years the dominant research into what causes dyslexia has focused on phonological processing, on the ability to break language into its component sounds. Most researchers today acknowledge that impairments in phonological processing are at the core of dyslexia. These impairments occur at the level of phonological awareness and at the level of phonics. It is this phonological difficulty at the level of single word decoding that distinguishes between children with reading delay, between dyslexia and other reading difficulties.

Phonological processing describes how the sounds of a language are perceived. It presumes a degree of awareness of the elements of sounds within words such as rhyme and rhythm, and then how to recognise the visual manner in which sounds of words are linked with their visual counterparts by way of letters and words. The ability to recognise same and different sounds not only in themselves but also in key positions in a word e.g. onset and rhymes, and to play around with sounds e.g. spoonerisms, as well as quick recall of sounds and words (Rapid Naming) are all part of what is called phonological awareness.

Phonological awareness predates the study of phonics. Phonics describes the system where auditory information (sounds) and visual information (alphabet, letters, words) merge in a coded system for conveying thoughts (written language).

Phonics is the skill of mapping sound onto corresponding letters and patterns of letters. It describes how sounds are represented by a system of symbols that are called letters. Usha Goswami[10], Director of the Centre for Neuroscience in Education at Cambridge, observes that learning to read changes the brain. The child must conceptualise words differently when they have a written form. She concludes that the difficulty in making the transition from oral to written language is a consequence of the child with dyslexia not having the auditory distinctions efficiently in place for phonics instructions to work.

Most researchers are in agreement that phonological deficit is now regarded as the core 'marker' of dyslexia.

Some researchers such as Marianne Wolf[11] maintain that the deficits that create dyslexia are twofold. In addition to the underlying difficulty in phonological awareness she identifies the second as Rapid Automatic Naming. This is the speed with which one can identify the patterns of letters. If the mechanisms that regulate speed act differently and if the processing of auditory and visual tasks is not simultaneous then one has difficulty with the automatic recognition of words. One of the results is staccato rhythm while reading, which is likely to impair comprehension.

Defining/Describing Dyslexia

If each of these theories is looked at, it is evident that they have identified a number of core areas that block the easy access to the written word and delay the child's reading development. These include visual processing, whether of visual memory, automatic apprehension of the patterns (orthographic representations), phonemic awareness or rapid naming.

How then is dyslexia to be defined or described? It can be described from a number of different perspectives which include how one learns (cognition), what parts of the brain are involved (neurology), what genes are involved (genetics) and behaviour. What is known at the neurological and genetic levels is incomplete and the research is on-going. Beyond these, at each level, is the influence of the environment in which the child grows.

The processes identified affect how one learns, organises a task and deals with many everyday tasks. One lives with dyslexia. It is not a medical problem: it does not call to be cured. It is genetic: it does not go away. The child and adult can adapt and find new ways to deal with information processing, thus getting around the original difficulties, often exploiting their strengths to do this.

There are many definitions. In fact everybody who writes about it, be it an organisation such as a dyslexia association, or classification manuals such as the Diagnostic and Statistical Manual of Mental Disorders (DSM) and the International Statistical Classification of Diseases (ICD), each has a different way of defining dyslexia.

Defining dyslexia is of most importance to children when by doing so one recognises that dyslexia exists and consequently the child with dyslexia will have access to special accommodations and tuition within the school system. The definitions used by Education Authorities are the bases for establishing rights under law and putting in place appropriate support systems in schools. They are descriptive and pragmatic rather than theoretic.

The following are three definitions:

■ The report by Sir Jim Rose, *Identifying and Teaching Children and Young People with Dyslexia and Literacy Difficulties* published by the UK Department for Children, Schools and Families (DCSF 2009)[12.]

■ The Research Committee of the International Dyslexia Association (2002)[13].

■ The Irish Department of Education and Science *Report by the Task Force on Dyslexia* (2001).[14]

The DCSF *'Rose' Report* defines dyslexia as follows:

■ Dyslexia is a learning difficulty that primarily affects the skills involved in accurate and fluent word reading and spelling.

■ Characteristic features of dyslexia are difficulties in phonological awareness, verbal memory and verbal processing speed.

■ Dyslexia occurs across the range of intellectual abilities.

■ It is best thought of as a continuum, not a distinct category, and there are no clear cut-off points.

Dyslexic difficulties can occur along a continuum from mild to severe. In any group of people with dyslexia there are a range of abilities and difficulties both within the individual and between the individuals. Some will have greater difficulty. Some will have greater ability. Usually the reading and writing delay is quite unexpected, given the individual's alertness and good ability in other aspects of learning.

The definition of dyslexia from the Research Committee of the International Dyslexia Association (2002) includes more exact information such as the concept of single word decoding and the fact that dyslexia is constitutional in origin. The report states:

Dyslexia is one of several distinct learning difficulties. It is a specific language-based disorder of constitutional origin characterised by difficulties in single-word decoding, usually reflecting insufficient phonological processing abilities. These difficulties in single-word decoding are often unexpected in relation to age and other cognitive and academic abilities.

The Irish Task Force on Dyslexia defined dyslexia as follows:

Dyslexia is manifested in a continuum of specific learning difficulties related to the acquisition of basic skills in reading, spelling and/or writing, such difficulties being unexpected in relation to an individual's other abilities and educational experiences. Dyslexia can be described at the neurological, cognitive and behavioural levels. It is typically characterised by inefficient information processing, including difficulties in phonological processing, working memory, rapid naming and automaticity of basic skills. Difficulties in organisation, sequencing and motor skills may also be present.

This definition describes dyslexia in terms of what is observed and what is recognised by researchers as being the salient features of dyslexia which include the following key points:

■ Unexpected difficulty with literacy and number.

■ Difficulties in phonological awareness i.e. ability to recognise the sound structures of a language.

■ Poor auditory working memory.

■ Delay in finding the right word (rapid naming).

■ Delay in becoming automatic in a skill.

Children with dyslexia often experience other difficulties, such as poor co-ordination and fine motor movement, ability to sequence and organise, delay in learning time, mixed laterality and problems with accurate direction. A number of these **indicators** are common to many learning difficulties including dyslexia, dyspraxia, attention deficit hyperactivity disorders and specific language impairment.

The features described above may be seen as the main characteristics as far as they can be identified at this time. The *Report of the Task Force on Dyslexia* acknowledged that it is not known exactly how visual processing is part of the picture. Children with dyslexia often experience difficulty with visual memory, eye tracking and reading speed. Clearly, a reader must be able not only to know that language consists of combinations of sound and that words can be broken into sounds at different levels but also that these sounds are represented visually by series of letters and letter-patterns. This recognition requires visual memory of words. If words are not adequately stored in the visual word memory area accurate recall, failure to recognise words automatically, writing letters in the wrong order and/or slower reading speed will result. The work of John Stein and other researchers into visual processing in reading is important. As with all activities, the brain works in a co-ordinated and integrated way. It is not yet fully understood how it draws together multiple processes to enable the child to read fluently.

Main Characteristics/Indicators of Dyslexia

It was noted earlier that dyslexia *does not go away.* It is a way in which a person processes information. In the traditionally valued areas of linear thinking, order and sequencing and in the tasks of reading and writing, the person with dyslexia can be significantly impaired. However, one must always remember that many individuals with dyslexia are very efficient/above average in how non-language information is processed.

The ways in which dyslexia has an impact on day-to-day living tend to change according to age and stage of development. In the early years difficulties with motor co-ordination, attention, learning phonics and the elementary tools for reading and writing predominate.

As the primary school child moves from junior to senior classes, issues around self-esteem and motivation may arise. Frustration and lack of self-confidence may interfere with social and emotional development. Difficulties with memory and organisation may compound delay in reading and writing.

In secondary school the challenge is to be able to deal with the range of subjects, the volume of reading and writing required and to prepare for and manage timed examinations. In addition they need to be able to look ahead to the future with confidence, knowing that they have opportunities equal to those of their peers of following the education and training courses that will best suit their talents and abilities. Literacy difficulties can dent their confidence, impair their level of performance and result in underachievement.

There are aspects of dyslexia which are constant and which do not go away when one leaves school. These include:

- Slower processing of auditory and visual information;
- Difficulty with working memory;
- Phonological difficulty;
- Poor spelling and, sometimes;
- Halting reading.

Most adults with dyslexia have to use memos and calculators and a host of strategies to remind them of tasks to be done, names and numbers to be remembered and directions to be followed. Many continue to have difficulty attending to a long sermon or lecture or listening and writing simultaneously. Some will continue to be slow and halting when reading aloud. They can have difficulty remembering people's names, addresses or telephone numbers.

However, they will also have developed other learning skills and characteristics that stand them in good stead. Many adults with dyslexia are very thorough, because they leave nothing to chance. They plan carefully because they have to be prepared. Having had to spend a much longer time learning work at school, they have developed habits of diligence and know how to work much harder, if necessary, to accomplish a task. Often having struggled with their disability, they believe in their ability to achieve their goals.

While dyslexia is a difficulty, aspects of which are enduring, these are significant strengths. They also often have particular strengths in visual perception and reasoning. The task for children, though, is to break through the barrier that delays their full access to knowledge in all its forms and to develop their innate abilities.

As well as finding a variety of definitions for dyslexia one also finds lists of indicators which may show that a dyslexic difficulty is present at the different stages in life. There are check lists and no one child or adult will have all the indicators. Dyslexia is complex and individual in its manifestation and so lists can be used as warning systems of risk factors rather than conclusive confirmation of having dyslexia.

The first four lists given below are adapted from the *Report of the Task Force on Dyslexia*. The last list is taken from the Dyslexia Association of Ireland information booklet.

The lists are as follows:
- For children age three to five.
- For children age five to seven.
- For children age seven to twelve.
- For children age twelve plus.
- For adults.

Each child/adult with dyslexia has a unique profile of strengths and weaknesses. The lists of indicators help parents and teachers identify children who may have a dyslexic difficulty. An educational assessment will still be required to make a diagnosis. What the lists do is help to confirm the suspicions that there is a difficulty present and therefore help in making the decision to obtain an assessment.

When looking at the lists of indicators, remember the following:

- No child will have all the indicators.
- Many children will have several of the indicators.
- Some indicators are more common than others.
- The number of indicators observed in a child does not indicate whether the child's dyslexia is mild, moderate or severe.

Indicators of possible learning difficulty arising from dyslexia (ages 3-5 Years)

- Is later than most children in learning to speak.
- Has difficulty pronouncing some, especially multi-syllabic, words.
- Has difficulty separating spoken words into sounds and blending spoken sounds to make words (i.e. has difficulty with phonological awareness).
- Experiences auditory discrimination problems.
- Is prone to spoonerisms (e.g. *Fips and chish* for *fish and chips*).
- Has difficulty with rhyming.
- Has difficulty maintaining rhythm.
- Is unable to recall the right word.
- Is slow to add new vocabulary.
- Exhibits delays in acquiring emergent literacy skills (e.g. understanding that written language progresses from left to right, discriminating between letters, words and sentences).
- Experiences problems learning the alphabet.
- Has trouble learning numbers, days of the week, colours and shapes.
- Has trouble learning to write and spell his/her own name.
- Is unable to follow multi-step directions or routines.
- Is developing fine motor skills more slowly than other children.
- May have difficulty telling and/or retelling a story in correct sequence.

Indicators of a possible learning difficulty arising from dyslexia (ages 5-7 Years)

Slow to learn the connection between letters and sounds.

■ Has difficulty separating words into sounds, and blending sounds to form words (phonemic awareness).

■ Has difficulty repeating multi-syllabic words (e.g. *emeny* for *enemy, pasghetti* for *spaghetti).*

■ Has difficulty decoding single words (reading single words in isolation).

■ Has poor word-attack skills, especially for new words.

■ Confuses small or easy words: *at/ to; said/ and; does/ goes.*

■ May make constant reading and spelling errors including:
   • Letter reversals (e.g. *d* for *b* as in *dog* for *bog)*
   • Letter inversions (e.g. *m* for *w)*
   • Letter transpositions (e.g. *felt* and *left)*
   • Word reversals (e.g. *tip* for *pit)*
   • Word substitutions (e.g. *house* for *home).*

■ Reads slowly with little expression or fluency (oral reading is slow and laborious).

■ Has more difficulty with function words (e.g. *is, to, of)* than with content words (e.g. *clouds, run, yellow).*

■ May be slow to learn new skills, relying heavily on memorising without understanding.

■ Reading comprehension is below expectation due to poor accuracy, fluency and speed.

■ Reading comprehension is better than single word reading.

■ Listening comprehension is better than reading comprehension.

■ Has trouble learning facts.

■ Has difficulty planning or organising.

■ Uses awkward pencil grip.

■ Has slow and poor quality handwriting.

■ Has trouble learning to tell the time on an analogue clock or watch.

■ Has poor fine motor co-ordination.

Indicators of a possible learning difficulty arising from dyslexia (ages 7-12 Years)

■ Has continued difficulty reading text aloud or silently.

■ Reading achievement is below expectation.

■ Still confuses letter sequences (e.g. *soiled* for *solid*; *left* for *felt*).

■ Is slow at discerning and learning prefixes, suffixes, root words and other morphemes as part of reading and spelling strategies.

■ Poor reading accuracy, fluency, or speed interferes with reading comprehension.

■ Spelling is inappropriate for age and general ability (e.g. spelling the same word differently on the same page, use of bizarre spelling patterns, frequent letter omissions, additions and transposition).

■ Poor spelling contributes to poor written expression (e.g. may avoid use of unfamiliar words).

■ Use avoidance tactics when asked to read orally or write.

■ Experiences language-related problems in Maths (e.g. when reading word problems and directions, confuses numbers and symbols).

■ Is unable to learn multiplication tables by rote.

■ Still confuses some directional words (e.g. left and right).

■ Has slow or poor recall of facts.

■ Lacks understanding of other people's body language and facial expressions.

■ Has trouble with non-literal or figurative language (e.g. idioms, proverbs).

■ Forgets to bring in or hand in homework.

■ Has difficulty remembering what day or month it is.

■ Has difficulty remembering his/her own telephone number or birthday.

■ Has poor planning and organisational skills.

■ Has poor time management.

■ Lacks self-confidence and has a poor self-image.

Indicators of a possible learning difficulty arising from dyslexia (ages 12 Years+)

- Is still reading slowly and without fluency, with many inaccuracies.
- Misreads words (e.g. *hysterical* for *historical*) or information.
- Has difficulty modifying reading rate.
- Has an inadequate store of knowledge due to lack of reading experience.
- Continues to experience serious spelling difficulties.
- Has slow, dysfluent and/or illegible handwriting.
- Has better oral skills than written skills.
- Has difficulty planning, sequencing and organising written text.
- Has difficulty with written syntax or punctuation.
- Has difficulty skimming, scanning and/or proof reading written text.
- Has trouble summarising or outlining.
- Has problems in taking notes and copying from the board.
- Procrastinates and/or avoids reading and writing tasks.
- Does not complete assignments or class work or does not hand them in.
- Is slow in answering questions, especially open-ended ones.
- Has poor memorisation skills.
- Still mispronounces or misuses some words.
- Has problems recalling the names of some words or objects.
- Has poor planning and organisation skills.
- Has poor time management skills.
- Has more difficulty in language-based subjects (e.g. English, Irish, History) than in non-language based subjects (e.g. Mathematics, Technical Graphics).
- Lacks self-confidence and has poor self-image.

Indicators of a possible learning difficulty arising from dyslexia in adults

- Difficulty with reading aloud.
- Difficulty with reading unfamiliar material.
- Tendency to mispronounce or misread words.

- Slow pace of reading.
- Reading for information only, not for pleasure.
- Understanding more easily when listening than when reading.
- Difficulty with spelling.
- Finding it hard to visualise words, or remember the sequence of letters in a word.
- Difficulty with sentence construction and punctuation.
- Difficulty putting information on paper.
- Difficulty in spotting mistakes made in written work.
- Finding it easier to express thoughts in words than in writing.
- Underachieving at school, particularly in exams.
- Having immature or ill formed handwriting.
- Tendency to be clumsy and unco-ordinated.
- Confusing left and right.
- Finding it hard to remember things in sequence.
- Difficulty in remembering new information or new names.
- Getting phone messages wrong.
- Confusion with times and dates and appointments.
- Getting phone numbers wrong by perhaps reversing digits.
- Making 'silly' mistakes in calculations.
- Having 'good' days and 'bad' days.
- Poor short-term memory.
- Having close family members with dyslexia.

Specific Learning Difficulties

The term dyslexia is often written as being synonymous with the terms specific learning difficulties/specific learning disability. This can be very confusing. The term specific learning disability includes dyslexia as one of a number of specific, as distinct from general learning disabilities. Dyslexia is specific to certain aspects of learning. The difficulties are not the result of overall general learning disability although dyslexia can also be present when one has general learning difficulties (see *Rose Report* definition). Psychologists in reports often describe a child as having a specific learning difficulty of a dyslexic nature.

The term specific learning disability has a meaning wider than the term dyslexia. It is used to encompass a number of specific disabilities. Since the mid-1990s the term has been used to include dyslexia, dyspraxia, specific language impairment (SLI), attention deficit disorder (ADD)/attention deficit hyperactivity disorder (ADHD) and autistic spectrum disorder. When observing and, later, assessing for each of these syndromes, one is aware how often features and, subsequently, difficulties co-exist and how much overlap there is with dyslexia. Thus the child with dyspraxia has difficulty similar to that of the child with dyslexia in processing information, with memory, laterality, following instructions, attention, sense of direction, sequencing, copying from the board and concept of time. However the core deficit of dyslexia, co-existing with some or all of the above, is difficulty with decoding the written word and with spelling. The core deficit in the child with dyspraxia is difficulty with motor-co-ordination. The core deficit for ADD/ADHD is with attention and impulse control. The core deficit with specific language impairment is with specific aspects of receptive and expressive language.

As a response to this awareness that a great number of difficulties are common to several co-occurring disabilities, researchers are considering the possibility that there may in fact be one underlying impairment rather than separate conditions. Kaplan in *Dyslexia in Context*[15] suggests the term 'atypical brain development'. He sees the need to assess pupils and students across a wide spectrum of tests because of the difficulties of not having discrete indicators for each disability. A wide and full assessment is necessary to make sure the child is appropriately diagnosed. This may sometimes require the child to be seen by the educational psychologist and one or more of the following: the speech and language therapist, the occupational therapist or the psychiatrist. Studies indicate that the co-occurrence of one or more disability is relatively high. Madeleine Portwood (1990)[16] suggested that between 40% and 45% of children with dyspraxia have co-occurring dyslexia. George Hynd (2004)[17] suggests that around 50% of children with dyslexia also have ADHD. Snowling's[18] work on reading has indicated the overlap between language impairment and dyslexia. Her research showed that children with reading impairment at age eight showed a pattern of oral speech and language delay in pre-school years.

Of these disabilities dyslexia is probably the most recognised.

However, because many parents may be unsure of how these co-existing conditions present, the following brief explanations are included here. More detailed information about these specific learning difficulties, assessment and support can best be obtained from the relevant organisations. Details of contact addresses can be found at the end of this chapter.

Dyspraxia

The term dyspraxia comes from the root **dus/dys** meaning bad or difficult and **praxis** meaning movement or action. Developmental dyspraxia is the term used to describe a condition whereby the child has more than usual difficulty with co-ordination, with organising movement and also often has significant visual perceptual difficulties. In some literature it can be referred to as developmental co-ordination disorder (DCD). The difficulties the child experiences are not caused by other recognised conditions, such as cerebral palsy, multiple sclerosis or hemiplegia. In early childhood the features most noticeable include:

- Difficulty articulating words;
- Difficulty dressing oneself;
- Limited concentration;
- Difficulty following instructions;
- Sensitivity to noise and changing light;
- Difficulty with spatial perception resulting in bumping into things, being clumsy and falling over easily.

Attention Deficit/Hyperactivity Disorders (ADD and ADHD)

Attention deficit disorder (ADD) / Attention deficit hyperactivity disorder (ADHD) describes a condition where the child has more than usual difficulty maintaining attention for any length of time, is highly distractible, disorganised, forgetful and appears not to listen to instructions. These children may also be over-active, fidgety, want everything instantly and be impulsive. Many people associate ADHD with hyperactivity. They focus on the most obvious indicator which is the child's difficulty with staying still and the need to be constantly on the go. However, since 1994, a significant distinction has been made between ADD (Attention Deficit Disorder) and ADHD (Attention Deficit Hyperactivity Disorder). In ADD the child does not exhibit the

hyper-activity which is associated with ADHD. In both cases the core difficulty is with ability to control attention.

The following is a checklist of some of the items which describe a child with ADD.

- Difficulty concentrating, except on activities of personal interest;
- Highly distractible;
- Inconsistent - good days/bad days;
- Disorganised;
- Difficulty following through instructions;
- Poor perseverance except on tasks enjoyed;
- Pays little attention to detail;
- Forgetful and dreamy.

In addition to the above, the child with ADHD manifests behaviours such as the following:

- Unable to stay seated for any length;
- Fidgety, restless and constantly touching things;
- Asks questions impulsively, interrupts, makes inappropriate comments and/or makes vocal noises;
- Needs to be moving most of the time;
- Has difficulty in controlling impulses;
- Can be impatient and demanding of instant response;
- Cannot queue in lines;
- Acts first, thinks later.

As with dyslexia and dyspraxia, any two children with ADHD/ADD may have quite different profiles because their combination of difficulties places them at different points along a continuum of difficulties. It is important to note that their poor reading and writing development may not be rooted in dyslexia but result from their difficulty focusing attention long enough to get a grasp of basic instructions.

Asperger's Syndrome

The term Asperger's Syndrome came into use as recently as 1983, in a paper published by Burgoine and Wing[19] which describes the features that are considered to characterise the disability. In the 1940s a Viennese paediatrician, Hans Asperger,[20] had already identified these, hence the name. Asperger's Syndrome is usually classified under the Autistic Spectrum Disorders. In the United States and in some English-speaking countries it is referred to as 'high-functioning autism'. Asperger's Syndrome/Disorder describes the social components of autism but without the significant impairments of learning and language that characterise autism.

The following are the core features of Asperger's Syndrome:

- Lack of empathy;
- Poor ability to form friendships;
- One-sided conversations;
- Intense absorption in a special interest;
- Poor verbal communication;
- Odd postures and clumsy movements.

It should be remembered that the presence of any one or any cluster of these features do not in themselves indicate Asperger's Disorder. For example, poor communication skills, and consequently poor ability to hold a two-sided conversation, may be caused by a language disorder. The only way to get a true diagnosis is to have an appropriate assessment which is wide-ranging and thorough. Aspire, the Asperger's Syndrome Association, will provide advice on where to look for this.

Specific Language Impairment (SLI)
Although specific language impairment (SLI) is not strictly classified as a specific learning difficulty, many children with dyslexia have experienced specific language delay. They may have required speech therapy, usually at the pre-school and kindergarten stage. Specific language delay can occur in either or both of the areas of expression and reception. The difficulties may be at the level of phonology (discrimination of different sounds, recognition of similar sounds), semantics (understanding meaning), syntax (grammatical structure of sentence), pragmatics (using language suited to what they want to communicate) and fluency. Recent studies in Britain by Professor Margaret Snowling from the University of York have identified reading comprehension difficulties in significant numbers of children. The studies also suggest that children with poor oral language skills are at high risk of literacy failure. Dyslexia and language difficulties often co-exist. This is why a psychologist assessing for dyslexia may

sometimes recommend a further assessment by a speech and language therapist. Prof. Snowling maintains that the highest risk factor for developing dyslexia is a speech and language disorder, where oral language is disordered.

REFERENCES

1. Kussmaul, A. (1877) *Disturbances of Speech*

2. Hinshelwood, J. (1895) *Word Blindness and Visual Memory* The Lancet 2, 1564-1570

3. Morgan, W.P. (1896) *A Case of Congenital Word Blindness* British Medical Journal

4. Kerr, J. (1896) *Congenital Word Blindness* British Royal Statistical Society

5. Orton, S. (1963) *Specific Reading Disabilities – Strephosymbolia* Reprinted in Annals of Dyslexia 1, 9-17

6. Stein, J. (2001) *Dyslexia 7; 12-36*

7. Stein, J. (2010) *World Dyslexia Forum, Unesco, Paris.*

8. Rose, J. (2009) *Identifying and Teaching Children and Young People with Dyslexia and Literacy Difficulties* Report presented to DCSF (UK)

9. Nicolson, R. and Fawcett, A. (1994) *Dyslexia: The Role of the Cerebellum* Electronic Journal of Research in Educational Psychology No. 2 (2) 35-58

10. Goswami, U. (2008). *Cognitive Development: The Learning Brain.* Psychology Press, Taylor & Francis Hall.

11. Wolf, M. and Bowers, P. (2000) *The Question of Naming Speed Deficits in Developmental Reading Disability: An Introduction to the Double Deficit Hypothesis* Journal of Learning Disabilities 33, 322-324

12. See 7 above

13. Annals of Dyslexia Vol. 1, 2003.

14. Department of Education and Science (2001) *Report of the Task Force on Dyslexia*

15. Kaplan, B.J. (1998) *Human Movement Science.* Elsevier. See also Reid, G., Fawcett, A. (2004) *Dyslexia in Context* British Dyslexia Association

16. Portwood, M. (1999) *Developmental Dyspraxia: Identification and Intervention* David Fulton Publishers

17. Hynd, G. Research studies quoted in Reid, G. & Fawcett, A. (2004) *Dyslexia in Context* British Dyslexia Association *327*

18. Snowling, M. & Bishop, D. (2004) *Developmental Dyslexia and Specific Language Impairment: Same or Different?* Psychological Bulletin 130(6):858-86. See also Snowling, M & Hulme, C. (Ed.) (2005) *The Science of Reading* Blackwell Publishing.

19. Burgoine, E. & Wing, L. (1983) *Identical triplets with Asperger's Syndrome* British Journal of Psychiatry 143

20. Asperger, H. (1944) *Die Autistischen Psychopathen im Kindesalter*

Contact Details

- Aspire (for Autistic Spectrum Disorders), Carmichael House, North Brunswick Street, Dublin 7. Ph. 01 8780027: Website: www.aspireireland.ie

- The Dyspraxia Association, 69A Main Street, Leixlip, Co. Kildare. Ph. 01 2957125: Website: www.dyspraxiaireland.com

- HADD (for Attention Deficit Disorders), Carmichael House, North Brunswick Street, Dublin 7. Ph. 01 8748349 (Wednesday/Friday mornings) Website: www.hadd.ie

- INCADDS: Irish National Council for AD/HD Support Groups. Unit 17A Ballybane Enterprise Centre, Galway. Website: www.incadds.ie.

CHAPTER 2

SCREENING, ASSESSMENT AND INTERVENTIONS

This chapter will be of most use to parents and teachers and is about formally identifying dyslexia. What should happen when concerns are raised that the child is having more than usual difficulty with sounds, letters and words? In this chapter you will read about the following:

- Identifying dyslexia through a staged approach;
- The Psycho-educational Assessment;
- Understanding the assessment report;
- Questions following assessment;
- Review of progress; standardised testing in school; re-assessment.
- Interventions at home
- Non-teaching interventions.

Identifying Dyslexia through a Staged Approach

Early intervention is recognised now as offering children with dyslexia the best chance of circumventing their difficulties. Consequently there is increasing emphasis on the need to monitor a child's progress and possible signs of reading delay and to start intervention some time before one considers assessing for dyslexia or even screening. This way of proceeding is known as the staged approach and is set out clearly in the Department of Education and Science (2000) *Learning Support Guidelines*[1]. Monitoring begins in the classroom. There is much greater awareness now than previously of behaviours that may be consistent with dyslexia such as difficulty remembering letter sounds, poor ability to recognise rhyming words or guessing at words. If a child's progress appears delayed and this is evident from evaluations carried out by the class teacher the child will be referred to the learning support teacher, a plan of work will be drawn up and the child will be given some hours of remediation within a small group of students. This will continue for a reasonable length of time before further action may be thought necessary. One of the indicators of dyslexia is that difficulties persist and are difficult to remediate, in spite of good tuition. Thus, if the child is struggling to make progress, the learning support teacher will probably carry out a screening test to gather more detailed information about how the child processes information.

Screening tests are instruments used to identify the possible cause of the reading delay. They consist of a series of subtests designed to target areas of cognitive processing (the specific abilities used when attempting a particular learning task, such as working memory, sequencing, or processing speed) that are known to be part of the dyslexic profile. Their purpose is to point out children 'at risk', but their use is not to be confused with full psycho-educational assessment. They can be very accurate in identifying that a child has dyslexia tendencies but, because the range of their testing is more confined, they cannot be definitive. The surest way to identify dyslexia is by means of a full psycho-educational assessment, which is carried out by an educational psychologist. In addition, the full assessment will be required to avail of support structures such as accommodations in examinations, language exemptions, learning support in second and third level education.

It is important that parents are involved at all points of the process. A child who constantly forgets work or who appears not to be putting in the effort may be easily misunderstood. However, if parents are able to vouch for the nightly struggle with homework, are able to communicate what they observe when reading together, feel they can freely express their concerns and may have undisclosed or undiagnosed dyslexia themselves, this knowledge is intrinsic to the care that is owed to the child. It is also an important part of the screening process.

Not all reading delay is caused by dyslexia and, as children develop at different rates, psychologists are reluctant to **diagnose** dyslexia before the child is seven years old. However, once the parent or the teacher begins to feel there is a possible reading delay, it is wise to talk about it and put interventions in place. Some children are more at risk, such as those who have other members of their family with dyslexia.

The following outlines the staged approach described in *Learning Support Guidelines*:

- Stage One is when the classroom teacher administers one or more screening tests to identify the particular nature of the difficulty in relation to the learning which is expected to have taken place at this stage of the child's development. Based on the information gained from this an individual pupil learning programme (IPLP) is drawn up. The guidelines contain detailed information about such programmes and recommends that the school involve the parent in 'contributing to the development and implementation of their child's IPLP'. An IPLP is a record of relevant information. It notes present levels of attainment and identifies learning strengths and needs. It forms the basis for setting goals to be reached and the means to achieve them. It should be revised at frequent intervals.

- Stage Two involves putting learning support in place. This means that the child is withdrawn from the general classroom for a short period of the day and given additional tuition. Progress is monitored and the level of progress is assessed by objective tests at the end of a period of specific instruction, usually thirteen or twenty weeks. The IPLP is revised according to the progress registered.

- Stage Three is when the parent and the teacher are relatively sure that there is more than maturational delay responsible for the child's struggle with sounds, letters and words. The school requests written permission to have the child referred for psycho-educational assessment by the psychologist assigned to the school under the National Educational Psychological Service (NEPS). The psychologist carries out the assessment in the school.

The staged approach is designed to ensure that the child's progress is carefully monitored and appropriate intervention is put in place. Ideally, it should lead to children with dyslexia receiving a better service. In reality, the delivery of the service is uneven. It may work smoothly and effectively in some instances and less well in others. With the increased awareness of such learning difficulties among teachers and with the changes that have been implemented in how learning support teaching hours are allocated within schools, children can access learning support more readily, certainly in the early years.

Children with dyslexia are categorised as being in the high incidence of disability. This means that there are large numbers of pupils in any one school who are likely to have dyslexia. Because of this categorisation intervention will be given in small groups rather than one-to-one. This is not necessarily a bad thing, provided that children in the groups are well matched according to their needs. There is significant research to indicate the benefits of group learning, which included peer learning. In other words, children learn from one another. In addition there is considerable solidarity which helps the child who may be struggling to feel less alone. {See the *Rose Report UK (2009)*[2] and Singleton; *Intervention for Dyslexia UK (2009)*[3]}

One of the gaps between the ideal and what happens in practice is the difficulty of having an assessment carried out within a reasonable length of time, or if the child is older, carried out at all. While the National Educational Psychological Service has been growing since 2000, it is still not able to carry out all the assessments that may be required.

Consequently many parents look for an assessment from psychologists working in the private sector. It is not necessary to wait for Stage Three of the Learning Support procedures. A list of practising psychologists may be obtained from the Psychological Society of Ireland: website: www.psihq.ie. The Dyslexia Association of Ireland has several educational psychologists and provides psycho-educational assessments. Appointments can be made by phoning 01-6790276. There is usually a waiting list for private assessments.

Private assessments can be costly, but there are several ways in which the full cost may be alleviated. It is possible to claim tax back on part of the cost on the MED.1 Form from the Revenue Commission. Secondly, agencies such as St. Vincent DePaul Society often fund or part fund assessments on the basis of economic need. Schools may have a fund which may be used to meet needs such as paying for or subsidising assessments. The Dyslexia Association of Ireland has a similar scheme.

The Psycho-Educational Assessment

Assessment serves more purposes than just naming the cause of a child's difficulties. It provides a snapshot of the child's abilities and competencies as they are at that time and should be used to guide the child's learning not just to put a name on a difficulty they are experiencing. Because parents and teachers usually only require an assessment when there is a difficulty, it is most often used as a way of pin-pointing where the difficulties lie in order to determine what aspects of literacy or numeracy learning need to be targeted for additional tuition. However, the assessment aims to explore how the child learns and to identify strengths in how learning and information processing takes place. Children suspected of having dyslexia often display an incongruous mix of abilities and disabilities.

Dyslexia is not all negative and the assessment is about more than identifying deficits. These children may have considerable strengths and may be very creative, adept at non-verbal pursuits, at finding ways around problems and using strategies. However, the difficulties may significantly affect how a child learns. Identifying learning strengths and weaknesses is the key to opening up different ways of learning. The psycho-educational assessment is essentially an exploration of cognitive functioning looking at how faculties such as memory, assimilation, reasoning and language are developing. It tries to measure the child's abilities and compare how that child is functioning with what is the norm for that child's age group. More importantly, perhaps, it indicates how particular abilities, known to be weak on the profiles of children with dyslexia, compare with the child's other abilities.

Over the years the structure of cognitive tests has changed, as more is learnt about the brain and what is understood by 'intelligence' is clarified. The best known test materials have been developed under rigorous scientific methods and are considered to be valid in that they test what they set out to test. They are also considered to be reliable in that they have been tested and retested on large populations so that the results are consistent.

What makes the psycho-educational assessment different from the tests of reading, writing, spelling and mathematics in school is the scope of the assessment. It measures not simply the level of attainment but tries to identify cognitive functions which make sense of patterns of reading and spelling behaviour. There are some tests of cognitive ability used in school also, such as the Non-Reading Intelligence Test (NRIT), but they are limited in their range.

A full psycho-educational assessment aims to gather as much background information as possible about the child. It is important to understand the child in relation to the family and progress at school. Thus a very important aspect of the assessment is the interview between the psychologist and the parents - both parents, if possible. Questions may be asked about family history and the child's early development, health, eyesight and hearing. Before diagnosing dyslexia, it is important to rule out any possibility that poor vision or hearing deficits are not the primary cause of the child's difficulty. For example, children who have had grommets inserted in their ears may have been slower to pick up the subtle differences of sounds.

It is also important for the psychologist to get as full a report as possible from the child's class and learning support teachers, in order to be informed about how the child works in a familiar setting and on a daily basis. Remember, the psychologist is meeting the child for the first time, for a limited amount of time and, sometimes, out of a familiar environment.

Parents may ask to be present throughout the assessment. If they wish to stay, they are placed to the back of the room, out of their child's field of vision and excluded from taking any active part or intervening in any way, unless the child is anxious. However, it is usually better for parents to leave, so that distraction caused by their presence is reduced. The psychologist guides the child through a series of tasks, some oral, some written, some practical and some visual with the intention of getting knowledge about overall ability, working memory, verbal and visuo-spatial ability. Tests to assess the level of word reading, reading comprehension, spelling and mathematics are also given and, if time permits, some exploration of ability to express ideas, both orally and in written form.

The assessment includes checking out the child's facility with the tools and structure of language and with phonological awareness. This means checking if the child can do the following:

- Understand that words are composed of sounds blended together;
- Identify similar/dissimilar sounds;
- Match sounds with corresponding letters or letter patterns.

The psychologist may look for other information if there are suspicions that features of co-existing conditions are present, such as dyspraxia, specific language disorder or attention deficit disorder. If this is the case, additional tests will be administered to check out attention levels or fine motor movement, visual difficulties and laterality. A full psycho-educational assessment may take one or two sessions to complete.

Following assessment there is often an opportunity for some immediate feedback. If the assessment is done in school this may not be possible for the parent. So, in this case, feedback is given to the teacher or school principal and an alternative date can be given for feedback to the parent. Often a psychologist prefers to work through the test results before making definitive diagnoses and recommend-ations.

The psychologist arrives at a conclusion deduced from all the information gleaned from the interview, test results, observed behaviours and school reports. It is important to remember though, that while the psychologist tries to have as near ideal conditions as possible, these tests are also subject to human error. In the end the results reflect how the child performed on that day, in the particular circumstances.

Understanding the Assessment Report

After the assessment the psychologist spends considerable time scoring and analysing the results before coming to a conclusion about what they mean. Sometimes no clear picture emerges and tentative conclusions are arrived at, which may lead the psychologist to recommend a reassessment within a reasonable length of time. It is recommended that reassessment does not occur within twelve months of the original assessment, because there is likelihood that results may reflect some familiarity with the test materials.

A report is written up and sent to the parent or to the school principal, if the assessment was done in school, in which case parents will ordinarily receive a copy of the report. This should be read carefully and kept safely as it will be useful to any tutor who will work with the child. However, the validity of a report is at most three years as children develop and the profile of abilities and attainments will change accordingly. It will be difficult, for example, to give appropriate learning support to a fifteen year old on the basis of a seven-year old report!

The original report will always remain important if it contains a statement of diagnosis or recommends a particular course of action such as applying for an exemption from the study of Irish and/or third language and applying for accommodations in examinations. Obtaining both an exemption and accommodations is subject to specific criteria laid down by the Department of Education and Skills and it is important to know what these are. Occasionally recommendations are made that these would be advisable. However, if the child does not meet the criteria, the application for these will be unsuccessful. For example, to obtain an exemption from Irish one must obtain scores on the IQ test in the Average range of ability overall and have scores on the Attainment tests that are below the 10th percentile. That means having standard scores on the IQ test greater than 90 and standard scores on one or more of the reading and writing subtests below 81. This situation is, however, currently under review.

Accommodations in examinations are discussed in Ch 3. What is important to know at this point is that an up-to-date assessment report is not required in order to seek accommodations in Junior Certificate examination. It is advisable to have a recent assessment report when applying for accommodations in the Leaving Certificate examination. For the Disability Access Route Education (DARE) which facilitates entry to third level colleges and institutions, a report of assessment carried out **no less than three years** previously is required. Thus for 2011 entry assessments must have been carried out after February 2008.

A report of psycho-educational assessment contains a variety of information. Some of the language may be technical and specialised and so a parent should not hesitate to ask for explanations. The report is written with two readers in mind: the parent and the teacher. Both want to know what conclusion the psychologist has reached and what interventions are needed. One may expect to find sufficiently detailed information, recommendations and guidelines for writing up the child's individual profile and learning programme. The report is a bank of knowledge, but a bank of knowledge about **one** aspect of the child, that of cognitive functioning, which gives some indication of potential and of present attainments in school-based tasks of literacy and numeracy. It does not usually give evaluation of attitudes, motivation, self-esteem, personality and specific talents – all the other aspects of the child's being. It is well to keep that in mind and in perspective.

In recent years reports have become much more detailed and perhaps are harder for the 'uninitiated' to understand. First time recipients get very confused with the range of scores that are presented and there is an increasing effort to clarify the way in which these are presented. Psychologists are at pains to provide as much useful information as possible to the different readers of the report. They are also endeavouring to give reliable evidence to support the conclusion they have reached. Parents should always feel they can ask the psychologist to talk them through the report.

There are some pieces of information which can be extracted very quickly, giving the broad outline of the report. The detailed scrutiny can follow. Look first at the conclusions, then at the recommend-ations to see if there is any action which needs to be taken, then revert to the tables of scores on the tests on general ability, usually the Wechsler Intelligence Scale for Children (WISC) and try to absorb these. Remember scores on the WISC are about cognitive functioning. They will guide parents to appreciate the child's strengths and weaknesses independently of school performance. If, for example, children have a good score on the Perceptual Reasoning Index, this is a signal to help them engage in tasks and learning experiences that require good visual skills and perhaps visual-motor skills, activities such as making objects, using space, colour and design.

Having absorbed this snapshot of their potential, the next section to study is their attainment scores in reading, writing and mathematics. This chapter hopes to give a good understanding of what the different numbers/scores mean.

It is also important to read the account of the child's behaviour because this will throw light on what may need to be included in interventions that follow.

A psycho-educational report will usually include the following sections:

Background
The report incorporates those pieces of information which relate to the reasons why an assessment was requested, what background and family information is relevant and salient information from teachers'

reports. The psychologist wants to know if other members of the family have similar difficulties and how the child behaves in the home. Also included is the child's own perception of school learning and difficulties. Developmental history, medical conditions or history of sensory deficits and language development are noted. Reports from teachers with regard to difficulties, results of tests administered and reports of progress, the intervention programmes in place and whether or not the child is receiving additional tuition in or outside school, all form part of this background. It is useful to include also an account of perceived strengths.

Besides the parent and teacher, this report may need to be seen by other specialists, such as other teaching staff members or professionals to whom the child needs to be referred for further assessment. The report is required by the Department of Education and Skills if the decision is taken to apply for an exemption from the study of Irish and/or reasonable accommodation in exams. It is also needed by the Disability Support Service at third level if application is made to access these services. There may be some information which parents share with the psychologist which they do not wish to be written into the report. It is important to indicate this at the time of interview.

Observations
This section includes observations made by the psychologist about the child with regard to such features as ease of separation from the parent, interaction with the psychologist, problem-solving approaches, ability to persevere at a task, writing, taking in spoken instructions, learning strategies being used, clarity of oral expression and ability to sustain attention over time. Each of these gives valuable information to support test results and ultimately helps the psychologist to arrive at a final conclusion. Remember they are observations, not judgments.

Tests Administered
This section contains a list of the various tests administered. Some test materials have greater reliability than others. This is because they have been tested on differing numbers of children of all ages and backgrounds before being released for general use. One can have a high degree of confidence that those which have been normed on

large populations give an accurate indication of the child's current functioning.

There is no standard battery of tests used by all psychologists. All educational assessments include one or other of the major 'intelligence' tests or test of general cognitive functioning. They will also include an in-depth exploration of literacy attainments. Usually, but not always, a mathematics test is also included. As indicated above, sometimes psychologists may include additional tests if they want to get further information regarding a particular aspect of behaviour or functioning.

The psycho-educational assessment is not an assessment of dyslexia only. It is testing general intellectual ability or what is called 'cognitive functioning'. It conceptualises intelligence as a global entity that can be subdivided into related but relatively discrete groups or 'factors'. Therefore it can help to identify where there are strengths and weaknesses in the 'factors'. These factor scores are called '**Indexes**' on the Wechsler Intelligence Scale for Children, now in its fourth edition, familiarly known as WISC IV. This is the most widely used intelligence test in this country. There is an adult version also, the Wechsler Adult Intelligence Scale (WAIS), also in its fourth edition. Both of these have been adapted for the United Kingdom, with norms derived from populations in that jurisdiction. The UK version is preferred in this country. Other Intelligence tests include the British Ability Scales, the Stanford-Binet intelligence Test and the Woodcock-Johnson® Tests of Cognitive Abilities. There are some differences in the way in which they subdivide the 'factors' of intelligence but the final result is to produce an overall Intelligence Quotient (IQ) score.

The psycho-educational assessment by itself is not adequate for all situations. It does not provide sufficient information about use of language, visual-motor movement or attention control if these are suspected to be specific areas of weakness. These will need to be assessed by specialists in these areas. What the psycho-educational assessment does give is a very good picture of a person's learning potential at that time.

Test Results

This section of the report describes the results of the tests administered. IQ tests are constructed in such a way that each subtest consists of a number of items that are ranged in order from easy to difficult. Thus the same test can be used for all ages, except that, the older the children are, the more items they are expected to complete.

When IQ tests are being constructed, they are piloted on very large numbers of children. As a result, it is possible to ascertain a level of functioning which is average for each age group. It then becomes possible to describe a child's level of intelligence as being in the average, high average, or low average range. These categories relate to what might be expected in a general population and the terms relate to how the scores fall along the Normal Distribution Curve.

The Normal Distribution Curve is a statistical concept based on the fact that if a normal population of people, chosen at random, were tested, their scores would fall across a range of scores according to a very specific pattern. This pattern, or distribution, applies to any normal population. On a graph the results form an even curve which is called the Normal Distribution Curve. In terms of scores, the range along the curve is from approximately 40 to 130+ . A score of 100 is considered to be the mid-point of the curve. The largest occurrence of scores will fall between the scores of 90 and 109. Half the population might be expected to obtain scores in this range. Hence this is designated as the **average** range. Scores on either side of the curve will be designated **above** or **below** average.

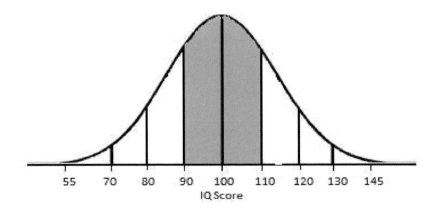

Diagram 1. The Normal Distribution Curve

Full Scale IQ scores, index scores and standard scores are all calculated in terms of the Normal Distribution Curve. The full range of scores along the curve is divided into **descriptive categories** that relate to the percentage of a population that might be expected to achieve similar scores. These are set out below.

Table 1: Normal Distribution Curve Scores, Population Percentages and Descriptive Range

IQ Score	% of population	Descriptive range
130 and above	2%	Exceptionally high
120-129	7%	High
110-119	16%	High Average
90-109	50%	Average
80-89	16%	Low Average
70-79	7%	Low
Below 70	2%	Exceptionally low

When reading the report it is well to remember that the term **range** is broader than **score** and allows the test results to be interpreted more realistically. It allows for a margin of error on the day, given that both the psychologist and the child are fallible beings!

Scores can also be calculated as **Percentiles**. Percentile scores range from 1 to 100. They calculate where, in a typical group of 100 children of the same age, the child would be placed in terms of achievement on a particular task, group of tasks and ability. Thus the child placed at the 90th percentile will achieve as well or better than 90 children out of the 100. Similarly, if the child is at the 45th percentile, achievement will be as good or better than 45 in the group of 100.

Most reports also quote **Scaled Scores**. These refer to the scores which are obtained on the individual subtests. For example the WISC Verbal Comprehension Index is obtained by administering the Vocabulary, Similarities and Comprehension subtests. Each subtest is marked on a scale 1 to 19. The mid-point on this scale is 10. Average is in the range 8-12. Any scaled score above 12 is above average. Any score below 8 is below average. As scores approach the score of 19, this is an indication of increasing strength of ability. Similarly as scores approach 1, they are indicators of increasing difficulty. The scaled scores are added up and converted to obtain the Index scores. Scaled scores are calculated for each age group. If a child aged eight years and five months gets ten items correct, a scaled score of fifteen is attained, but if a child of twelve years and three months gets those same ten items complete, the scaled score will be considerably less, because the expectation is that the older child will have more knowledge or developed ability.

The WISC, as do most of the major intelligence tests, draws on the Cattell-Horn-Carroll (CHC) theory of cognitive abilities, which recognises there is a fairly large number of distinct abilities in cognitive functioning which can be grouped together and measured. The fourth edition of the Wechsler tests does this under **four headings** or **Indexes**: Verbal Comprehension, Perceptual Reasoning, Working Memory and Processing Speed. In terms of scores, each of these Indexes is the sum of scores on a number of **subtests**.

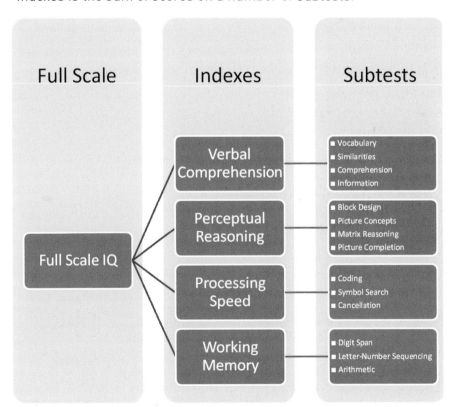

Full Scale IQ score is obtained from the combined Indexes scores.

From this section of the report it is possible to get a good idea of where the child's strengths lie and also where there may be a need to develop abilities. It gives an idea of the relative strengths of the different 'factors'. This is pertinent information. Teaching methods will be more successful when a child's strengths are used to best effect and when weaknesses are recognised and remediation put in place. It is through the strengths a child will be able to make good progress, maintain self-confidence and learn ways around the difficulty. For children with dyslexia part of the valuable information is also to identify weaknesses so that one can work to turn weaknesses into strengths.

Working Memory and Processing Speed are likely to be weak areas on the profile of children with dyslexia. On the other hand many people with dyslexia often have highly developed visual spatial and reasoning abilities. Language may be well developed in some, while very weak in others. The Index scores give very good indications of the child's cognitive development. The individual subtest scores on their own are less reliable as indicators of an area of ability or disability. At the same time, as research uncovers more information about the differences in dyslexic processing, test instruments are becoming more refined and better able to identify these areas.

The following is typical of the kind of table of results to be found in a report, where the WISC has been administered.

Table 2: Example of Table of Results on WISC

	IQ/Index Scores	Percentile	Confidence Interval 90%	Descriptive Range
Full Scale IQ	94	34	88-100	Average
Verbal Comprehension	102	55	99-105	Average
Perceptual Organisation	105	58	100-106	Average
Working Memory	90	25	90-97	Average
Processing Speed	88	21	85-92	Low Average

A table of the subtest scores is given below. Remember that a scaled score between 8-12 falls in the Average range.

Table 3: Example of Table of Subtest Results on WISC

Verbal Comprehension	scaled score	Perceptual Reasoning	scaled score
Vocabulary	08	Picture Completion	11
Similarities	11	Matrix Reasoning	09
Information	07	Block Design	14

Working Memory	Scaled score.	Processing Speed	Scaled score
Digit Span	09	Coding	06
Letter-Number Sequencing	08	Symbol Search	09
Arithmetic	07		

Attainments

The term attainments refers to the levels of reading, spelling and numeracy that the child has attained. This section of the report contains analysis of tests of word recognition, spelling, reading comprehension and word attack skills. It is possible for the psychologist to check from statistics the reading and mathematical scores that are appropriate for each ability and age level.

As with the IQ tests, literacy and numeracy test scores have been standardised. This means they have been tried out on large numbers of children across all sections of a society. In this way it becomes possible to say what the average child of any given age should be able to read, spell and calculate. The results of these literacy and numeracy tests are quoted in standard scores. These are similar to IQ scores in that a standard score of 100 is the mid-point of the **Average** range.

Attainment tests results are also often quoted in age equivalents. This means, instead of giving a standard score, the report records a reading age. While reading ages are useful, they can also be very misleading. Usually reading ability corresponds to level of intellectual functioning. Thus, a child of age six with an average IQ would be expected to have a reading age of six years. But if the child's ability is above or below average, the reading age may not be the same as the chronological age. A six year-old child with an IQ of 115 would be expected to have a reading age of seven years.

It is possible to predict from an IQ score what standard score in the attainment tests could be expected from a child at any particular age. If there is a **significant** gap/discrepancy between the predicted score and the score attained on the day's testing, which cannot be explained by any other cause such as a long absence from school on account of illness, then a diagnosis of dyslexia is most likely.

Significant means that the discrepancy is **unusually** wide. Some discrepancy is allowed for but there are cut-off points beyond which the psychologist concludes that this discrepancy needs to be explained by more than the usual variations found among children of this age. This ability/attainment discrepancy has long been an important feature in the diagnosis of dyslexia. It is not without controversy but it is used widely to help diagnose dyslexia by most education authorities in Ireland, the United States and Britain.

One would expect children's discrepancy to become less significant as they become better able to read. Many children retain a discrepancy but the important point to make is that they are also maintaining progress if the discrepancy does not become wider. Modern interpretations in the diagnosis of dyslexia look at the pattern of abilities and deficits on a person's profile as a surer guide than a discrepancy or than a discrepancy alone. However, the discrepancy is still used widely by most education authorities, included in their definitions for the purposes of access to learning support, reasonable accommodations in examinations and exemption from the study of Irish.

While scores and reading ages are necessary, it should also be remembered that at every assessment the psychologist is looking at how the child is functioning. This is a much more important question than what score does the child achieve. Scores in themselves are very inadequate descriptions of a child's learning ability and potential. The purpose of the assessment is to make recommendations to improve the child's way of learning. Thus attainment scores should be read in conjunction with a description of **how** the child is reading or writing.

The types of reading tests given may vary according to the age of the child. With older children the psychologist needs to assess their reading rate as well as accuracy. It is necessary to check out how automatically children can sound out a letter, a syllable and a polysyllabic word. These are called word-attack skills and testing is usually done by asking children to read nonsense words, which are made of patterns similar to real words. This ensures that children are not reading from the memory of a word but can actually relate sound with symbol and patterns of symbols. The reading test checks children's ease of word recognition and a reading comprehension exercise checks how efficiently they can read sentences and if they are using context to read. The end goal of learning to read is being able to use and enjoy reading. Comprehension, then, is an important factor to measure, as is reading speed. Reading speed affects comprehension if it is slow and staccato. Language difficulties also impair comprehension. If word recognition and understanding of punctuation and syntax are impaired, comprehension is likely to be reduced.

The assessment also tests the child's spelling knowledge. The advantage of standardised tests which are not in general use in school is that they test the child's long-term memory of spelling of words which are in familiar usage but not directly related to the day's or week's classroom activities. Passages of free writing and dictation may also be given to see if knowledge of spelling transfers to these activities. Writing speed is an important piece of information about the older children and is essential when looking at their need for supports in examinations or at third level.

Tests of level of numeracy may or may not be included in every assessment. The general ability subtests include an oral arithmetic test which gives some indication of the child's understanding of number and numerical operations. Of course, if maths is an area of difficulty in school or when doing homework, this should be reported to the psychologist in the initial interview. Today there is much greater awareness of difficulties with mathematics. Some of these relate to difficulties of language or memory. Others are more deep-seated, relating to the whole concept of number. This is a learning disability called dyscalculia and is distinct from dyslexia, although it may co-exist with dyslexia.

Phonological Awareness, Sequencing, Laterality, Directionality.
Further sections in the report may discuss other abilities such as phonological awareness, sequencing, laterality and directionality. Investigating these throws much light on aspects of the child's abilities. These are often areas of difficulty which can be indicative of dyslexia, though not peculiar to dyslexia only, it must be added.

Phonological awareness is the ability to break down words into separate sounds, to play with sounds, to recognise similar sounds in words, to exchange sounds, to add and subtract sounds from words such as *slight/sight* and to hear the difference. Difficulties in the area of phonological awareness are now recognised as one of the core features of dyslexia. As noted elsewhere, phonological awareness predates the study of phonics.

Tests of memory such as reciting the order of the days of the week, months of the year, arithmetical tables and the alphabet are recorded as sequencing ability.

Laterality refers to which hand, foot or eye a child uses in preference to the other. Sometimes the child may not yet have established dominance. With others there may be cross-laterality. They use right hand and foot but left eye. Recognising this may be important for the direction their eye follows when presented with tasks such as reading.

Directionality is noted in the report when the psychologist refers to the child's ability to identify direction such as right/left.

Summary and Recommendations
The final section of the report states the conclusion at which the psychologist has arrived and the recommendations made in the light of the child's needs. These recommendations should be incorporated into the school's plan for the child. Recommendations will fall into several categories:

Changes that need to be implemented at the **systemic level** such as:

- Put learning support in place;
- Apply for place in a reading unit;
- Look for an exemption from the study of Irish;
- Apply for reasonable accommodations in examinations.

Further investigation of difficulties such as a **referral to other specialists** such as occupational therapists, or clinical psychologists. Apart from recommendations for remediation at school and implementation at home, the psychologist may recommend that specialists in other areas are consulted in order to investigate further some issues raised by the assessment. Dyslexia is only one of a number of learning difficulties. There tend to be a number of these difficulties which co-exist. Some dyslexic children may have aspects of dyspraxia or attention deficit disorder or Asperger's syndrome. In this case it will be necessary to make an appointment with the relevant specialists. The psycho-educational assessment may well be only the first of a number of assessment procedures. The diagnosis of Attention Deficit Disorder is usually made in a medical context. Dyspraxia is identified through occupational therapy. Some children require speech and language assessments.

Interventions for implementation at school level. This is usually the longest section. A psychologist aims to direct the learning support teacher about the elements to be included in an intervention programme, the methods to use and sometimes useful resources. Recommendations may also target areas beyond the academic difficulties such as social or emotional development and what programmes or exercises are helpful.

Interventions for implementation at home. The report is not only for the school. There are many ways a child's abilities can be developed at home in a less formal way through games and family activities (See Chapter 5). The report and the recommendations should be read carefully and a home plan of action drawn up which complements what will happen at school. This is where working very closely with the school is the best approach. Parents are not expected to take on the role of teacher and the school cannot substitute for the emotional and practical support only a parent can give to the child. Parents and teachers can help one another by

- Sharing information;
- Reinforcing lessons;
- Creating structures;
- Negotiating volume of work;
- Making sure that all the other aspects of the child's life are being developed.

The psycho-educational assessment is the most accurate way to identify learning difficulties at this time. It is not infallible. Remember, no test instrument is perfect. The psychologist will encourage children to do the best they can and to be at ease. However, both child and psychologist can be influenced by such factors as tiredness, anxiety or even environmental factors such as the noise level, time of day or the comfort of surroundings. In the assessment procedure one tries as much as possible to keep these external variables to a minimum. The language used to introduce the various subtests is laid down by the test constructors so that the instructions given to a child do not vary from psychologist to psychologist. There are time rules for many of the items. When these have been observed to the best ability of child and psychologist, the assessment is deemed to be valid. In the end, the judgements made and conclusions arrived at are, at best, good estimations based on reliable test materials, the psychologist's knowledge and experience and how the child presented on the day. Children develop and the next time an assessment is carried out the picture may be different.

Review of Progress

In the primary school, once the child has had dyslexia identified through assessment, it should happen as a matter of course that an individual profile and learning programme (IPLP) will be set up, in which case review of progress will be part of this programme. The difficulty may be that, in some cases where a child does not receive additional support, this may not happen and the main testing in school may be through the standard end of year tests. In reality the child would benefit from a more detailed assessment of gains and losses over the year and this needs a more diagnostic review. The learning support and resource teachers can do this by administering an individual test to the child. However, a parent may still wish to have a review carried out by the psychologist. A full re-assessment is not always necessary.

At second level the student's needs are different from those in primary school. However, there is need to continue to identify these as the child goes through the school system. The progress of students should be discussed regularly with their teachers. If a review cannot be facilitated in school, a specialist tutor or the psychologist who made the diagnosis could be asked to review progress.

Reassessment

Some people like to have their children re-assessed regularly. In general, a full re-assessment should be necessary only at critical points in the child's academic career. It may be advisable before transferring from primary to secondary school, particularly if the first assessment was carried out when the child was in first or second class. Profiles tend to change as the child becomes older.

A recent assessment (one less than three years old) must be available when applying for the Disability Access Route to Education (DARE) for entry to third level colleges. It is advisable to have a recent assessment when applying for reasonable accommodations in the Leaving Certificate. Other than on these occasions a full assessment should only be considered in the light of individual cases.

Questions Following the Assessment

After the assessment these are some questions which may arise for parents.

How am I likely to respond when my suspicions that my child has a learning difficulty are confirmed by the psychologist?

For most people knowing is more comfortable than not knowing, even if it means one is in for the 'long haul' and that there are no 'quick fixes'. The essential facts about you and your child have not changed. You have always lived with a child who learns in a definite way. What is going to change is the way that learning style must be accommodated in the family and in the classroom. You and the family members will probably need to learn more about dyslexia. As already suggested, you will have to work even more closely with teachers. You may have to find out what additional supports may be available in and outside school. You may have worries about how other people will accept and deal with the idea that your child has dyslexia. Knowledge and information are the best tools for countering fears. Fortunately discussion about dyslexia is much more in the public domain now, so one can expect greater acceptance and understanding in society. The video/ CD/ROM *Understanding Dyslexia*[4] should further heighten awareness and understanding.

How am I going to explain to my child what dyslexia is?

Your child already knows that learning is a struggle when many in the class group are speeding ahead. How much you can tell children depends to a degree on their level of understanding and psychological readiness. In general it is better for you to explain in a positive way before somebody else does, perhaps in not so supportive an environment. Dyslexia is about different ways of learning. Your child has strengths, not only those which were assessed but many others which were not included in assessment. What is essential is that you remain positive: positive about your child's ability and potential and the long-term outcomes, about your ability to provide guidance and to encourage your child to grow in confidence. There are available some stories and films about children who discovered they had dyslexia, which will appeal to children, such as *Tom's Great Talent*[5] and *It's Called Dyslexia*[6], which can be used to talk through the diagnosis. Both are available from the Dyslexia Association of Ireland.

How do I explain to the child's brothers and sisters?

As with the child, the more siblings are encouraged to respect difference, the more they understand. Dyslexia should be presented not so much emphasising the difficulties but allowing the child with dyslexia to demonstrate abilities. It is necessary to reinforce the knowledge that everyone has **disabilities,** just as they have abilities. They may need to understand that the ability to learn to read and write at an early age is not the only, or the most important, aspect of being a capable person.

Standardised Testing in Schools

Standardised testing is very much part of monitoring of progress of students at primary school. Parents would expect to receive a report card detailing how their child has performed in relation to national averages. Tests such as Micra-T and Drumcondra Test are standard in all schools. They can cause considerable distress to pupils with dyslexia, not least because they encourage comparisons with their peers.

However it is important to realise that there are very real limitations to the use of standardised testing for students with dyslexia.

Standardised tests are tests given under very strict conditions. The purpose of each test is to give a result which shows how a student achieved in relation to the population of students of the same age and sex. This is done by comparing the result to norms that have been researched. Standardised tests in use in Irish schools include the Micra T tests, Drumcondra Tests, Differential Aptitude Tests (DATS), AH2 and AH4. These tests do not give information of reading achievement relative to cognitive ability and academic potential.

For some of these tests timing is critical. Students are not meant to finish the test in the time allocated. The score is derived from how far they get through the test in the time allotted. In other tests the time is not so important. The allotted time is so generous that the vast majority of students will have answered all the questions with plenty of time to spare.

It is worth noting that the Public Appointments Service allows applicants with dyslexia additional time when taking standardised testing for recruitment and promotion purposes.

It may be difficult to get an accurate result on such tests for the student with dyslexia for the following reasons:

- Students may be slower in processing information. Here is an example based on the DATS (Differential Aptitude Testing). There is a generous time allowance for completing all but one section of the DATS. The vast majority of students finish the questions well within the time allotted. On the Numerical Reasoning section the student completed twenty-seven out of the forty questions consecutively and then ran out of time. All of his answers to that point were correct. It was obvious that with more time this student would have completed more questions and obtained a higher score. His result is different to the student who has completed the full forty questions within the allotted time and got thirteen incorrect. Yet both students will be given the same result.

- These students may be slower in reading the instructions or in deciphering the sequence of instructions. This is critically important in maths testing. Here is an example of a maths question from a standardised test.

  John spends three times as much as Michael on bus fares each week and Michael spends three times as much as Martin. If John spends 45p, how much does Martin spend?

  For some students with dyslexia such a question is more a test of their English skills than their maths abilities. They may need time to work out what the words mean and to interpret the sequence of instructions correctly. This makes their work much slower and sometimes they may not successfully decode what it is they are meant to do.

■ They may lack the vocabulary to be able to do the task required. An example from another standardised test is as follows. It is a test of the student's ability to classify. They have to choose the odd one out from a series of words such as the following: **Butcher, vicar, grocer, baker**. The students are given forty such problems, and a limited amount of time in which to answer. No student is expected to complete the entire test. The score is based on how far they progress in the test. Lack of vocabulary and slowness in decoding the words on the page can slow down answering of students with dyslexia.

It is important that parents, students and teachers realise the limitations and unreliability of these tests for students with dyslexia and other learning difficulties. **They are not valid predictors of the student's ability**. For students with dyslexia the psychological assessment is a far more valid instrument for assessing their ability.

At primary level, no critical decisions are made based on standardised tests. However the results could affect the child's self image. Despite being told not to, students do compare the results achieved. Therefore it is important that the child understands the results are not reliable. Also, if teachers have not received training on the topic of learning difficulties, they also may form expectations of the child based on the results of standardised testing and not see the child's real potential. This is why it is so important that the psychological assessment report is brought into school and the student's profile with its strengths and weaknesses is discussed with the teacher.

Far more important is the fact that these tests may be used at entrance assessment at second-level. Crucial decisions may be based on the student's performance in entrance assessment such as class placement and selection of options. Students who are placed in weaker classes due to a poor result in an entrance examination may find that taking subjects at higher level is not open to them. This will have major consequences later in second level and affect results in both Junior and Leaving Certificate and, therefore, points in the CAO system.

Standardized tests of attainment for classroom use may be useful as baseline measures at seven years of age, and as measures of progress made, at eleven years of age. They may identify teaching/learning targets met or not met but they present real difficulties for the learning disabled child. As not all low achievers are learning disabled, under this system there will continue to be the possibility of confusing dyslexic difficulties with low achievement. Therefore the importance of full psycho-educational assessment should not be underestimated.

Interventions in the home

The following are some activities that can be used when a particular subtest score is lower than expected or average or when one wishes to develop what may be a strength on a child's profile.

Verbal Abilities – Vocabulary

- Familiarity with and rapid recall of the names of everyday items, such as pictures;
- Matching words and pictures;
- Classification exercises such as picking the odd one out;
- Use headings and ask the child for naming words, 'doing' words etc.;
- Describing an object, 'Show and Tell';
- Retelling stories which have been listened to;
- Games based on naming things that are the same or different; use of thesaurus and dictionary, synonyms and antonyms, charades;
- Word games, Scrabble, crossword puzzles, Hangman, Card games with sight vocabulary - When children draw a card, they have to talk about the word;
- Meaning of prefixes, suffixes; finding words within a word.

Verbal Abilities - Similarities and classification/concepts

- Matching pictures that have similar features: How are they alike? How are they different? Explain in own language. Repeat with sound. Tabulate in chart;
- Games with homonyms and synonyms: look up word, say it. Second child has to supply similar or different word;

- Cloze procedure orally e.g. January is the first, December is the —————-- They are both —————————;
- Classification: supply heading, child must supply the name of an item;
- Recognising concepts. Have discussions and reading material that explore more abstract ideas such as love, hate, success, failure, conservation, global village.

Verbal Abilities - Comprehension

- Activities that encourage understanding of working together and understanding the 'other' and social norms;
- Role play;
- Discussing stories;
- Reading about people in public and community services e.g. police, firemen nurses, teachers;
- 'What if...' games that bring out the consequences of behaviour.

Non-Verbal Abilities – Block Design

- Work from the concrete to the abstract;
- Copying exercises;
- Making large shapes from group of different shapes (including letters made of lines, half circles etc. words are shapes also - Indicate relationship between parts;
- Colouring letters;
- Copying from model;
- Find hidden figures in larger designs;
- Word searches;
- Separate real words from non-words;
- Making words from syllables or sentences from words;
- Making models, costumes etc.;
- Classification exercises with materials and words.

Non-Verbal Abilities - Matrix Reasoning

- Sequencing exercises;
- Spot the Difference exercises;

- Drawing by Number games;
- Word wheels;
- Use road map to plan a journey, pointing out interesting features along the way.

Non-Verbal Abilities - Picture Concepts

- Use general classification e.g. Animal, Vegetable, Mineral – have a collection of pictures -child must pick out a specified group e.g. cats, made of iron etc. This can be played in the reverse. The child must name categories of pictures that share a common feature such as a common use such as a candle and a lamp.
- Pictures can be used to develop abstract concepts such as transportation, travel, or good and bad.
- Books can be classified under types of writing such as biography, science, travel, fiction.

Non-Verbal Abilities - Processing Speed

- Setting time targets – use with caution!
- Good handwriting;
- Making associations e.g. pictures, tunes, salient feature;
- Skimming and scanning techniques.

Working Memory

While Susan Gathercole[7] has stated that 'We have no direct evidence that general working memory capacity can be improved by training in low memory children', the following strategies may help:

- Make a list of the different ways child can learn new word/new concept such as picture association, writing on computer, using it in crossword, applying it in different contexts, checking dictionary/thesaurus, and discuss it.
- Develop child's own strategies...ask them;
- Using markers and colour coding;
- Training to have a system and order of activity e.g. come in, sit down, take out book, relax;
- Unspoken code such as pointing to spot or gesture in order to draw attention back;

■ Working to pattern: Do five sentences. Take a break. Another five sentences. Another break.

Non-teaching Interventions

In Chapter 1 the theoretical explanations for dyslexia were examined. The advent of neuro-imaging has proved to be an important means of exploration. Neuroscience in education is the new and exciting discipline. However, while new sites where language, oral and written, are processed can be observed within the structure of the brain, there is still a considerable gap between the knowledge which has been gained and the knowledge needed about what procedures actually remediate and change the patterns when there are deficits/differences in some areas. There is a constant bombardment by commercial interests which claim, to greater or lesser degree, that their product or plan, if followed, will make significant improvement in the competencies of the person with dyslexia. Consequently, this section is included so the parents may be aware of the range of interventions. While some interventions may be of benefit to some individuals, the research evidence is not yet decisive about why this benefit happens and if it does allow one to read and write with greater ease.

Each of the main causal theories (see Chapter 1) has given rise to the development of practical programmes of intervention. Many of these address aspects of functioning other than the activity of reading and writing. They may be considered as non-teaching interventions, to differentiate them from the traditional process of learning to read and write in school. They do not replace it. Most claim that, by providing additional stimulus and a systematic programme that develops an aspect of the child's functioning, their therapy also results in improved literacy skills. The level of scientific research upon which they base their claims is a crucial factor in evaluating the possible efficacy of any one particular programme.

Dyslexia is a complex syndrome. People with dyslexia will have a range of difficulties along a continuum of degree of difficulty. The particular programme may have very beneficial results for the child in improving perhaps visual perception or motor skills. When these skills improve, they may well contribute to a greater reading readiness for a host of reasons such as increased one-to-one time with parents. What is not clear is the link with dyslexia. It is important to remember that developmental dyslexia is a condition the effects of which can be ameliorated, but usually is a life-long part of self.

Reading is a secondary, not a primary skill. This means it is a taught skill for all people and thus, while non-teaching interventions can help some children who have deficits in particular areas of processing, they will still continue to need great support and informed teaching methods to allow them to become expert readers and writers.

There are a number of types of interventions, each emanating from a particular theoretical viewpoint, not all of which have been proven by sound scientific research.

Interventions Based on Neuro-Developmental Delay
Many children with developmental dyslexia are clumsy and have difficulty with co-ordination and, in particular, with fine motor control. Several kinds of therapies have emerged that claim that specific learning difficulties are related to delay in attaining developmental milestones and omission of developmental steps such as crawling and poor sensory-motor development. One group of interventions is based on the theory that certain primary reflexes may not have been inhibited as the child develops, resulting in a variety of difficulties, many of which are observed in children with dyslexia. The scientific evidence of the relationship between such neuro-developmental delay and dyslexia is not yet available. One research group in TCD Smyth and Doyle (2003), for example, found no evidence of a link between 'retained primary reflexes' and dyslexia.

As one would expect, interventions based on these theories focus on remediating fluency of movement, blocking primary reflexes, integrating sensory co-ordination and improving balance. There are a number of such therapies available in Ireland and Britain. There is no doubt that many children benefit from such programmes, as other children benefit from, say, speech and language development programmes or counselling.

Vision Therapies
There are a significant number of persons with dyslexia who experience significant difficulty with visual processing when reading. When developmental dyslexia was first being researched, Orton called it 'strephosymbolia', which means a mixing up of symbols. The

classic caricature of how a person with dyslexia writes is with inversions and reversals of letters. This characterisation of dyslexia focused on the visual aspects of processing. Later researchers have categorised dyslexia as **deep** when phonological difficulties are particularly pronounced and as **surface or eidetic** when visual processing difficulties are to the fore. Some therapies specifically address visual processing difficulties. There is no doubt that some people with dyslexia experience difficulty maintaining smooth eye movement across the page and moving from line to line. Poor visual memory for letter patterns is not uncommon. Some people experience light sensitivity and respond better to background colour other than white and print colour other than black. A significant number have difficulty with visual perception, which may suggest the presence of co-existing dyspraxia.

Helen Irlen[8] developed a method of testing for what was called **scotopic sensitivity**, later known as Irlen Syndrome and now called visual stress. Subsequent studies have identified visual differences that can be alleviated by the use of coloured lenses or acetate overlays. Visual stress is not unique to persons with dyslexia

There are many unanswered questions around the area of visual processing and there is much ongoing research attempting to address them. John Stein's magnocellular theory, which implicates visual processing, is currently one of the most influential of the causal theories of dyslexia and because reading must of necessity be a visual as well as an auditory process, it is not unexpected to find programmes which also concentrate on developing visual memory and other visual processes. But visual and auditory processing have been shown to be jointly implicated in the reading process, so it is unlikely that targeting one only of the channels will effect the necessary change in neural pathways and connections.

Auditory Therapies
The third category of interventions addresses the auditory and phonological deficits that are seen as core indicators of **deep** dyslexia. These include programmes aimed at auditory stimulation through music and structured listening techniques. They may help to some degree to attune the ear more readily to rhythms and sound. One leading neuroscientist, Prof. Usha Goswami[9] has carried out detailed research on how people with dyslexia hear the opening sound of a

word and has measured the rise and fall pattern of sound in words. This is a function of phonological processing. As with the above, there is a need for more scientific research to demonstrate the effectiveness of these therapies.

Nutrition and Diet

A fourth category of alternative therapies uses the information derived from research into the relationship between diet and brain functioning. There is a body of research that has been examining the role of essential fatty acids (EFAs) and highly unsaturated fatty acids (HUFAs) in brain function. There appears to be a higher than average level of deficiency of essential fatty acids (omega three) among many people who have dyslexia, and/or dyspraxia and attention deficit disorder. Dr Alex Richardson[10] (Oxford) has presented very thorough research findings on the beneficial effects of taking fish oil supplements. It should be pointed out as well that many people, not only people with dyslexia, benefit from increasing their intake of Omega 3. A balanced diet, rich in natural sources of omega oils such as oily fish (salmon, tuna and mackerel) and vegetable oils and seeds (sunflower, flax/linseed, pumpkin and sesame) may be all that is needed. Prof. John Stein[11] argues that increased function in the cerebellum resulting from increased intake of fish oils, for example, does minimise some of the difficulties of dyslexia.

Combined Teaching/Other Therapies

Some interventions combine theory-based therapy with teaching. These include techniques to develop speed-reading and the ability to visualise.

Parents and teachers often ask about specific information technology programmes. Because of the possibilities that neuroscientific data has opened up and with the explosion of technology as a channel for learning, it is not surprising that new programmes are coming on the market regularly. A number of well researched programmes aimed at improving working memory, for example, are available, though in each case the trial populations have been somewhat limited in number and questions such as 'Does the improvement maintain over time?' have not been fully answered.

Programmes to develop phonological, reading and writing skills have proliferated and offer good support to the learner, in attractive and modern formats. These programmes are as good as the way in which they are used. There is no fail-safe programme that will 'cure' dyslexia. Programmes of remediation need to be individualised and the work needs to be directed, to ensure maximum benefit from the programme.

All programmes come with a warning to proceed with caution and circumspection. Many of these will cite neuroscientific evidence for their programme. The commercial interests promoting these programmes may sometimes result in exaggerated claims being made for their efficacy. In reality, at present, while great strides have been made in neuroscience in education, claims for training the brain in specific areas may not be fully justified by sufficiently rigorous or widespread testing. Besides, there still remains a gap between neuroscience, particularly what has been learnt of the processes of reading and writing through neuroimaging, and programmes that positively account for improvements in literacy. The brain is a complex organ and reading and writing are very complex activities. To do either activity, multiple sites and networks in the brain are implicated. The brain processes information in an integrated way, so that no one area acts independently and thus cannot be responsible for either of these activities. There is still a great deal of research to be carried out.

Good programmes are most likely to emerge through the dialogue between research scientists and effective classroom practitioners, whose success is evident. Working with children with dyslexia calls for increased attention to the individual, a programme of remediation that matches the child's profile, creative teaching, perseverance, an eclectic mix of strategies, multiple repetitions of a particular task and a lot of good common sense,

Alternative therapies and intensive programmes based on 'brain training', particularly ones that are directed by a tutor, can be expensive. When financial resources are limited it may be wise to consider whether a less expensive but more long-term support such as combined teaching and support software might be an equally good investment. It is wise to check out the claims independently before opting for an expensive course of action.

Because dyslexia affects a cluster of abilities and because each person's dyslexia is so individual, it is likely that any one of these therapies may address a particular area on the child's profile. The child may well benefit from what is on offer, sometimes not by improving their literacy or number skills specifically but by greater ease in using their senses. As a result, developed ability to listen and monitor attention should make staying on task easier. Movement exercises that make handwriting more fluid can be of great benefit to the child. Exercises to develop greater ocular control should certainly improve reading.

However, a particular course may not be needed by the child. In many cases good nutrition, good exercise and physical education programmes, more explicit listening exercises at home and the ordinary helps tailored a little more individually to your child may be just as beneficial. However, when exploring an alternative route, ask these relevant questions:

- Is there solid scientific evidence that this method is effective?
- What is the known link between the theory and dyslexia?
- Does this intervention claim to cure dyslexia?
- Is there evidence that the effects of the intervention persist into the long term and are not simple short-term improvements that disappear when the intervention stops?

In the words of Professor Rod Nicholson, when summing up the proceedings of the 2004 BDA International Conference on Dyslexia:

> There is growing (but still disputed) evidence that at least some dyslexic children benefit from non-reading support aimed at eliminating problems that make it especially hard for them to learn to read. These complementary approaches include dietary improvements, use of tinted lenses, elimination of primitive reflexes and use of exercise treatment. One can see them as trying to equip the climbers (children with dyslexia) with better footgear so that, whichever path they're on, they will climb more easily and more safely.

References

1. Department of Education and Science (2000) *Learning Support Guidelines*
2. Rose, J. (2009) *Identifying and Teaching Children and Young People with Dyslexia and Literacy Difficulties* Report presented to DCSF (UK)

3. Singleton, C. (2009) *Intervention for Dyslexia. A Review of Published Evidence on the Impact of Specialist Dyslexia Teaching*

4. Department of Education and Science (2004)   CD/DVD *Understanding Dyslexia*

5. Gaynor,K. (2009*)   Tom's Special Talent*   Dublin: Special Stories Publishing

6. Moore-Mallinos, J. *It's Called Dyslexia.* Dublin: O'Brien Press.

7. Gathercole, S.E. & Packiam Alloway, T. (2008) *Working Memory and Learning.* London: Sage Publications

8. Irlen, H., *Reading by the Colours ,(2001)*, Penguin Putman Pub.

9. Goswami, U. *Dyslexia Conference, University of London, June 2010.*

10. Richardson, A. (2006)   *Nutrition Practitioner.. Omega 3 for Child Behaviour, Learning and Mood: ADHD, Dyslexia, Dyspraxia, Autism and Related Conditions.*

11. Stein J. *World Dyslexia Forum, Unesco, Paris (2010)*

CHAPTER 3
PROVISION IN THE IRISH SCHOOL SYSTEM

In this chapter you will read about the provision for students with dyslexia in the Irish school system. Such provision includes:

- Educational legislation;
- State agencies;
- Government publications;
- Additional teaching support;
- Other supports.

Educational Legislation

The Education Act 1998
Among the provisions of this Act are the following:

- The school shall provide education for students appropriate to their abilities and needs.

- The school shall use its available resources to ensure the educational needs of all students, including those with a disability or other special educational need, are identified and provided for.

- The Board of Management of the school shall publish ... the policy of the school concerning admission to and participation in the school including the policy of the school relating to ... admission to and participation by students with disabilities or who have other special educational needs and ensure that, as regards that policy, principles of equality and the right of parents to send their children to a school of the parents' choice are respected.

- The Board of Management shall make arrangements for the preparation of a school plan. This plan shall state the objectives of the school relating to equality of access to and participation in the school and the measures the school proposes to take to achieve those objectives including equality of access and participation in the school by students with disabilities or who have other special educational needs.

A grievance procedure is set out in the Act. It provides that the parent of a student or, in the case of a student who is 18, the student may appeal against the decision of a teacher or other member of staff of a school. It also provides an appeal procedure when a student is permanently excluded from school or a school refuses to enrol a student. The parents have the right to appeal to the Secretary General of the Department of Education and Skills after they have been informed of the decisions by the school and have gone through any appeals procedure offered by the school.

The Education (Welfare) Act 2000

This Act safeguards every child's entitlement to an appropriate minimum education. It focuses particularly on causes of absenteeism. Included in its provisions are:

- The establishment of the National Educational Welfare Board, which has the lead role in implementing the Act. The Board deploys Educational Welfare Officers at local level who promote regular school attendance and prevent absenteeism and early school leaving. These officers focus in particular on children at risk who are experiencing difficulties in school with the purpose of resolving impediments to their regular attendance. Alternative schooling is sought for students who have been expelled, suspended or refused admittance to a school.

- School managers have the responsibility of adopting a pro-active approach to school attendance by maintaining a register of students and notifying the Educational Welfare Officer of particular problems in relation to attendance. They should also prepare and implement a school attendance strategy to encourage regular school attendance.

- The Act makes specific provision for the continuing education and training of young persons aged sixteen and seventeen years who leave school early to take up employment.

- The central role of parents in providing for their child's education is recognised. Parents should send their children to school on each school day or otherwise ensure they are receiving an appropriate minimum education. If the child is absent, the parents should notify the principal of the school of the reason for the absence.

The Education of Persons with Special Educational Needs Act 2004
This Act provides for the inclusive education for the child with special educational needs (SEN) in mainstream schooling. It defines a child with SEN as one who learns differently. This definition positively includes children with dyslexia. The Act set up the National Council for Special Education (NCSE). Among the duties of the Council are the following:

- To communicate to schools and parents information on best practice concerning the education of children with SEN;
- To plan and co-ordinate provision for the education and support services for children with SEN;
- To assess and review resources required for the educational provision for children with SEN.

The Council employs Special Educational Needs Organisers (SENOs) who give advice and assistance to schools. They have a role in planning an individual education plan (IEP) for the student with SEN in collaboration with the teachers and parents of the child. They decide on applications from schools for extra resources for students with SEN.

The Act sets out that if the principal of a school is of the opinion that a student is not benefiting from the educational programme provided in the school and that these difficulties arise from a special educational need, the principal, in consultation with the parents, shall arrange for an assessment of the student as soon as possible and not later than one month.

If the assessment establishes that the student has special educational needs, the principal, within one month of receipt of the assessment, will ensure an education plan for the student is drawn up. The contents of such a plan are specified in the Act. The principal should give parents and the SENO a copy of the plan.

The Council has the power to designate the school that a child with SEN is to attend and that school shall admit the child on being so directed by the Council. The Council has to take into account in making such a designation the needs of the child, the wishes of the child's parents and the capacity of the school to accommodate the child and to meet their needs.

The Act contains an appeals procedure for parents if they believe the special educational needs of their child are not being addressed.

When the Act was introduced in 2004 there was a five year time band given for its implementation. By 2009 only a few sections of the Act had been implemented. The key provisions remained unimplemented. The decision was taken in April 2009 to postpone indefinitely the implementation of the Act.   In the *Revised Programme for Government* agreed by the Green Party and Fianna Fail in October 2009, a commitment was given for the implementation of the Act, but now progress on its implementation will depend on the new Government in 2011.

State Agencies

National Educational Psychological Service (NEPS)
The National Educational Psychological Service was established in 1999 and is an executive agency of the Department of Education and Skills. The development plan for NEPS provides for the gradual expansion over a period of years, with the number of psychologists increasing to two hundred.

NEPS has been delegated authority to develop and provide an educational psychological service to all students in primary and post-primary schools and in certain other centres supported by the Department. NEPS provides the following services to schools:

- Consultation and casework about individual students;
- Work of a more preventive or developmental nature.

Each psychologist is responsible for a number of schools. The school authorities provide names of children who are giving cause for concern and discuss the relative urgency of each case during the psychologist's visit. This allows the psychologist to give priority to urgent cases. Where cases are less urgent, the psychologist, as a preliminary measure, acts as a consultant to teachers and parents, and offers advice about educational/behavioural plans and monitor progress. The psychologist is also involved in assessing students for reasonable accommodation in state examinations.

Until NEPS becomes adequately staffed, there will be a backlog of assessments. Priority is given to those students in greatest need. As a result there may be waiting lists. Consequently many parents opt for private assessments. Tax relief was introduced on the fees paid on private assessments. This is claimed by using the MED 1 form.

The NEPS website is found on the Department of Education and Skills website: www.education.ie.

Special Education Support Service (SESS)

The aim of the service is to enhance the quality of teaching and learning with particular reference to the education of children with special needs. It is targeted at teachers in mainstream primary and post-primary schools as well as special schools.

SESS provides this service through the following initiatives:

- It provides teachers with professional development. An example of such support is subsidising the cost of on-line training courses offered by ICEP Europe on topics such as dyslexia, ADHD, autism and inclusion;
- The provision of in-service training on special education topics;
- Telephone and on-line query service;
- Local Initiative Schemes, where schools can apply for assistance to meet their needs on special education. This assistance may be financial, professional or advisory.

The SESS website is www.sess.ie. It is a comprehensive website offering information on categories of special needs, resources available, courses available, latest developments in special education and a quick reference to official documents such as Department of Education and Skills circulars and legislation on the topic of Special Education.

National Council for Special Education (NCSE)

The National Council for Special Education was set up under the Education of Persons with Special Education Needs Act 2004. The details of the work of the Council were outlined at the beginning of this chapter in the section on the Education of Persons with Special Educational Needs Act. The NCSE website is www.ncse.ie.

Government Publications

Report of the Task Force on Dyslexia

In 2000 a Task Force on Dyslexia was set up whose brief was to examine the current range of educational provision and support services available to children with specific reading disabilities in Ireland, to assess the adequacy of current educational provision and support services and to make recommendations for the development of policy approaches, educational provision and support services.

The report was completed in 2001 and published on the Department of Education and Skills website at www.education.ie. The Task Force looked for submissions from the public and received 399 written submissions. The Task Force also decided to look for oral submissions from the public. This recognised the fact that some individuals with dyslexia would find it easier to make an oral submission than a written one. Adverts quoting a free telephone number were made on the radio. As a result 896 oral submissions were received.

The Task Force gave a definition of dyslexia that recognised the broad range of difficulties which arise from the condition and which also took into account recent research findings. It is a common misperception of dyslexia that it has to do only with reading and spelling and so this definition is very useful as it acknowledges the wide range of difficulties that may be present.

A welcome statement in the report is that 'each student with learning difficulties arising from dyslexia should receive a level of provision appropriate to his/her needs'. The Task Force recommended that since the difficulties presented by students with dyslexia range along a continuum from mild to severe, there is a need for a continuum of interventions and other services.

The Task Force suggested a scheme that would involve class teacher, learning support teacher and parents working in co-operation to support the child. The role and contribution of parents is emphasised throughout the report.

The first recommendation of the report was that appropriate printed and electronic material on dyslexia be distributed to all schools. This has resulted in the publication of the video/CD ROM/DVD *Understanding Dyslexia.*

Understanding Dyslexia Video/CD ROM/DVD
This video/CD ROM/DVD is a joint initiative of the Departments of Education in Ireland, North and South, and was issued to all schools in 2005.

- The video has eight sections and features professionals, parents, students and adults with dyslexia. This is a very good introduction to the topic of dyslexia in Ireland. Topics covered include the signs and facts about dyslexia, recognition of dyslexia, interventions and how parents and teachers can help.
- The CD ROM is a comprehensive and invaluable resource for teachers, other professionals dealing with dyslexia, parents and students. The contents are too extensive to list here, but to give some idea the following are included:
  - The Task Force Report;
  - A discussion on the definition of dyslexia;
  - Advice and strategies for teachers, both primary and post-primary and for parents. These can be downloaded as booklets
  - A self-help section for the pupil;
  - Comprehensive listing of resources such as books, websites, tests and teaching materials.
- The DVD includes both the video and the information on the CD ROM.

Learning Support Guidelines

The *Learning Support Guidelines* were published by the Department of Education and Skills in 2000. The primary purpose of these guidelines is to provide practical guidance to teachers and parents on the provision of effective learning support to pupils with low achievement/learning difficulties. The guidelines address the following topics:

- The principles of good practice in the provision of learning support in schools;
- The need for a policy statement on the provision of learning support in the context of a whole-school plan;
- The adoption of a collaborative approach by those involved including the principal teacher, class teachers, the learning support teacher and the parents;
- Screening and identification of pupils, selection of pupils for supplementary teaching and evaluation of the progress of the pupil at the end of each term;
- Details of the individual profile and learning programme that should be drawn up for each pupil receiving additional help.

Post Primary Guidelines on Inclusion of Students with Special Educational Needs

These guidelines were published by the Department of Education and Skills in 2007. An important aspect of the policy of the Department is to support the development of inclusive school environments. The guidelines are a support to assist schools in the provision of appropriate education for these students.

The guidelines set out advice for school management and teachers in relation to the education of students with SEN in post primary school. Specific guidance is given on planning at the whole-school level and for the individual student. Suggestions are made about school organisation, teaching methodologies and teaching approaches that reflect best practice.

In Section 2 it discusses policies and procedures on attendance, enrolment, behaviour and discipline, bullying and transfer of students from primary to post-primary and from post-primary to post school settings. Also it discusses class placement arrangements such as mixed ability, streaming, or banding. It also discusses how to provide additional teaching for students, which could be provided through in-class support or withdrawal of the student from class.

Section 3 discusses the roles and functions of all those involved in the school from the board of management, the principal, the SEN support team, mainstream teachers, the resource teacher, year heads, guidance counsellor, class tutors, special needs assistants and parents.

Section 4 is devoted to planning for the student with SEN and detailed information on the individual education plan.

Section 5 is a very practical overview of how to teach in an inclusive school. It discusses and gives examples of different teaching approaches such as co-operative learning, peer-tutoring, active learning, multi-sensory instruction, the use of ICT and student involvement in their own learning.

Additional Teaching Support

The Department of Education and Skills provides additional teaching support for students with dyslexia in three different ways:

1. Extra teaching support through the provision of learning support or resource teaching;
2. Special classes attached to a mainstream school;
3. Special schools for children with specific learning difficulties.

This support is targeted at those students in greatest need as defined by the Department of Education and Skills criteria. As a result not all students with dyslexia qualify for such support. The *Report of the Task Force on Dyslexia* described dyslexia as occurring in a continuum from mild to severe. It recommended the adoption of a model of provision based on meeting the needs for each student. A continuum of interventions should be available to students matched to the severity and persistence of their learning difficulties.

Extra Teaching Support
The terms resource, learning support and remedial have been used to describe additional teaching support provided for children.

Resource teaching is granted based on an individual application for a child with special educational needs to the SENO for the school. Such applications have to be accompanied by relevant psycho-educational/medical reports.

Learning support teaching is provided to children with low achievement. It was formerly called remedial teaching. It does not need an individual application. Assessment for access to such help is done in school through the use of standardised testing. The *Learning Support Guidelines* state that when selecting pupils for such help, priority should be given to those who achieve scores that are at or below the 10th percentile on a standardised test of English reading or mathematics.

Increasingly the term special needs teacher is being used which describes both learning support and resource teaching.

The Department of Education and Skills Circulars SP ED 01/05 and SP ED 09/04 set out new arrangements for the allocation of special education resources at primary level. In May 2005 the then Minister for Education and Science, Mary Hanafin, announced further changes in the allocation of these resources. A weighted allocation has been introduced to cater for pupils with higher incidence special educational needs and those with learning support needs, i.e. those functioning at or below the 10th percentile on a standardised test of reading and/or mathematics. The circular states the higher incidence special educational needs are borderline mild general disability, mild general learning disability and specific learning difficulty.

The weighted system meant that special needs teaching posts are granted on the following basis:

- In all-boy schools the first special education teaching post at 135 pupils, a second post at 295 and so on;
- In mixed schools one post for 145 pupils, a second post at 315 pupils and so on;
- In all-girl schools the first post at 195 pupils, the second at 395 pupils and so on;
- In disadvantaged schools the first post at 80 pupils, the second at 160 pupils and so on;
- There was also increased provision made for smaller schools.

In addition there are specific allocations in respect of pupils with low incidence disabilities. The low incidence disabilities include physical impairment, hearing impairment, visual impairment, emotional disturbance, severe emotional disturbance, autism, autistic spectrum difficulties, moderate general learning disability and specific speech and language disorder. Applications for these pupils are made on an individual basis to the SENO.

This new model of provision means that there are more special needs teachers in the schools. It also means that, in the future, the child with dyslexia will be covered by the general allocation to the school. There will not be individual allocations to children with higher incidence special educational needs.

This new system is designed to put resources permanently in place in schools and therefore facilitate early and flexible intervention. It allows better planning as schools know the resources available. One of the advantages of this model is stated in the Department of Education and Skills press release to be that it will reduce the need for individual applications and therefore the need for assessments to support such applications. While teachers may have well-founded suspicions that a student may have dyslexia, an assessment is required for a diagnosis to be made. It is not clear whether this means that fewer children will be referred for assessment. This could result in the child getting extra teaching support, but the reasons why such help is required will not be investigated. In order to provide the most effective intervention, it is necessary to understand the causes of the difficulties. A child with mild general learning difficulty requires different teaching strategies to those required by a child with dyslexia. Assessments are still necessary when applying for supports such as an exemption from Irish, reasonable accommodation in exams or access to the support services at third level.

At second level, Circular PPT 01/05 advises school authorities of the establishment of the National Council for Special Education. It also refers to three other circulars: M 08/99, SP ED 07/02 and SP ED 08/02. These circulars form the basis for determining if a child has a special educational need and what extra teaching or other supports should be put in place. Circular SP ED 08/02 states that for students to qualify for resource teaching under the heading specific learning difficulty, they must have been assessed by a psychologist as:

- Being of average intelligence or higher;
- Having a degree of learning disability specific to the basic skills in reading, writing or mathematics that places them at or below the 2nd percentile on suitable, standardised, norm-referenced tests.

Application for resource hours is made in February. Parents of students entering second level should ensure that the school has psychological reports by this stage if an application for resource teaching is to be made. It means that, in the case of students for whom resource teaching is appropriate, the school can apply to the Special Educational Needs Organiser for the necessary resource allocation and have it in place by the September of entry.

The learning support teacher provides learning support to children with low achievement. The *Learning Support Guidelines* set out that supplementary teaching should be provided to students who have not yet achieved basic competence in English and Mathematics i.e. those performing below the 10th percentile on nationally standardised tests of literacy and numeracy.

These criteria for resource and learning support mean that students with dyslexia whose scores are higher than the second percentile or the tenth percentile respectively do not fall within the criteria for additional teaching support.

This is an area of rapid change in education. The Department of Education and Skills website: www.education.ie and the SESS website: www.sess.ie provide access to circulars for those who want to follow the ongoing developments in the provision of extra support for students.

Education Plans

Under the *Education of Persons with Special Educational Needs Act*, an individual education plan (IEP) should be drawn up for the child who has been assessed as having special educational needs. For the child who falls within the criteria for learning support an individual profile and learning programme (IPLP) is drawn up. Both are very similar and record information about learning attainments and learning strengths of the student. Both contain an outline of the learning programme that sets out learning targets and activities. The learning support/resource/special needs teachers have a key role in such planning. However, it is strongly recommended that an inclusive approach involving class teacher(s), parents and students themselves be adopted in both the diagnostic and planning stages and later in implementation and monitoring of such plans.

Special Classes attached to Mainstream Schools

Special classes (units) for children with specific learning difficulties (including those arising from dyslexia) have been established in designated schools where there are a sufficient number of students with such difficulties to form a class. The pupil-teacher ratio for these classes is 9:1. Students are placed in the classes for one or two years and then return to mainstream classes. There are nineteen such units throughout the country. The Department of Education and Skills website gives details of locations.

The criteria for access to such special classes which are set out in the Department of Education and Skills document *Revised Guidelines for the Enrolment of Children with Specific Learning Difficulty* (June 1998) are as follows:

> Assessment by a psychologist on a standardised test of intelligence should place general intellectual ability within the average range or above ... There must be an obvious discrepancy between general intellectual ability and performance on a standardised test of reading ability ... It would be expected that

not more than two per cent of the overall student population would be found in this category. Performance in basic literacy skills as measured by a standardised test should be at a very low level compared to the vast majority of students in a similar age cohort. Consideration should also be given to the child's speaking, writing and spelling skills as well as to his/her level of adaptation to learning within mainstream education, to his/her progress in other aspects of the curriculum and to his/her social and personal development ... Students transferring to a special school or support unit for students with specific learning difficulties should have completed second class in a primary school or be at least eight years old on the first day of the school year.

Special Schools for Children with Specific Learning Difficulties
The Department of Education and Skills has established four primary schools for students with specific learning difficulties including those arising from dyslexia. These schools are as follows:

- St Killian's, Bishopstown, Cork;
- St Oliver Plunkett's, Monkstown, Co. Dublin;
- Catherine McAuley's, 59 Lower Baggot Street, Dublin 2;
- St Rose's, Balrothery, Tallaght, Dublin 24.

The criteria for access to these schools are similar to those for access to special classes.

Support for Students Who Do not Qualify for Additional Teaching
Some students with dyslexia do not meet the criteria set by the Department of Education for access to extra teaching supports such as learning support/resource teaching or special classes or schools. However, they may still experience varying degrees of difficulty in school. The *Report of the Task Force on Dyslexia* recognised that since the difficulties presented by students with dyslexia range along a continuum from mild to severe, there is a need for a continuum of interventions and other services. Some students with mild dyslexia may need minimal intervention and yet this intervention is essential if the student is to reach full potential and achievement. An example from second level is the student who may only need interventions such as a waiver of spelling and grammar in the State examinations and that his teachers are informed of the presence of dyslexia. If the

student does not fall within the learning support/resource remit, whose responsibility is it to ensure that such interventions are in place? Whole-school planning should clearly set out the roles and responsibilities of the staff involved.

The *Report of the Task Force on Dyslexia* stressed the key role of the class/subject teacher in providing support. Even if students are receiving learning support/resource teaching, they spend the vast majority of the school day with the mainstream teacher. The student, who receives no additional teaching, relies totally on the class/subject teacher. For this reason it is vital that all teachers receive pre-service and in-service training on the topic of dyslexia.

The Dyslexia Association of Ireland (DAI) workshop classes and exam preparation classes provide an example of the targeted help that can be provided for such students. These workshops are run throughout the country. Details of the workshops are available on the DAI website www.dyslexia.ie.

Other Supports

Exemption from the study of Irish

Irish is a compulsory subject for students in primary and post-primary schools. However, students with specific learning difficulties including those arising from dyslexia may be granted an exemption from the study of Irish. Such an exemption is given to students who function intellectually at average or above-average level but have a specific learning difficulty of such a degree of severity that they fail to achieve expected levels of attainment in basic language skills in the mother tongue. The guideline for such exemptions is that the student is achieving at or below the 10th percentile on a standardised norm-referenced test of reading or spelling. Circular M10/94 sets out the details regarding the exemption from Irish.

The procedure for gaining an exemption involves the parent submitting a written application on behalf of the child to the school principal along with a copy of a report from a psycho-educational assessment that is less than two years old and which recommends that the student should be exempt because the criteria are met. If the school authorities grant an exemption, a certificate is issued and the

Department of Education and Skills is informed. The exemption granted at primary level will be recognised at second level and for entry to the National University of Ireland (NUI) colleges. The exemption should be taken into account at entrance assessment when students are transferring to second level if Irish is included as part of the assessment.

Students who attend the special schools referred to in the previous section of this chapter may apply for an exemption from Irish when leaving these schools.

Some students may fall within the guideline of the 10th percentile at one stage, but with additional tuition, may develop their skills in English. Therefore at one stage they may qualify for such an exemption and, if assessed at a later stage, may not. If the student qualifies for the exemption at a particular point in time, it would be prudent to get the official certificate. Parents may decide to let the student continue to participate in Irish class in order to benefit from the cultural aspects of the subject. By having the official certificate they then have the option further on in the educational system to withdraw the student from Irish. This could be of major benefit to senior cycle students who intend to apply to the Central Applications Office (CAO). Entry to CAO colleges is determined by points. Senior-cycle students should be able to present their best subjects for examination to maximise points and be able to compete on even terms.

Take the case of a student in 2004, with very good Maths and technical ability but poorer verbal abilities, who applied for an Engineering degree in one of the National University of Ireland (NUI) colleges. The entry requirements for NUI colleges state that students must have English, Irish and a third language. This student began his Leaving Certificate course taking nine subjects. He did not qualify for an Irish exemption as he was outside the 10th percentile. He was studying English, Irish and French at ordinary level due to weaker verbal skills. He then had to take six other subjects at higher level in order to maximise his points. His higher level subjects were Maths, Applied Maths, Physics, Geography, Technical Graphics and Accounting. Most Leaving Certificate students do seven subjects. This student, who has a learning difficulty, was in the position of having to take two additional subjects outside school time. He applied for and received an exemption from the NUI third-language requirement in the course of fifth year.

This reduced the number of his subjects to eight. He achieved 475 points based on his six higher level subjects. He therefore got a place on his chosen course. If he did not have two additional subjects he would have received 365 points, a difference of 110 points. Many students with dyslexia have a similar profile of ability and could face the same difficulties in maximizing their performance in the very competitive points race that exists for places in the CAO system.

There are some careers where a certain standard of Irish is required. A 'C' in higher level Irish in the Leaving Certificate is necessary for primary teaching. It affects a small number of career choices if the student does not study Irish. Irish used to be a requirement for the Gardai. However this was changed in 2005 to a two language requirement. An applicant must have Irish or English and another language in the Leaving Certificate.

Sometimes a teacher at primary level, recognising the child's difficulties, allows the child to do extra English work during the allocated time for Irish. However, the official exemption is not issued. If the student is not studying Irish at primary level, it is very important for a parent to ask the school for the certificate of exemption. Otherwise the child will be required to study Irish when attending second level.

If the student is exempt from Irish, there should be provision for this class time to be used constructively such as learning support withdrawal, additional English reading or computer time.

Exemption from the NUI Third Language Requirement

The National University of Ireland (NUI) comprises the colleges of UCC, UCD, UCG and Maynooth. The entry requirements for NUI colleges specify that a student must pass six subjects in the Leaving Certificate, two at higher level, and that the student must include English, Irish and a third language.

NUI recognises the exemption from Irish granted at primary or post-primary and also allows a student with such an exemption to be exempt from the third language requirement for entry to NUI. This means that students do not have to take Irish and a third language as subjects in the Leaving Certificate. It is important to apply to NUI, preferably during fifth year, for recognition of the Irish exemption and to apply for the third-language exemption.

If students are not exempt from Irish, they may still qualify for an exemption from the third-language requirement. NUI considers applications for such an exemption from students who are certified by a qualified professional as having a serious dyslexic condition. The application should be made prior to entry to senior cycle at second level, before subject choice for the Leaving Certificate has been made. Forms are available from NUI at 49 Merrion Square, Dublin 2.

It is vital when applying to the CAO that information about such exemptions is provided and that it is mentioned on the statement of application that each applicant receives in April/May from the CAO.

Special Arrangements/Reasonable Accommodations in State Examinations

Reasonable accommodation (RACE) is the phrase used to describe the various types of support provided for students in the state examinations. The types of help include:

- *Extra time to be given for the examination.* An additional twenty minutes is given for each examination session in the subjects Irish, English, History and Geography in the Leaving Certificate examination. All students taking the examination can avail of this time. Other than this provision, extra time is not granted to students with dyslexia.

- *Reading assistance.* A reader should only be granted where a candidate is unable to read the question paper. This means the candidate must have a severe reading difficulty and that in the absence of the assistance of a reader the candidate would be unable to take the examination. The explanatory note on the certificate and statement of results will read, 'All parts of the examination in this subject were examined except the reading element'.

- *Tape recorder or computer.* The use of a tape recorder or computer is appropriate where it can be established that the candidate has good oral ability, good knowledge of the course content, a score well below average on a spelling test and more than 20 per cent of the target words unrecognisable under test and on written samples. The explanatory note on the English result will read, 'all parts of the examination in this subject were assessed except spelling and written punctuation elements'. In the other language subjects it will read, 'all parts of the examination in this subject were assessed except for the spelling and some grammatical elements'.

- *A waiver from the spelling and grammatical components in language subjects.* This exemption is considered appropriate where it can be established that the candidate has good oral ability, good knowledge of the course content, a score well below average on a spelling test and that the target word is easily recognisable as the target word, although mis-spelt. The explanatory note is similar to that for the tape recorder or computer.

- *A scribe.* The accommodation of a scribe appeared on the application for RACE in the Junior Certificate in 2011 for the first time. Reasons must be given when applying for a scribe as to why the student cannot use a computer or use a tape.

Students who are given the accommodation of taping, use of reader, use of scribe or use of word processor take the examinations in a centre by themselves with a supervisor. Students who have been granted the accommodation of a waiver from spelling and grammar take the examination in the main examination centre.

Applications for reasonable accommodation are made by the school. Applications for accommodations in the Leaving Certificate are made in late May for the following year. There is a detailed application form to be completed by the school which is sent to the State Examinations Commission and should include a psycho-educational assessment report and three samples of the student's work. Students should keep examples of their work under examination conditions such as the Christmas exams in 5th year or examples of long written answers in subjects where there are essay type answers such as English which show what their difficulties are. It is important that they realise that such examples will be needed in May in 5th year and form part of the application process for accommodations. Parents are asked to sign this form. It is important that the applications are in by the due date. As part of the application, the school may be required to carry out additional testing. The application is processed through NEPS. The NEPS psychologist may come to the school to interview the student. The psychologist decides if the accommodation is granted. If an application is turned down, there is an appeals procedure.

For the Junior Certificate applications are made in October/ November prior to the examination. For Junior Certificate students, there is a less rigorous application process. The form is simpler and there is no need for an assessment to accompany the application. The school may be required to carry out further testing as criteria are set out in the documentation issued by the State Examinations Commission. These criteria are defined scores in specified standardised testing. The following is the criteria that apply when applying for a spelling and grammar waiver.

'Such an exemption for a candidate with a specific learning difficulty is appropriate when it can be established that the candidate has significant difficulties with spelling that are attributable to a specific learning difficulty as distinct from his/her general intellectual functioning and where the level of difficulty does not require mechanical aid. Such indications are

- Good oral ability
- Good knowledge of the course content
- A score well below average on a spelling test
- 15% to 20% of words mis-spelt but easily recognisable as target words
- The observed score and mis-spellings are inconsistent with the candidate's ability as demonstrated in knowledge of course content and knowledge of other areas of the curriculum.

A standard score of 70 or below is likely to be eligible for spelling and grammar/writing accommodations when considered in light of information on ability. A score of between 71 and 85 will normally merit further investigation. A score of 85 plus is likely to be of average spelling ability and hence not likely to be eligible'.

The use of criteria as cut-off points for RACE make access to such supports more problematic. Eligibility for support is based on a standard score of 85. A score of above 85 is considered to be in the average range and hence not eligible for accommodations. A standard score of 85 is the 16th percentile. The application of such criteria takes no account of the discrepancy between the scores for general ability and literacy scores. Take a student with general ability at the 90th percentile and a spelling score at the 20th percentile. The discrepancy in the scores is 70. The performance of this student in examinations will be affected by this discrepancy and yet they will not be able to access RACE.

If an accommodation is not granted, there is no way for examiners to be aware of the student's difficulties. There is no warning that spelling may be phonic. Examiners need to slow down for phonic spelling to recognise if the word is correct. An example is a student who lost 6 marks in a Science Mock paper for spelling 'bend' as 'bouend'. The student correctly stated that a bimetallic strip would bouend when heated. The answer was not recognised as correct. At higher level English in the Leaving Certificate the student is in danger of losing the 10% of marks awarded for mechanics of language. 10% can make a difference in the points achieved in the CAO system. Also having examiners aware that they have difficulties can also reduce students' tension/anxiety about facing an exam where they know their spelling or handwriting may be a problem.

The use of these criteria facilitates the system in making decisions quickly and all that needs to be checked is the criteria. It does not take into account the individual difficulties of students and multi-faceted ways in which dyslexia affects the students. Also students and teachers are involved in time-consuming form filling. At Leaving Certificate the form has eight pages to be filled and is a time-consuming exercise for the school. Is this information used or are the decisions based on the criteria alone?

In the past schools filled in the application forms for RACE and submitted them to the Examinations Commission for consideration. In recent years the forms have looked for much more information from the schools and asked for up-to-date standardised test scores. The suitable tests are listed in documents which are issued with the forms. This involves the school in time-consuming testing and also puts them into the situation where they are involved in deciding on the accommodation, since they have to check if the student meets the criteria.

Approximately 110,000 students sit State examinations annually. The numbers granted reasonable accommodations in 2010 were:

	Leaving Cert.	Junior Cert.
Reading Assistance	1685	3620
Tape Recorder	144	303
Word processor	141	313
Waiver spelling & grammar	2679	4970

It is important that there is an objective assessment by the school of which reasonable accommodations, if any, would be appropriate for a particular student. Sometimes parents may be looking for any possible help and yet such help might not be appropriate or helpful to the student.

If the use of a word processor might be appropriate, a preliminary step is the development of excellent keyboarding skills early on at second level. Otherwise it is not possible to ascertain if the use of the word processor would be of benefit.

If a particular form of reasonable accommodation is considered appropriate, such accommodation should be given in the house exams in the school. Indeed it is essential that the mock exams prior to the state exam be taken using the accommodation granted. This is very demanding on school resources to provide such accommodations as it may mean that a teacher has to be freed to supervise such exam students on a one-to-one basis. Very often the necessary number of staff may not be available. It may be possible to use parental assistance to help out or to train transition year students to act as readers or supervisors of taping of the exams.

The student will also need training in the use of the accommodation granted. It may be a stressful experience to take an examination alone with an adult present. Repeated practice can reduce this stress. The student also needs to know the role of the supervisor and the help that can be given. In reading aloud the supervisor can only read what is on the paper, but the student can request particular sections to be reread as frequently as needed.

When using a tape recorder, the student needs practice in giving the exact details such as the number and section of the question being answered. Taped answers may be too short, possibly because it is difficult to check over what has already been said, whereas with a written answer, it is possible to scan the answer quickly. The student can use some blank paper to help structure the answer by making a list of the points to be included before speaking to the tape. The student should also ensure that the tape recorder is turned off when it is not being used. It is also important to start the taping session by checking that the tape recorder is recording clearly and that the answers are audible.

Another reason for short answers may be because of embarrassment in the one-to-one situation with the supervisor. The school appoints the supervisor for exams taken with a reader or taping and it can be someone with whom the student is familiar. This may reduce the embarrassment.

In the case of the reasonable accommodations of reading assistance, use of a tape or word processor, the student is in a special exam centre within the student's school. The fact that the student is separated from the rest of the student body during the exams is a very public statement. This is at a time of development in adolescence when many young people want to be part of the peer group and do not want to be considered different. As a result some students may be reluctant to use such accommodations. However, when it is made evident to them the difference in grades they may achieve, it may help them to overcome their initial reluctance.

The introduction of the explanatory note on the certificate is a cause of concern to the Dyslexia Association of Ireland (DAI) and to parents. It is a permanent statement on the certificate of the student. For future employers, who may not be familiar with dyslexia and its effects, the wording of the different explanatory notes might imply the student cannot read, spell or use grammar at all. This is more important for the student who opts for employment directly after second level. There is no such explanatory note on the qualifications granted by third-level colleges and PLC courses and, in all probability, employers will not ask to see the Junior or Leaving Certificates of applicants who have further or third level qualifications.

The examiners of scripts in the state examinations are second level teachers. Many teachers have not received formal training in how dyslexia presents in written work in either pre-service or in-service training. As a result they may not be aware of how bizarre the phonic spelling of some students with dyslexia can be. Correcting exam papers for students with dyslexia takes more time than the usual. Poor handwriting, unusual spellings and poorly expressed facts can mean the teacher has to decipher the script to see if the student has the correct answers. If examiners do not have experience of dyslexic scripts, it is quite possible that the student may lose marks. Such a concern is noted in the *Report of the Task Force on Dyslexia (2001)*.

The DAI has requested the State Examinations Commission to include such training in the conferences that are held in June when examiners receive guidelines on the correction of scripts in state examinations until the time comes when all post-primary teachers have received adequate training.

Grants for the purchase of equipment

There is a scheme for the purchase of equipment for pupils with a disability. It applies to pupils who have been diagnosed as having serious physical and/or communicative disabilities of a degree that makes ordinary communication through speech and/or writing impossible for them. The purpose of the scheme is to provide the pupils with equipment that is deemed necessary and of direct educational benefit to them. Examples of such equipment include computers, tape-recorders and word processors. The application is made by the school to the SENO and must be accompanied by a comprehensive professional assessment.

Department of Education Acts and Circulars

The Education Act 1998

The Education (Welfare) Act 2000

The Education of Persons with Special Educational Needs Act 2004

SP ED 01/05 & SP ED 09/04 on provision of additional teaching support at primary level

PPT 01/05, M08/99, SP ED 07/02 & SP ED 08/02 on provision of additional teaching support at post primary level

M10/94 on the exemption from the study of Irish

Guidelines for Psychologists on Assessment and Reporting.

Publications available from Government Publications Office

Report of the Task Force on Dyslexia 2001

Understanding Dyslexia video/CD ROM/DVD

Learning Support Guidelines 2000

Post Primary Guidelines on the Inclusion of Students with Special Educational Needs 2007.

CHAPTER 4
DYSLEXIA – THE EARLY YEARS

This chapter will be of most use to parents and in it you will read about:

- Early signs of dyslexia;
- Screening tests for young children;
- Developing the skills necessary for reading;
- Helping the young child with social skills

There is a certain 'Catch 22' element about early identification of dyslexia. All experts agree that the earlier the difficulty is identified and remediation begun, the more likely it is that the child will cope with school and learning. However, as dyslexia shows itself most clearly as a reading difficulty, it is not usually suspected until the child has tried and failed to learn to read. By that time the child may be seven or older. Much valuable learning time will have been lost and the child's confidence in his/her own ability will probably have been damaged. So the question arises, how do you identify a reading difficulty in a child who has not yet been taught to read? And should we put so much emphasis on learning to read at an early age?

Early identification is, undoubtedly, very important for children with dyslexia but one has to beware of making a premature diagnosis. Children develop at very different rates and, while one child is ready to read at age four, another may not be ready until much later. Many Irish children start formal schooling at age four and teaching of reading commences soon after. In many countries reading is not taught until age six or even seven. Studies show that these children have caught up with Irish children by age nine. So we must ask – are we putting too much emphasis on early teaching of reading? There are many skills which children must master before they can begin to read and some children need longer to acquire these. Therefore before the age of seven, it is hard to say whether a child has a dyslexic type reading difficulty or is simply developing at a different pace to other children of a similar age?

Early Signs of Dyslexia

While reading difficulty may be the most obvious sign of dyslexia, there are other more subtle indicators. Many parents worry that, because their five or six year old reverses letters or writes some numbers backwards, they have dyslexia. Happily, this does not usually indicate a problem. Most children do this until the age of seven or even later. One swallow does not make a summer and one sign does not mean a child has dyslexia.

There are a number of indicators and, unless a child checks positive for several items on the list, no further action is needed.

> It is the severity of the trait, the clarity with which it may be observed, and the length of time during which it persists which give the vital clues to the identification of the dyslexic learner. (Augur, 1997)[1]

Below is a list of possible indicators of a dyslexic difficulty. See also the indicators listed in the *Report of the Task Force on Dyslexia* in Chapter 1.

- Delay in the development of speech and language.
- Problems with naming (i.e. mislabelling).
- Difficulty in doing simple jigsaws.
- Difficulty in copying shapes with pencil.
- Difficulty in colouring pictures within the lines.
- Difficulty with simple sequences such as days of the week.
- Difficulty in identifying and remembering rhymes.
- Enjoys being read to, but shows no desire to learn to read.
- Inability to remember the order of simple instructions.
- Clumsiness, poor co-ordination, trips up and bumps into things.
- Difficulties getting dressed, fastening buttons, tying laces, putting shoes on the correct feet.
- Poor concentration, easy distractibility and does not seem to listen.
- Delay in establishing dominant hand, eye and foot.
- Family history of dyslexia or specific learning problems.

If a consistent pattern of the above difficulties emerges, then positive actions should be taken. Children do not 'grow out' of dyslexia. It will not go away if ignored. Some professional advice may be necessary, either in the area of language development, dyslexia screening or full psycho-educational assessment.

Speech and Language

The presence of an early speech and language difficulty should alert parents to the possible existence of other difficulties. Before reading even begins, language development must take place. If a child has difficulty in understanding spoken language, there is a risk of written language difficulty. A professional assessment may be necessary to determine the cause of the problem. Factors such as hearing loss, general developmental delay, social, cultural or emotional problems need to be investigated. If a specific speech and/or language delay is diagnosed then speech therapy may be necessary before reading or spelling can be taught successfully.

Speech and language assessment is provided by the Health Boards and referral is normally through the family doctor or the school. As there is great demand on this service parents may opt to seek private assessment. The Irish Association of Speech and Language Therapists can supply names of qualified therapists.

Visual Perception

Often children have some delay in visual perceptual development. While children's visual acuity is checked out in the school, there may be more subtle features of perception that are not revealed by these tests. Children with poor spatial awareness, clumsiness and poor hand eye co-ordination may be experiencing difficulty with visual rather than motor functioning. Many children confuse directions of letters and numbers and are slow to read consistently from left to right. These difficulties may be evident in a dislike for making jigsaws, difficulty colouring within lines or catching balls. Visual perceptual delay is not necessarily an indication of dyslexia but may be implicated. Persistent visual perceptual difficulties may need to be examined by an optometrist.

Screening Tests for Young Children

If parents or teachers find cause for concern in younger children, there are some screening tests which can be given to children as young as four. These screening tests can be used to decide if a child needs a full psycho-educational assessment from a psychologist. They can also be useful in providing information about the child's learning strengths and weaknesses, and in devising an individual education programme. Such tests usually include diagnostic tests and attainment tests. Diagnostic tests examine how the child performs on tasks which are known to be affected by dyslexia and the attainment tests look at how the child has assimilated what has been taught to date.

Probably one of the most widely used tests is the Dyslexia Early Screening Test (DEST), devised by Dr. Rod Nicholson and Dr. Angela Fawcett of Sheffield University. It is one of a series of three that can be used from early childhood to adult screening. The DEST is intended for children between the ages of four and a half and six and a half. The advantage is that it can be given by the class or special needs teacher. It is available from ETC Consult, 17 Leeson Park, Dublin 6.

Computerised programmes are also available as another screening device. An example of such tests is Lucid CoPS (Cognitive Profiling System) which can be given to children between the ages of four and eight. This is a fully computerised programme which teachers can administer. It includes nine tests which are said to predict dyslexic type difficulties. It provides teachers with a profile of the learner which can assist in the preparation of the individual pupil learning profile.

An early screening test based on Irish data and geared to the Irish educational system has been piloted in over 200 primary schools. Work is ongoing on this test and it may be on the market in the next few years.

Definitive assessment of dyslexia by a suitably qualified psychologist is not usually obtained until the age of seven or older. This means that a child may be attending school for three years before full diagnosis is reached. Early identification is beneficial because it makes parents and teachers aware of any difficulties and so enables them to use the child's early school years to the best advantage. Many parents, particularly those with a family history of dyslexia, have a shrewd idea that a potential difficulty exists even before a screening test is carried out. Parents are well advised to follow their own intuition in relation to requesting screening and/or assessment. They may be discouraged from seeking assessment as it no guarantee of securing learning support, but the wider benefits of formal identification should not be ignored.

Developing the Skills Necessary for Reading

So what can parents and teachers do to help a child with dyslexia before a formal diagnosis has been made? There are many activities which can help a child to develop important pre-reading and other skills. Some of these activities are outlined below but many parents and teachers devise their own. This list offers a variety from which parents and/or teachers can pick and choose. It would not be possible to attempt all of these activities. The most important thing is for parents and children to find something which they enjoy and which does not put pressure on child or adult. Children enjoy activities which challenge them a little, particularly when parents, childminders, grandparents or friends are involved. These activities benefit any child, whether dyslexic tendencies exist or not. They may take a little time and organisation but they do not require special equipment or expertise and can be carried out at any time and in any place. In this regard grandparents are often a wonderful resource. They may have more free time than other adults in the child's life and they can offer a great deal simply from their own life experience.

General Activities

- Talking to children is something we all take for granted, but the words used, the range of vocabulary, the ideas expressed, the tone of voice, all contribute not only to the understanding of language and communication but also to their own feeling of self-esteem

- Listening to a child is equally important. A child with dyslexic difficulties may well have some expressive language problems and may take a long time to tell a story or may get the order of events confused. A busy parent could be tempted to hurry the child or to finish sentences, but encouraging the child to tell a story in sequence and to give all the relevant information, develops vital language skills.

- Saying nursery rhymes together is a great way to improve vocabulary and develop an awareness of rhythm and rhyme.

- Games involving mime and drama develop the child's visual skills.
- Games and songs where the child has to follow instructions, such as *Simon Says* or the *Hokey Cokey*, help a child to follow instructions and learn that certain things have to be done in sequence.
- Television can be a very stimulating and entertaining medium if used intelligently. There are some excellent programmes which can be watched together and discussed. If a parent watches a programme with a child and shows interest in it, this makes it more important in the child's eyes and more likely to be remembered. Even quite young children can be interested in news events of the day and they benefit from discussion and explanation of what is happening in the world.
- Introduce children to computers as soon as they are ready. There are now many early learning computer programmes designed for pre-school children. These provide a fun way to learn as well as introducing children to computers. It is important to note that computer programmes are not a substitute for appropriate teaching programmes delivered by a trained and experienced teacher. **A word of warning**: Video games do not fill the same function as computer programmes which develop skills. They do not have real developmental or educational value. Research indicates that children who spend long periods of time playing repetitive games derive no benefit, other than entertainment, from the activity and may indeed hinder their development in other more useful areas.
- Finally, the old games which develop hand-eye co-ordination and develop motor skills should not be forgotten. Many children with dyslexia tend to be clumsy and may not perform as well as their peers at games. Parents can help greatly by encouraging the child to master activities such as cycling, roller skating and skipping in a non-competitive environment. It is very important to the child's self-esteem to be able to do these activities but it may take longer to acquire the skill. Parents can help by encouraging perseverance and teaching that all skills improve with practice.

Some of the following activities may be more familiar to the pre-school or infant class teachers but there is no reason why parents should not try some of them. The most important thing is for these activities to be presented in a relaxed setting and that the child does not see them as a chore, or worse still, another task at which they may fail.

Listening (Auditory) Activities

- With eyes closed, try to get the child to identify everyday sounds such as the clock ticking or traffic going by.
- Tape everyday sounds and play a game where the child has to identify the sounds.
- With eyes closed, try to get the child to recognise the speaker from the voice.
- Clapping out syllables in words or tapping out the rhythm in a poem develops auditory awareness.
- Songs like *Old McDonald* and *Ten Green Bottles* involve memory and sequencing.

Looking (Visual) Activities

- Play card games like *Snap* and *Pairs* with both pictures and symbols and then move on to using letters and words. It is important to avoid the competitive element in games, so playing with an adult rather than a peer can be helpful. Nothing deflates a child's self-esteem more than having a younger sibling outperform them.
- Sorting pictures by colour, shape and size helps develop awareness of the visual appearance of objects. This concept is useful when reading, as the shape and length of a word can be useful clues.
- Get the child to look at a picture and remember all the details they can. Then cover it and ask questions about it.
- Provide a tray with several objects on it. Give the child a few minutes to study what is on it. Then take it away and ask them to name what was on the tray.
- Draw basic shapes on cards. Lay out a series of these cards and ask the child to remember the sequence and then draw it. Gradually increase the length of the sequence.
- Cut up basic cartoon strips and mix them up. Then ask the child to rearrange the parts to recreate the story.
- Provide several pictures and ask the child to create a story around them.

Play *Odd One Out* games with pictures or objects such as an onion, carrot, orange and potato.

Kinaesthetic Awareness
- Encourage the child to trace shapes, letters and words.
- Make letters and words with pipe cleaners or play dough.
- Make letter shapes and words on a rough material such as sand, carpet, sandpaper or even on the child's palm.
- Feel and name wooden or plastic shapes or letters with eyes closed.

Jigsaw puzzles are very important.

Co-ordination and Balance
- Don't forget about physical skills. Throwing, catching, skipping, hopping, jumping and balancing are all important skills to master. Some children will need to consciously practice these skills. The little skills which many children acquire naturally may have to be taught to children with dyslexia.

Introducing Books
- An early introduction to books is an advantage to any child. It is important to read to children, to talk about the story, to look at pictures and ask the child questions such as, "What might happen next"? "Why did that happen"? or 'Why did he say that"? If the child has even a limited reading range, simple books with tapes can be very helpful as the child can read the words while hearing them spoken.

Helping the Young Child with Social Skills

Many children with dyslexia develop somewhat more slowly than children who do not have the condition. They also appear to have more difficulty in acquiring information about everyday things which other children pick up quite naturally. Difficulties with time awareness may lead to confusion about dates of birthdays or whether Christmas comes before Easter. They may get the names of everyday objects mixed up or confuse relationships. One child, for example, thought he had three grandmothers. Adults may not even notice such little discrepancies but children are very quick to pick up on any perceived lapses by their peers. A simple mistake on the child's part may lead to teasing or worse. Therefore parents of children with dyslexia may need to devote some thought to how they can ensure that their child has appropriate social skills and does not lose face before other children. Parents who observe how a child interacts with peers may be able to intervene quietly and diplomatically in cases where the child may be at a disadvantage.

Bullying

It is unfortunately true that a five or six year old who is not reading at the same level as classmates may already be seen by them as different and may be a target for bullying or exclusion. This danger may be lessened by a very pro-active parent who ensures that the child's self-esteem is maintained and who takes care that siblings or classmates are not allowed to tease or mock reading difficulties. Talking to the child about the reading difficulty, putting it in context and not letting it dominate the child's life is very important.

It is also true that a child who experiences a difficulty at school may react by bullying other children or younger siblings. Developing self-esteem and learning to control frustration will be helpful in this situation. Parents need to seek the reason for behaviours in order to deal with them effectively.

Emphasising the positives

Children, who show indications of reading difficulty, should be encouraged to develop any skills or talents which they possess in other areas such as drawing, dancing, swimming or drama. A child, who is good at sport for example, will often achieve sufficient success in that area to counterbalance any loss of esteem due to a reading difficulty.

Teachers will deal with the formal teaching process. It is important for parents, child minders or grandparents to remember that their teaching is informal. Sometimes the most important things are learned in that way. Doing the shopping, baking scones, chatting, playing word games while sitting in traffic or commenting on television programmes can be entertaining and educational at the same time. Helping the child with dyslexia to acquire the skills needed to cope with school-based learning does not have to be a grim and boring task. Parents sometimes feel that unless they have a pencil and a workbook in hand they are not helping the child to learn. Nothing could be further from the truth. The grandmother who has time to tell stories, the grandfather who plays draughts, the parents who talk and listen to their child are all likely to contribute more to that child's development than the parent who insists on completing three pages of reading come hell or high water.

Discovering that a child has, or may have, a dyslexic type problem can be very upsetting for a parent. There may be a temptation to focus in on the difficulty, to the exclusion of other aspects of the child's life, but it is important not to let that happen. The overall development of a healthy and happy child is the main priority. The fact that a child is not reading as well as little Jimmy who lives next door is not important. What matters is that the child gets all the help possible, and is not made to feel that parental love and approval are conditional on good school performance.

Useful Resources

Dyslexia Early Screening Test, Nicholson and Fawcett,

Lucid CoPS (Cognitive Profiling System)

www.dyslexic.com

Parents courses offered by Dyslexia Association of Ireland
Website: www.dyslexia.ie

References

1. Augur, J. (1997) *'Early Indicators of Dyslexia'*, *The Dyslexia Handbook*, London: BDA.

CHAPTER 5
THE CHILD AT HOME
- FAMILY MATTERS

This chapter will be of most use to parents and in it you will read about:

- Preparing the child for assessment;
- Dyslexia and family life;
- Supporting the younger child in the home;
- Supporting the older child in the home;
- Helping with homework – the primary school age;
- Supporting the child through the school system;
- Mediating with the outside world;
- Caring for the carers

Preparing the Child for Assessment

If parents, in consultation with teachers, believe that a child may have dyslexia it is very important that the child should have a full psycho-educational assessment. Having such an assessment should be a pleasant event in the child's life. Some commonsense points to bear in mind are listed below.

- Find out as much as you can about the assessment procedure in advance. The more prepared you are, the more relaxed you will be and this will be beneficial for the child.
- Be as honest and frank as you can. Note down points you consider relevant beforehand so that you do not forget them on the day. Note down any questions you would like to ask.
- Tell the child why you are visiting the psychologist. The reason is often because the child is having some difficulty in reading, writing or spelling.
- Present it in the most positive way you can – as something you have arranged to do so that you can help the child. Explain that the assessment will be of help to teachers in school in understanding how the child learns.

- Explain what the psychologist will do. The child will be asked questions about school experiences and will be asked to do tasks like making designs with blocks, finding missing parts of a puzzle and some reading or spelling.
- Explain that it is not an exam. The child cannot fail. The psychologist is only interested in finding out how the child thinks and learns.
- Tell your child where you are going, at what time and how long it will take.
- Try to ensure the child is well rested.
- Bring a nutritious snack and if possible, build in a little treat afterwards.

After the assessment, the psychologist will probably give you some brief feedback. Using your own good judgement, tell the child as simply as possible what the psychologist has said, always stressing the most positive things. If you are upset or anxious about what you have been told, wait until you are feeling more positive before saying very much.

Dyslexia and Family Life

Nothing is nearer to the heart of parents than the welfare of their children. An illness or disability in one child affects the entire family. This is equally true of dyslexia. While dyslexia may not seem to be a big issue to people unaffected by it, it can have major implications for all the members of a family when a child is diagnosed with dyslexia.

It can be quite shocking for parents when they first get the diagnosis of dyslexia. They may feel angry with the school for not identifying the difficulty earlier. They may blame each other for things they did or did not do. They may worry that the child will never learn to read or write. They may feel embarrassed or ashamed of the difficulty.

They may feel sad and fear for their child's future. They may over-react to the situation, thereby putting pressure on the child and get the difficulty out of proportion. Whatever the immediate reaction, parents should allow themselves some time to come to terms with the fact that their child has a learning problem and to acquire as much information as possible about the condition and what they can do to help. The way in which the child reacts to the difficulty will be largely determined by the way in which parents approach the problem. If parents take a matter-of-fact approach, accepting that the child needs practical educational help and all the love and support they can provide, then the outcome is likely to be favourable. Children can, and do, cope with dyslexia. They grow up to be happy, useful and productive adults and the most important role in securing this outcome is played by parents.

Fathers sometimes have more difficulty in accepting the diagnosis than mothers. Dealing with schooling and homework often falls to the mother in the family. Fathers may not be quite as involved, particularly when the child is young. High-achieving fathers may have high expectations for their own children and be unwilling to admit difficulties. Fathers, who have succeeded in life despite their own learning difficulties, may think that too much fuss is being made of a dyslexic condition. However, it is very important that both parents are committed to whatever strategy is adopted to support the child at home and in school.

The child with dyslexia has special educational and emotional needs. Meeting these needs may involve spending extra time and money on the child. If both parents are in full agreement about the necessity for this, then it may be difficult but it can be done. If parents disagree about the management of their child's learning problem, this can cause conflict. Many parents report tensions arising from differing views on how much time is spent on homework, how much support is given, what effort is required from the child and how relations with the school and class teacher are to be managed. If money is scarce, the added expense of extra classes can add to the strain. Other children in the family may resent the fact that money is spent on tuition for the child with dyslexia but is not available to them for their hobbies or sports. These difficulties can be minimised if the family, as a whole, agree that the child with dyslexia needs extra support. Energy should, therefore, be put into providing this support and not diverted into issues of blame or allegations of favouritism.

Supporting the Younger Child in the Home

The first task that parents face is that of explaining dyslexia to the child. In order to do so, parents need to inform themselves. They then need to translate that information into simple language which the child can understand. There is a charming little book *It's Called Dyslexia* now available from the Dyslexia Association and good book stores. It is designed to help children aged 8 – 12 years to understand the concept of dyslexia through a story format. The book also includes a section for parents with some simple tips and advice.

Parents may be surprised to learn that many children are very relieved to be given a diagnosis of dyslexia. They are often aware that a difficulty exists, and may worry that they are stupid or even ill. The following are some hints which may be helpful when talking to your child.

- If your child is diagnosed as having dyslexia, then tell your child this. There is no reason to hide it.

- Explain that dyslexia is a very common condition and several other people in the school and maybe one or two in the class or in the family also have it

- You can tell the child that dyslexia is just a big word to explain why some people find it hard to learn to read, write and spell. Everyone is different. We all have different strengths and weaknesses. Identify something the child does very well, whether it is sport, music, art or cooking. It could be that the child is good with animals, generous, popular, funny, loving - whatever. Find some real strength which the child has. This is most important. Then say that the child does not find reading and spelling as easy as these other things but that is how life is.

- Explain that this is not the fault of the child, the parent or the school. It is something that happens - like having fair hair or freckles or brown eyes.

- Let the child know that this explains why school learning is difficult.

- You can explain that it will be necessary to work very hard, maybe harder than others in the class to succeed but that it can be done, with proper help and support.

- Be prepared to discuss the problem with your child more than once. Do not assume that they will take it all in the first time. You may need to return to the subject over the coming years.

- If you have been angry with or critical of your child in the past because of home-work/school difficulties then this is the time to apologise. Don't be afraid to say that you were wrong. Children can be very forgiving.

- If extra help is needed, either with a learning support teacher or outside of school, present this in the most positive light - as help rather than punishment.

- If extra help clashes with an activity which brings the child success, think very carefully before disturbing this arrangement.

- Make sure the child knows that while school work is very important it is just one aspect of life.

- Ensure that the child knows that your love is not dependent on good results in schoolwork, that you value all of your children for their own sakes.

If you are telling relatives or friends about the diagnosis of dyslexia in the child's hearing, be careful to be as positive as possible and not to tell them a different story than you told the child. Children very quickly pick up on discrepancies between what they've been told and what you really think.

It is also important that other children in the family understand about dyslexia. Sometimes a child may not want friends or siblings to know about the difficulty. This wish must be respected but it must be balanced by the fact that brothers and sisters need to know, so their support can be enlisted. It can be very demoralising for a ten year old who is struggling with homework to have a much younger child provide the answers or comment on the older child's mistakes. If the dyslexia is acknowledged openly and siblings know that they all learn differently, then this is less likely to be a problem. Equally, other children in the family may feel neglected if too much parental energy goes into supporting the child with dyslexia. Children have a natural sense of fair play. If they see that a sibling is getting attention because of need and are re-assured that if they needed the extra care they too would receive it, they are likely to be supportive.

Supporting the Older Child in the Home

Increasingly, children are being diagnosed with dyslexia in early primary school. This is a very good development because younger children accept such events without too much questioning. However, it still happens that dyslexia is not identified in some students until entering secondary school or even later. This is most unfortunate because it means they may have already experienced failure and may have lost a great deal of confidence and self-esteem by then.

Secondary difficulties such as school refusal, behavioural or emotional problems or withdrawal may have emerged. While most children are relieved to discover that there is a reason for the difficulties which they experience, some react badly to being told that they have dyslexia. They may have no understanding of the condition. They may even fear that it is a psychiatric illness. They may deny it and refuse support, saying that there is no point. They may become angry with parents or school for not having identified the problem earlier or they may even want to opt out of school altogether. This reaction is understandable. Adolescence is a time when it is very important to be part of the group and any trait which makes one different is to be avoided. Any sign of weakness is to be hidden and self-consciousness and embarrassment cause agonies.

Teenagers who have had bad school experiences as a result of their dyslexia may need some formal or informal counselling before they begin to receive tuition. In order to benefit from remedial help, they must be mentally and emotionally ready. Students need to regain confidence in their own ability and to believe that they can succeed.

The guidance counsellor at school may be able to help in this situation or parents may seek the advice of the assessing psychologist for referral to an outside counsellor. The family doctor should also be in a position to give advice on referral.

Parents can help by explaining dyslexia to the student, emphasising that it is not a defect but a learning difference and that it does not preclude school success. Second level students should be able to read through their own psycho-educational assessment reports and begin to understand their own learning style. Adolescents, no less than their younger brothers and sisters, need to be reassured that parental love is not dependent on school success and all achievements are to be celebrated. At the same time, a fine line has to be walked between appreciating students' difficulties with academic work and allowing them to use dyslexia as an excuse for not trying.

Keeping a young teenager with dyslexia motivated to stay in school, to attend regularly and to work hard at schoolwork can be a challenge. Students, particularly those who did not receive help in their early years can become disillusioned with school and pessimistic about their own chances of examination success. They may miss a great deal of school time or want to drop out completely. Parents report that getting through second and third years are probably the most difficult in this regard. Many parents achieve this by taking a short term approach. To an unhappy fourteen year old student, the idea of spending another four years in the school system may be unbearable, but staying on until Christmas may not seem so bad. By breaking up the school year into segments, say September to mid-term, or mid-term to Christmas, and using a system of goals and rewards for each section, a year or two could be completed without too much trauma. The aim is to keep the student within the school system because dropping out before sitting the Leaving Certificate really limits a person's career choices. It must also be borne in mind that the legal school leaving age is sixteen.

Students who see themselves as failing in school desperately need to experience success in other aspects of life. Students with dyslexia may excel at science or maths, art or computer studies. On the other hand there may be no school subject for which they show a special aptitude. In such cases it is very important to maintain self-esteem by encouraging any out-of-school interests which bring satisfaction.

Students who experience no success at school may well be disruptive in class or engage in unacceptable behaviour. They may be suspended from school or at the least be regularly in trouble.

Parents may have to exercise great imagination and ingenuity to find areas where their young teenagers can shine. Involvement in sports activities is an obvious area but many young people with dyslexia have poor motor co-ordination. Chess, debating, drama, scouting, youth clubs, involvement in community and voluntary groups such as Junior Red Cross, or Young Citizens Parliament could all prove valuable. The most important thing is to identify an area where the student can gain feelings of competence and self-worth. Of course, at all times the love and belief of their own families will be of paramount importance. Home is where each student should feel safe and unthreatened, where there is no need to prove oneself to gain acceptance. More detailed information for supporting the student through second level education is provided in chapters eight to ten.

Helping with Homework – Primary School Age

Helping a child with dyslexia with homework can be a challenge, even for the best-organised parent. Sessions can end in tears and tantrums or with a smile and a sense of achievement. These two outcomes may be experienced on successive nights. Volumes have been written on the topic but in the end parents will work out the best system for themselves and for their child. Perhaps the most important thing to remember is that you are the parent, not the teacher (even if you have a doctorate in dyslexia), and that nothing is achieved when you and your child are tired, frustrated or upset. The common themes in all advice manuals are listed below:

- Children with dyslexia often find it difficult to copy material from the blackboard, so the very first problem with homework may be that your child is not sure just what homework has been set. Questions to be answered may not have been fully copied, maths questions may not have been noted accurately, and instructions given may have been forgotten.

- To cope with this problem it may be possible to enlist the help of the class teacher who would kindly agree to check the child's homework notebook after work has been assigned. You might arrange with the parent of a classmate that you can phone to get any missing information. Choose wisely, of course. Be sure to pick the parent of a child who takes accurate notes of homework. It is also worth checking with other parents whether information about trips, free days or special activities has been given out. Children with dyslexia are notorious for not remembering to pass on oral messages and even for losing printed ones. This is not deliberate. It is part of the difficulty.

- Having ensured that the correct homework has been identified, the child then needs to be settled comfortably at a table or desk, in good light and with the minimum of distraction. Some children may manage to complete homework while watching *The Simpsons* or feeding the cat but children with dyslexia generally can not. They often have difficulty concentrating and once disrupted it may take some considerable time to get back on track. A supply of pens, pencils, erasers, rulers, notebooks, copies and number squares needs to be available, as these items tend to go missing. In extreme cases a second set of schoolbooks might be secured, particularly if some books are kept in a school locker. That way there is always a set of books to hand. For the slightly older child, biros which can be erased such as the Papermate Replay are very handy. Child-friendly dictionaries with large print are also invaluable.

■ The role of the parent ideally is to support by getting the child organised and then staying nearby to keep an eye on progress. It is not a good idea to sit at the child's elbow and oversee every word written. It is best to be available, if required, but not to assume responsibility for completion of the homework. That is the child's job. The older child may manage to complete homework in privacy but the younger child almost invariably needs some support.

■ If a child asks for help to read or explain a word or to spell a word, it is wise to do just what the child asks. It may be tempting to enter into a reading or spelling lesson, urging the child to sound out the word or to recall it from a previous task, but resist the urge. If a child finds that every time they ask a question the parent goes into teacher mode then the child may well stop asking questions.

■ It is quite common for children with dyslexia to have days when learning comes easily and days when they seem to have forgotten everything they ever knew. It is very frustrating for a parent who has carefully explained something on Monday night to find that on Tuesday night it is as if the child has never heard of the concept. Don't despair and don't be angry. Eventually the learning will take place.

■ On the subject of teaching – this is the job of the teacher. Homework is intended as a review or exercise on work done in the classroom. If the child does not understand, the parent may explain but should try to avoid teaching. The role of the parent is much too important in the child's life to confuse it with that of the teacher. A child has many teachers in the course of school life but only one Mum and Dad.

■ If the child has a major problem with an item of homework, perhaps a note to the teacher in the homework journal is the best option. The teacher then knows that the child has not grasped the concept and may be able to repeat the lesson.

■ Homework should not take up a child's entire leisure time. The class teacher can tell you how long homework should take. Children in primary school are not usually expected to spend more than an hour or so at homework. If your child is spending much longer on tasks than normal, then it should be possible to arrange with the teacher that the child will spend an agreed amount of time on homework. If the child is exhausted and the parent is frustrated and needs to clear the kitchen table for dinner, then not much learning will take place, so it's best to call it a day.

- It is worth remembering that children with dyslexia do get very tired. Schoolwork is often a struggle and takes more effort than is required from other children. They may also attend extra classes outside of school or may have homework from their learning support teacher. In general, they do have to work harder at learning than other children, so at times they must be given a little leeway. However, parents also need to be on guard that the child does not use dyslexia as an excuse for not trying. It is a very difficult line for a parent to walk and it is just not possible to get it right all the time.

- Parents can only do as much as their circumstances will allow. Most people these days have very demanding work lives and in many families both partners work full-time. There has to be time to enjoy your child and to have fun. A child with dyslexia may be extremely capable in many ways and it is important to acknowledge that fact. They may also have unique talents and ways of viewing the world. Enjoy that difference and remember that, like all others, children with dyslexia grow up very fast.

Learning to Enjoy Reading

The early school years are spent learning to read. The remaining years are spent reading to learn. Fortunate people learn to read for pleasure. Children with dyslexia run the risk of thinking of reading purely in terms of school work and do not easily associate it with fun. Parents can really help in this area. Reading to young children is a wonderful way of opening their minds to the wider world, increasing their vocabulary and their understanding of language. Even when children with dyslexia learn to read reasonably well, they still benefit from having an adult read to them. They hear a fluent reader, who pronounces words properly, who pauses at the appropriate places and who can explain the meaning of words or discuss the events in the story. This allows the child to appreciate the content of the story.

When a book or series is very popular, it is very important that the child with dyslexia keeps up with the trend. Parents can ensure that their child is up-to-date on the latest book by reading it with or for them. This will not make the child lazy or reluctant to read alone. On the contrary it will encourage a love of reading. Books on CD are a great way of passing a long car journey. Disputes about space, cries of "are we there yet?" and even travel sickness can be eliminated by listening to the children's choice of books, during the long holiday drive.

Paired Reading

Paired reading is an ideal technique for parents to use when reading for pleasure with the child and it is also very successful in improving reading ability. It has been recommended by learning support teachers for years and schools will usually have information leaflets and videos on how to do it. The thinking behind this technique is that daily practice of the art of reading, without any formal teaching strategy being used, helps the child to read while enjoying the process. The reading takes place at a different time and in a different atmosphere to homework. Curled up on a sofa in front of the fire would be ideal.

The child chooses a book. Parental guidance may be needed to ensure that the book chosen is not way out of the child's reading level but the important thing is that the child wants to read that book. Then parents set aside a particular slot of five to seven minutes every day, during which they read together with the child. The parent adjusts reading speed to match that of the child. They say the words together. If the child finds a word difficult the parent reads it. The child repeats the word. They move on and the flow of reading is not interrupted by any attempt to make the child sound out the word. If the child would like to read alone, an agreed signal (say, a tap on the book) can be given and the parent stays silent until the end of the session. This technique is beautifully simple, yet it is very effective. To get the most benefit from paired reading, it is important that it is done every evening over a period of weeks.

Of course, paired reading could also be done by grandparents or other adults with whom the child is comfortable. The idea is for a pleasant, entertaining and enjoyable reading session to take place.

Helping the Child to Learn Spellings

There are many suggestions about how best to teach spellings but they are all based on the same fundamental principles. It is widely agreed that children with dyslexia benefit from a multi-sensory teaching approach. This means that a combination of senses should be used, hearing, seeing and touching. The history books report that in the old monastic schools children were taught the alphabet by first making the letters in dough, baking them and then eating them. What a lovely way to learn and what a lot those early teachers knew about acquiring knowledge. Today a parent with the time and energy could use some cookie dough to help a child to 'internalise' a difficult word.

A simpler and less fattening technique is the following, often called the *Look - Say - Cover - Write - Check* method. Best results are obtained if no more than five words are learned at a time. The words can be written, formed with plastic or wooden letters, traced on sandpaper, rough carpet or on a sand tray. The child looks at the word until it is known. The word is spoken and explained if necessary. It could be put in a sentence. Then the word is covered and the child writes the word and says it. Next the child checks the written version of the word with the original. If the spelling is correct then the next word can be tackled. If the spelling is not correct then a little more time has to be spent on looking at and repeating the word.

Supporting the Child through the School System

Recent developments encourage much more participation by parents of children with special educational needs in the management of their children's education. The role of parents is recognised by the Department of Education and Skills in its legislation and in its recommendations. The Education Act of 1998 requires schools to produce a policy for pupils with disabilities, outlining how they cater for such students and setting up a grievance procedure which parents can use if they feel that adequate support is not provided. The Education for Persons with Special Educational Needs Act 2004, states its purpose is:

> To provide that people with special educational needs shall have the same right to avail of, and benefit from, appropriate education as do their peers who do not have such needs.... and

> to provide for the greater involvement of parents of children with special educational needs in the education of their children...

The *Learning Support Guidelines* issued in 2000 state:

> If, following diagnostic assessment, it is agreed that the pupil should receive supplementary teaching, the parents can

> contribute to the development and implementation of their child's individual profile and learning programme (IPLP) by discussing the learning targets for their child and by identifying activities that can be implemented at home to support the work of the school in achieving the agreed targets.

The underlying thinking is clear. Parents should be involved in discussing the supplementary teaching their children receive at school and how this can be best supported at home. Parents are to be involved in all aspects of their children's education and most schools welcome the input from interested and supportive parents.

When a child has a specific learning disability, supporting the child through the school system depends less on legislation perhaps, than on developing a good working relationship with the school and keeping informed on how educational policy impacts on the child with dyslexia.

Developing and maintaining a mutually trusting and understanding relationship between schools and teachers requires time and effort on both sides. Parents can best help to foster this by being honest, open and realistic about their child's needs and abilities. Information such as results of psycho-educational assessment, the amount of time spent on homework and the help which is given by parents or outside tutors is important to teachers. It helps them to evaluate the child's learning strengths and weaknesses and in preparing education plans for the child in school.

Keeping the school informed of your child's educational needs can be more difficult at secondary than at primary level. A copy of any psycho-educational assessment report should be supplied to the school principal but this will not necessarily make its way to all subject teachers. A brief summary of the report, with any relevant recommendations, could be sent in to all the child's teachers in September and also given to teachers at parent/teacher meetings. It may be necessary to make several copies and give one to every subject teacher every year.

It is important to be realistic about your child. A child, who has been assessed as of high academic ability but is achieving at an average or lower level, is likely to be frustrated and even angry. This child may not be easy to handle in a classroom situation. It is unrealistic to expect that a teacher with a large class will always be able to be as tolerant and accommodating of your child as you would wish.

A child who does not have great academic ability must be allowed to work at a pace suited to that ability, and parents must recognise that fact and not expect unreasonably high achievement. It is important to realise that every difficulty a child experiences in the classroom is not necessarily caused by dyslexia. There are other factors involved, such as the personality of the child, their overall ability, the attitude to work and to authority. Children with dyslexia can be forgetful, disorganised and even disruptive in class. They are normal children and vary enormously in both the degree of their dyslexia and in their other traits.

It is also important, of course, to act as an advocate for your child by explaining both needs and abilities. Parents may be told that each child in a class or a school has to be treated the same way in the interests of fair play. This is not necessarily the best approach. Treating children according to their own individual needs is much fairer. If one child feels ill and is sent home, the other children are not sent home too. This is not unfair. If children with dyslexia need some adjustments to the amount or type of homework which they do, this is not unfair. What would be unfair would be to make the ill child remain at school or to expect the child with dyslexia to spend three times as long on homework as the other children.

Children with dyslexia often have great competence and ability in a variety of areas. It is not boastful to make sure that teachers and other relevant people are made aware of this. At primary level, the class teacher will know your child well and be aware that while spelling may be a problem, maths is a strength. At second level this does not apply. Second level teachers may see three hundred students in a week and can't be expected to know the full profile of each one.

The other way in which you can support your child is by learning as much as possible about dyslexia and by keeping up to date on developments within the education system to support students. It is not wise to rely solely on the school to carry out this function. As a parent you should make this your business. There is a great deal of information out there and it pays to be aware. Books such as the one you are currently reading and *Lost for Words* by Wyn McCormack give you the basic information. Updated information is contained on the following websites:

- Department of Education and Skills: www.education.ie
- The Special Education Support Service: www.sess.ie
- The Dyslexia Association of Ireland: www.dyslexia.ie
- The Association for Higher Education Access and Disability: www.ahead.ie

The latest information on topics such as exemption from the study of Irish, reasonable accommodations in state examinations, assistive technology, up-coming conferences/parents courses and support services at third level can be obtained from these websites. This information is directly relevant to the child with dyslexia and their parents. At the least it may help to ease the student's progress through the system. At best it may make the difference between attaining entry to a desired course/career and settling for a second choice.

Mediating with the Outside World

If you think back to the time before your child demonstrated a learning difficulty, can you honestly say that you were aware of dyslexia? In all probability you had heard the word or some basic facts but never stopped to think what it might involve for a person who had that condition.

Other people are no different. Over the years your child will come across may people who do not know much about dyslexia or who may even have totally mistaken ideas about its effects. You may have to explain to grandparents, to the extended family, to your friends, perhaps even to teachers, that your child is a normal, healthy and capable child who just happens to have dyslexia.

Dyslexia can, as the cliché goes, "cause smart people to act dumb". To the uninitiated it may look as if your child is being careless, stupid, stubborn or downright uncooperative. Children with dyslexia may have great trouble in remembering quite simple things and in organising themselves. They may do the wrong homework, lose their belongings, forget to deliver messages, get details or instructions mixed up and be perpetually late for appointments. It is all too easy to say, "He may have a reading difficulty but why doesn't he do what he's told"? As a parent you may have to explain to a football coach, a scout leader or the parent of a classmate that dyslexia affects much more than reading ability. Poor short-term memory, short attention span, motor co-ordination difficulties, poor sense of time and a tendency to get names and dates mixed up are all part of dyslexia. If you can explain this to a person who is feeling frustrated by your child's behaviour, then they may look at the child in quite a different light and be prepared to see the child's ability as well as the disability.

Caring for the Carers

This is a very important topic. Parents invest time, money and a great deal of energy in rearing their children. This is even more true of parents of children with dyslexia. Caring and supporting is a demanding business but it does not have to occupy all your time and energy. You are entitled to leisure and some time for your own interests.

It can be difficult to keep the learning needs of your child in perspective but, realistically, there is a limit to what parents can be expected to do. In many households both partners work long hours and have other family duties and commitments. There will be times when you don't have the time, the energy or the patience to respond to your child's needs as you feel you should. There will be times when parents are quite frustrated and disappointed at the lack of a child's progress or at how quickly information is forgotten. There will be worries when tests and examination results are disappointing, despite the best efforts of everyone concerned. Parent/teacher meetings can be quite stressful. There may be differences of opinion between parents, between parents and child or between parents and school, about how the dyslexic problem is to be managed. All of this takes its toll on parents and on family members. Sometimes it is necessary to step back a little and distance yourself from the situation. If parents concentrate too much of their energy on dealing with a learning difficulty, it can interfere with their own normal lives, with sports, hobbies or social interaction. All of these are necessary to a balanced life and it is the right of every person to take some time for themselves. If you don't look after your own well-being, you will not be able to look after your children. You are often told not to be too demanding of your children. You should not be too demanding of yourself either.

Useful Resources

Parent courses offered by the Dyslexia Association of Ireland

Dyslexia Association of Ireland *All Children Learn Differently: A Parent's Guide to Dyslexia.*

McCormack, W. (2008) *Lost for Words, Dyslexia at Second Level.* Dublin: Tower Press.

Moore-Mallinos, J. (2010) *It's Called Dyslexia.* Dublin: O'Brien Press.

CHAPTER 6
THE PRIMARY SCHOOL CHILD
– CHILD DEVELOPMENT

This chapter will be of use to parents and teachers. In it you will read about:

- Stages of child development – early primary school years;
- Stages of child development – later primary school years;
- Emotional needs – developing a secure sense of self;
- Coping with bullying and anxiety;
- The efficacious student, self-esteem and self efficacy.

During their primary school years children are becoming more sophisticated in the way they think, learn and monitor their own learning, in how they recognise, name and manage emotion and how they relate to others. There are important milestones to be reached and hurdles to be negotiated. It is a time when they develop their sense of self and their belief about own capabilities.

The following section attempts to put much of this general introduction into the context of important stages of development which are taking place, cognitively and emotionally.

Stages of Child Development – Early Primary Years

During the early primary years young children are beginning to recognise their strengths and understand that they are individuals with abilities. They need to experience a sense of industry through trial and perseverance and accomplishment by being able to complete tasks successfully. On the emotional level they are eager to please and thus they need frequent recognition and praise. On the cognitive level children at this stage are becoming more capable of thinking, though still in a concrete manner rather than abstractly. They can think about situations and solve problems within their own experience. At this time their attitude to school and what it has to offer them is being established. Their roles within the group are being formed.

During these years the child is being introduced to reading and writing skills. A survey of the aims and objectives as outlined in the primary school English language curriculum indicates how far-reaching and ambitious these are. In the Junior and Senior Infant classes they are expected to develop 'concepts of language and print' and 'competence, confidence and the ability to write independently'. This includes activities such as listening to stories, learning nursery rhymes, playing language games with sounds, action songs and poems, writing and reading their writing aloud.

By the end of second class children are expected to 'pursue individual interests through independent reading of fiction and non-fiction' and are expected to discuss what they have read. They have been taught the basic strategies for comprehension. They are learning how to write in a variety of genres and how to make notes while they read.

By third class they are expected to use the library freely, be able to look at tables of contents, use a dictionary and find the pronunciation of words. They are expected to write regularly at some length. They are expected to present work with a clear sequence of ideas and to have begun to self-correct their work.

Children without a disability respond eagerly to each initiative because most children at this stage are keen to learn. Children with dyslexia, like their peers, are enthusiastic about learning but these are the very activities that present them with difficulties. Letter-sound matching, phonological analysis (sounding out words, recognising same/different sounds of letters and clusters of letters), handwriting, spelling, sequencing and order may all be problematic. They are experiencing varying degrees of success, depending on their form of dyslexia. At first they do not understand why they are falling behind. Later they may adopt unhelpful attitudes to protect themselves from further failure. The more advanced the learning task, the more noticeable is the difference between themselves and their peers. The danger is that the initial enthusiasm for learning begins to wane.

The support available for children is crucial. It is important at this stage to build up their sense of accomplishment through activities and skills that are not affected by dyslexia. Reading and writing are but two skills in a wide range of skills where children can be competent. The importance of literacy skills needs to be kept in proportion relative to the *whole* child's development. **They need to know that because such skills are considered important, they should try and they will eventually learn them.** That hope and inculcated self belief will give them the motivation to continue to persevere. It is important that they develop skills in other areas, too. Without seeing some measure of success it is difficult to keep motivation strong. Good teaching and step-by-step learning will make this possible. Parents and teachers can help the child to develop strategies for learning in informal and formal ways. By learning how they solve problems in activities other than reading and writing they can begin to apply such strategies to the task they find difficult. This demands an investment of effort and time from parents. Teachers need to use creative activities and teaching methods that have been found to bring about success for the child with dyslexia.

Under the staged plan of learning support in school dyslexia will, in all likelihood, not be formally diagnosed until children are nearer to seven-and-a-half years old. This is for two reasons. It can be difficult to be certain of the cause of delay and difficulty prior to that because the delay may be developmental, health-related or circumstantial and not as a result of dyslexia. Secondly, the school will operate on the principle of early intervention before formal assessment. Once children have been recognised as having a difficulty or a delay in learning to read and write, the school should put in place additional learning support for a fixed period and should review the progress at the end of the period. Then, depending on the results, the decision will be made to continue the learning support, to withdraw the support if they have 'caught up' or to refer children on to an educational psychologist for full psycho-educational assessment.

All this needs to be dealt with very positively. Parents may begin to feel anxious for the child and unsure about how to proceed. The following is a list of ways to help develop pre-reading skills:

- Reading for pleasure with the child;
- Playing visual games such as *I Spy* or *Spot the Difference*;
- Tracing;
- Copying activities;
- Model building;
- Word games;

- Memory tasks;
- Organising their materials;
- Playing rhyming games with them;
- Beating out the rhythm in nursery rhymes and poetry;
- Beating out a rhythm of sounds in words, using their names, for example;
- Playing 'Spot the Difference' with words as well as with pictures.

Since many children with dyslexia do not pick up new words as easily as children who do not have dyslexia, try to do the following which are all very ordinary but very essential ways of developing language:

- Speak clearly;
- Repeat new words;
- Explain what they mean;
- Encourage them to use them as part of their vocabulary;
- Engage them in conversation;
- Ask their opinion.

Other siblings may try to intervene when they see the child has difficulty in finding the right word but it is better to accustom them to wait for a reply. Insisting, tactfully, on full sentences and helping with word-finding will assist in developing an awareness of the structure of language.

It is also important to keep in close touch with teachers and consolidate at home some of the lessons being taught in school. There are a number of early learning programmes that can be used at home, with no teaching background required. Today's materials are bright and attractive and are intended to make learning fun, which it should be at this stage of a child's life. There are also many learning games that can be used as a family activity, which has an added advantage, provided that siblings are understanding.

Children are alert and register the attitudes of people who are significant in their lives towards their difficulty. At this stage children usually respect rules and look up to authority figures. This is a time when experiences where they feel they have not succeeded need to be talked about in a positive way, so that they learn that not succeeding on one occasion is part of a learning process that can be discussed. At home and at school the emphasis needs to be on what they can do. Homework needs to be tailored to their present competence so that it reinforces what they know and little by little they are stretched out towards the new level of attainment. The time given to homework should be limited to what is reasonable and within their attention span and not allowed to spill over into their play time. As they get older, rules about homework, such as about length of time or location, and which also encourage effort, can be made into contracts or mutual agreements.

Children at this stage are also beginning to be very sensitive to their place in the group and are adopting roles in relation to the group. With confidence, they will be active participants. Where there is a poor sense of competence and a perception of failure, they may well adopt attitudes of learned helplessness or withdraw from the group. Where children have begun to have a stable sense of self, which is evident when they can describe themselves as having certain characteristics, likes, dislikes and feelings, they are less likely to feel threatened in the group. This growth in self-awareness is closely related to how they value themselves that, in turn, has been learned from how they think others value them. If they are to develop a good self-image and self-esteem, children need to be regarded as individuals, without reference to the achievement of their peers.

At home parents can minimise situations where children may fail by making sure that tasks are structured and are within their capabilities and that they are rewarded for their effort. Similar criteria are relevant in school. The classic spelling test needs to be individualised for children with dyslexia so that there is a minimum number of spellings they are sure to remember and that their progress is marked by reference to their own previous spelling achievement and not with reference to achievement of others. If a child can accurately recall three spellings this week, try four the next week. Gradually increase the load when the child is ready to move on. Teach strategies such as:

- Visually remembering parts of words or even whole words;
- Making associations between words and objects;
- Grouping related pieces of information.

Such individualisation does need to be explained to the students to prevent them or one of their peers from interpreting it inaccurately. It should be clear that one is not individualising their learning because of a belief that they cannot achieve.

By the time children are ten, they have acquired most of the tools needed to be an efficient learner. Everyone has a personal, preferred way of doing things. Some educators think that it is best to go with this. Others suggest that there is much to be gained, in terms of learning problem solving skills, if the child works with the way things are less naturally acquired. For example, children who have keen visual memory may wish to aid their auditory memory by means of mindmaps and images. This is good and probably very effective. However, their skills will be enhanced if they also make a deliberate effort to find ways of developing auditory memory. Not all learning experiences can depend only on one way of doing things, so it is wiser to build up a number of ways of accessing and storing information and problem solving.

Some children may not automatically know how to solve a particular problem, such as how to learn the alphabet and the sounds that go with each letter. Efficient ways of doing things can be taught. This is what is meant by learning strategies. Often, children's time and energy are wasted because they insist on personally reinventing the wheel. Teach them:

- How to make mind-maps of information to be learnt. Such mind-maps could use pictures instead of words;
- Put the information on tape;
- Have them devise a story around the facts;
- Use colour coding for mathematical symbols and signs;
- If they cannot remember how to add and subtract 'in their head', then give them an abacus to count with;
- Apply **the use of such concrete materials** to mathematical shapes such as triangles and cubes until the child is ready to move on.

Stages of Child Development – the Later Primary School Years

Having successfully negotiated the first five years of primary school and having begun to develop a sense of self as competent, children in the senior primary school are becoming more interested in aspects of identity such as appearance and gender role. They will have developed an ability not only to generalise from individual experiences but also to generate hypotheses about how things might be. They can now think abstractly. They become more involved with the group and with co-operation. This means that rules are more meaningful when they are negotiated and agreed upon. Peer acceptance and the ability to take personal decisions are increasingly important. At this stage physical development can affect self-confidence and consequently behaviour. At the same time they are now better able to take another's point of view and understand it. Literacy and school achievement may have a lower place on the list of priorities.

For the parent, knowledge is power. The methods of dealing with the situation may need to change. Having a say, not losing out on group activities and being part of the group are all very important to the child at this stage. However, while some things can be negotiated, there remain basic non-negotiable ground rules. If this is understood for all activities then it will be easier to apply a similar method when encouraging habits of study and accepting additional support.

Children with dyslexia need greater support to become the confident, competent persons they have the potential to be. Characteristically, they may experience a delay in becoming automatic at reading and writing and the gap between academic potential and achievement may get wider as the work becomes more demanding. While they know and have developed skills in other areas, they realise deep down that ultimately the ability to read and write is important for their future. By the time they face into secondary school, it is important to have developed a curiosity about the world and some awareness of how they work best, as well as good strategies that help them to store information.

In the senior primary school days learning skills can be reinforced in a variety of informal ways. Basic to all learning is the ability to focus on information long enough to process it. One does not learn what one did not notice. First, one pays attention. Then one stores the information. Later, to recall the information, one has to find the file in which it is stored. Children with dyslexia experience difficulty with holding attention and storing information in a systematic way. Apart from reading and writing they need to develop ways and means of focusing their attention and connecting information. Techniques can be used to develop attention by using strategies such as:

■ Demanding eye contact;

■ Giving an instruction and asking for it to be repeated.

■ Developing a habit of zoning in before starting a task. The child should stop, think and question what is going to be answered while doing this task.

Later the student uses the strategy of recollecting or reminding themselves at the beginning of each study session of what they are about to do. Learning will not take place with a divided attention. All distracting stimuli should be eliminated, whether auditory, visual or postural. Not everybody can sit upright at a desk but nobody can learn efficiently with one eye on the moving frames on the television set!

Visual attention to detail can be developed by playing memory games when walking down the street. Questions can be asked such as, 'What colours were in the dress shop window?' or 'How many instruments were in the music shop window?' Develop habits such as:

■ Repeating information which was heard,

■ Associating it with a significant number, picture or detail such as recalling a person by the colour and shape of her handbag.

Children in the senior primary classes are expected to take part in discussions at school. The more they are included in family discussions, where their opinion is asked for and valued, the more confidently they will present themselves in class. When he can discuss in a **safe** environment, where everybody is expected to make a contribution and where everybody's opinion is valued, the child will learn how to take turns, to listen, to respect and probably to revise. When children are not listened to, they are more likely to be loud and uncompromising in their statements.

Emotional Needs: Developing a secure sense of self.

So far we have dealt with stages of development and processes for learning, specifically academic learning. But what happens when the stages are not being traversed as smoothly as the above would suggest? How does the parent deal with the **wobbles** of identity, the loss of self belief, the 'I'm stupid' period, the anxieties, the learned helplessness, the switching off and the bullying that may happen because the child is different?

Having dyslexia may be considered as an additional risk factor for the child's emergent sense of self. There is some evidence that children with dyslexia are at greater risk of developing low self-concepts and self-esteem. But beware of too easy an association. There is also evidence to suggest that they will not necessarily do so. Research by Robert Burden[1] for example, found that pupils with dyslexia in an environment where their disability was understood and where they were taught strategies to enable them to achieve academically, had strong and healthy self-esteem. If the environment at home is warm, affirming, supportive and pro-active, there is every chance that the children's development will be able to encompass the difficulties presented in the classroom when they try to learn to read.

It is useful to reflect on what contributes to the development of a healthy sense of self and to recognise what may be happening when a child's self-esteem is low, or to identify the underlying motivation behind some unhelpful patterns of behaviour, which are in fact signalling a confused or unhealthy sense of self.

Who we are and the emotions behind how we act out are shaped by many relationships. For the growing child, family, peers and school are significant influences.

The Concept of Self

The sense of 'Who I am' depends on two processes which are to create a self image and evaluate that image. Children create a picture or image of facts they come to **believe** about themselves such as: 'I have blue eyes, I am musical, I can play sport, I cannot read'. Self image is a set of these beliefs. Beliefs are formed through feedback from the environment; very often from how people who are important or significant to the child respond and say positive comments such as:

■ 'Well done! You have accomplished that well';
■ 'You tried really hard there. Well done'.

On the other hand, negative comments may well contribute to a lowering of self-esteem. These could be comments such as:

■ 'Go to your seat and stop looking for notice';
■ 'What do you think you are doing?'

Self evaluation is the **judgment** made about the importance of these facts or beliefs. If blue eyes are important, then having or not having blue eyes may be very important and individuals judge themselves accordingly. 'Reading is important; I cannot read...I judge myself accordingly'. These two processes, creating a picture and putting a judgement on, or evaluating, happen often without the individuals becoming aware of how they have associated them.

Beliefs and judgments are usually associated with strong feelings. What is generally meant when talking about **self-esteem** is self-evaluation associated with feeling. People weigh up what aspects of their beliefs about themselves are important and that evaluation is accompanied by a particular feeling.

Feelings tend to drive behaviour. The image held and the evaluation made is a guide to behaviour and how people understand what happens to them or what they may expect. If beliefs about people are evaluated and accompanied by a feeling of satisfaction, they are likely to behave in such a way that makes them feel even more satisfied and accepted. This is healthy self-esteem.

If on the other hand, faulty beliefs are formed about the person, their behaviour and expectations, these are likely to reinforce the poor image and increase the uncomfortable feelings held. This is low self-esteem.

People with low self-esteem tend to confirm their low opinion of themselves in some of the following ways:

- They select what details of an incident they choose to remember, usually the ones which illustrate to them their uselessness and failure;
- They use absolute judgments such as, 'I'm no good at anything';
- They make inaccurate associations: 'I can't read, therefore I'm stupid';
- They take all criticism personally.

This may result in a habit of responding in a certain way such as: 'I cannot read; reading is something everyone learns so I must be different and I don't like it'. The response to this evaluation may be **angry** behaviour. It may be manifested in behaviour which is directed inwardly: 'I cannot read so there must be something wrong with **me**'. This leads to individuals protecting themselves by not trying or by retreating into their shell. A healthier response may be: 'I cannot read, so what! I know I will'.

Children with dyslexia are faced with a number of possible ways of responding as they see their literacy tasks becoming more difficult and they begin to fall behind their peers. How they *feel* about the challenge may have a significant effect on how they behave. When self-esteem is low it is likely to be evident in expressions of anger, boredom, anxiety, being fed-up and being useless. These may translate themselves into *actions* such as:

- Evading doing the work;
- Excuses as to why it is not finished;
- Giving up easily;
- Being noisy and boisterous;
- Statements such as 'I can't do that';
- Hiding work;
- Attention seeking;
- Being easily led.

Thus, the base line beliefs held about the person are integral to developing a secure self-concept and the evaluations and the feelings and behaviours that evolve around these beliefs.

An aspect of self-esteem worth mentioning is that it is multifaceted. Children may have a general or global sense of self but may view themselves in different ways. Thus they can value (esteem) the part of themselves that plays music or gets on well with friends and family. They may not value themselves in the whole area of academic learning. Thus they can have one belief about their ability in reading and a different one about how they get on with their peers. One may be 'low', while the other may be 'high'. The risk is that a belief about school attainments like literacy or numeracy being very important can pervade the global image they have of themselves. Parents often observe that a child's self-esteem has plummeted in the second or third year after they have failed to keep up with their peers in the classroom when learning to read. The comment 'I am no good at .../ I am rubbish at reading' is cipher for 'I believe I cannot read' or 'I hate it that I cannot read' or 'I must be no good because I cannot read'. If this is the belief held and significant adults are stressing what a good and important thing it is to be able to read, write and spell, it is a short step to devaluing one's whole Self. The particular becomes the general and affects how children see themselves overall as people rather than how they see themselves in a particular area of 'Self'.

Building up self-esteem is a slow and painstaking process and requires ongoing reinforcement. The trap is lowering expectations for children when what they need is to be challenged in such a way that they learn to succeed and use failure constructively and in perspective. They need to know that parents and teachers believe they can and will succeed. 'Dumbing down' expectations of what they are capable of doing is one of the risk factors to their concept of self for a child with special learning needs. A significant fear experienced by parents where children have been diagnosed as having dyslexia, is that their future may be limited by their disability. When significant players in children's lives make up their minds what is the limit to which they can aspire, it usually happens that that is the limit. Limited expectations from a parent, caregiver or teacher may signal to the children that the feeling held is 'I don't believe they can'. One of the benefits of having a full psycho-educational assessment is the wide information it gives about a child's **potential** and about the difficulties that become the jumping off ground for appropriate intervention. Often, it would appear these reports are used only to confirm a diagnosis, get access to learning support or exemptions and accommodations and not as learning and teaching tools.

Behaviours associated with self-esteem
In the 1950s what has become a classical study, Coopersmith[1] and his associates outlined behaviours and attitudes that correlated with high and low self-esteem.

High self-esteem was associated with:
- Having a positive, realistic sense of self;
- Not being unduly worried by criticism;
- Enjoying participation;
- Setting realistic goals;
- Willing to take risks.

Low self-esteem was associated with:
- Feeling more isolated;
- More fearful;
- More reluctant in participate;
- Over-sensitive to criticism;
- More self-conscious;
- Setting unrealistic goals.

As adults watch children grow it is wise to listen carefully to comments children make about themselves and to challenge gently the underlying 'false' self belief. Help them to prove themselves wrong!

Dyslexia and self-esteem in the home

An important consideration for children developing within the family is how their specific need is explained, talked about, and managed. The whole family is involved with the children's emerging sense of who they are. Sometimes one hears stories of how dyslexia is not talked about or 'denied' by not wanting to name it. Efforts are made to keep it 'within the family'. If significant adults and peers do not adequately acknowledge and explain to children the special learning needs and differences, their interpretation of their difficulties and differences is likely to be that these are in some way negative things.

The self-esteem of children struggling to understand themselves and their learning difficulties can to be developed by giving them as much opportunity for discussion and decision-making within the family and that they participate as equally as their siblings.

A healthy home environment will contain to a considerable degree the qualities of:

- Family warmth;
- Openness;
- Listening;
- Consultation;
- Authoritative structure, firm but not rigid;
- Direction;
- Guidance;
- Clear boundaries for behaviour;
- Allow evolving levels of appropriate discipline and independence;
- Demonstrate cooperation and mutual support within the family.

In short, the optimum environment whether at home or school, for the developing child is one that is:

- Warm;
- Respectful;
- Accepting;

■ Supporting and enabling;

■ Consultative.

These qualities allow the child to feel loved, accepted, respected and secure.

School and home are more beneficial to the child's development when they work in tandem, such as in managing homework. The parent may discuss what needs to be done with the teacher and individualise it so that the aim is to make sure the child will be able to have at least 50% of homework accurately completed. In this way the esteem-destructive pattern of learning-failure-repeated failure is avoided.

Anything that reduces the fear of failure is appropriate. All concerned should understand that errors and mistakes are accepted as being part of the trial-error-strategy-success aim of the task. Remember that not every error needs to be pointed out in every written exercise or task. Pick judiciously and try to group mistakes so that the learning can focus on two or three points to be learned. The same applies to social learning and discipline breaches. 'To win the war, choose the battles' is an old adage still appropriate to today. Some possible strategies are:

■ Discuss what went wrong;

■ Encourage children to grow in the practice of monitoring how they proceed through a task so that they learn to be their own positive critic;

■ Give honest, constructive feedback;

■ Never allow/accept 'put down' comments from other members of the family or peers.

Back to the learning environment

As the child develops and tasks/learning challenges become increasingly more complex, the recurring question is not only how much do they know, since information known facilitates the learning of the new material, but what can they do? Have they the tools to access further knowledge? **What do they believe they can do?** One of a teacher's main tasks, is to provide the set of skills that will help the child to move from 'I believe I cannot' to 'I believe I can'. Warmth, respect, acceptance, support are abstract nouns. Effective teachers must make concrete – by their behaviour - these abstractions. Many people speak of the difference an inspirational teacher makes in one's life. Children have a better chance of making progress when they experience empathy, respect, understanding and belief from teachers and when parents and teachers are seen to be working together.

It is important to identify/recognise less acceptable behaviours that are in danger of being misinterpreted and which are in fact children's ways (albeit unwelcome) of signalling their loss of self worth or self competency. Sometimes behaviour, where children are achieving well but insist on drawing attention to the fact continually by boasting or needing to be acclaimed, is in fact a cover for poor self worth. In other cases behaviour is disruptive because children are **not** achieving in a particular area but they have plenty of confidence in their worth or 'value'. In this case low self-esteem has a different source. Confident in their 'worth,' they lack belief in their **ability** to attain. At times the parent and teacher may be challenged by the behaviour of the child.

It is very difficult to separate the different layers at which the individual functions. Feeling informs belief and vice versa. Belief and evaluation with feeling inform behaviour. Children with dyslexia need to understand the nature of their disability if they are to integrate it into their picture of who they are. Opportunities should be found to describe, discuss and point out the possibilities for adult life that are within their reach. Children are likely to be fearful as much as parents are, though they may not always express it. On the other hand, confidence in their potential to achieve is a strong motivator.

Often children are afraid of telling others about their difficulty for fear of the perceptions others may have of what it means to be dyslexic. Poor acceptance of the disability can take the form of denial. In particular teenagers often prefer to ignore their differences at school rather than avail of the supports that could improve their difficulties.

Giving them the opportunity to explain to others how it feels to be dyslexic can be an enlightening experience. It is a two-way transaction. Often they do not know that everybody does not experience the world as they do. How can others know how they feel if they do not listen to them? By giving them opportunities to explain to others, perhaps a class group, the message is given, 'It is all right to think and feel like this'. Sometimes an audience can be invited to perform a number of everyday activities that mime the difficulties experienced by people with dyslexia in order to get a deeper understanding. Similar exercises that are non-threatening might be used in class and with siblings to illustrate the point.

Bullying

At all stages the fact that children with dyslexia are different leaves them vulnerable both to being bullied and to perpetrating bullying behaviours. A common insult is to call children with dyslexia 'stupid' because they cannot get their spelling right, or because they are clumsy and cannot keep up at football or because the class has to wait for them while they look for the right page. However, low self-esteem generated by a sense of being 'no good' can result in aggressive, bullying behaviour. In each case the behaviour needs to be confronted and each party led to understand the impropriety of their behaviour. Parents and school need to work together at resolving the issues.

Children who are the victims of bullying behaviour will need to develop a stronger sense of self. How is this achieved? In the long term the beliefs they have formed about themselves may need to be re-stated since they are the baseline for behaviour. In addition, other strategies include getting them to focus on what they can accomplish, extending their range of activities and interests, or involvement in group activities where they are shown the rules of how to communicate well. A useful strategy is to create a **Positives** diary in which they record the personal achievements of each day such as, 'Finished my homework', 'Didn't give up when I couldn't solve the maths problem' or 'Held my tongue when I wanted to shout out the answer'. Establishing a reward structure where the achievement is recognised not only by the adult but claimed by children themselves is another method of helping them to a healthier sense of self.

And what of the child who becomes the bully? There are many underlying reasons why children bully other children. Top of the list must be a sense of powerlessness and the need to dominate. Bullies become expert at finding the Achilles heel of their victims and often appeal for the support of their gang of followers. Sometimes they are unaware of the hurt they cause. Helping them to take another's point of view is important for their social development. Denial and poor self-esteem can express itself in aggressive and inappropriate behaviour. Consequently, the underlying low self-esteem may have to be addressed. The social effects of bullying need to be made very clear to the child and a clear system of reward and reprimand put in place to reverse the behavioural patterns that may have become habitual.

In the case of both the victim and the bully, it may be necessary to involve professional counsellors to help address the issues. Counsellors may work out a programme of behaviour therapy. There are a variety of approaches that can be used. Some therapists deal with the individual situations and facts of a particular incident. They intervene with suggested solutions rather than a lengthy analysis of incidents and causes. Others take a 'no blame' approach, which allows early intervention without attributing blame to one side or the other. School counsellors, NEPS psychologists and HSE psychologists may be consulted. There is an Anti-bullying Unit in Trinity College Dublin.

However it is managed, bullying needs to be dealt with openly and in a concerted manner. School and home must work together with common, agreed policies and action. As with all abuse, secrecy is the lethal weapon of the abuser. Children who bully depend on others not speaking up and children who are bullied are often in fear of speaking up. Keeping the lines of communication open between parents and children may not save them from being bullied or from bullying others but these situations are less likely to occur if they know they can tell adults how they feel.

Anxiety in Children

Some people are born 'worriers'. Having a learning difference can exacerbate this trait, particularly if the environment is not fully understanding. Anxiety may be expressed by the child in the following ways:

- Self-doubt statements they make frequently or from time to time;
- Critical evaluations they make of themselves;
- Irritability;
- Over-sensitivity;
- Poor ability to sleep may also signal higher than usual anxiety.

In school these anxieties may transfer themselves into:

- A need for constant approval;
- Avoidance of activities;

- Poor concentration;
- Refusal to go to school.

Anxiety disorders such as obsessive-compulsive disorder and social phobia – which are persistent rather than occasional states - may co-exist.

For parents such worries can further increase their own anxiety. However, in spite of the feeling, the most helpful course of action is to keep calm and to try not to convey those feelings to children. Parents could model for them how anxiety can be dealt successfully.

Useful interventions include the following:

- Good listening skills that hear what children are saying without coming in too quickly to give advice or belittle their fears.
- In the face of a dreaded event, reassurance that the child has managed a previous similar situation is a reassuring reminder.
- Learning to take 'time out' and visualise a place of utter peace and security may well help to calm fears and anxiety.
- Children can be encouraged to take part in non-threatening activities which will distract them from the underlying anxiety.
- Talk to them about occasions when they successfully 'managed' a stressful situation and examine together the strategies they used.
- Praise regularly not just academic successes but also the way they are managing their fears and feelings.
- Discuss their fears with the school personnel in order that they may experience empathy and understanding. Ask that similar techniques for coping with anxiety are used within the classroom. This calls for adapting rules where necessary. It also calls for sensitivity when choosing topics and materials, finding time and place to talk personally to the child, getting to know what situations trigger anxiety and devising alternative strategies to help them cope. Group discussions or drama may be used to explore anxiety but this should be done sensitively and where possible with the consent and prior knowledge of the child.

The Efficacious Student: Self-esteem and Self efficacy

There is no reason why children with dyslexia may be any less likely than their peers to become great learners and to go on to adult life ready to use their qualities, skills and abilities to their potential. One goal of school experience should be to become an 'efficacious' student.

Self–efficacy is the belief that one has the competence to perform a task and to problem solve in the face of new tasks. The essence of the concept is belief about what the individual can do. Self-esteem (how I value myself) goes hand-in-hand with self efficacy (what I believe myself capable of) and these are part of the main power lines in the interconnected networks that create the sense of self. Students with a positive feeling about themselves and their ability are likely to be more motivated, put in more effort and feel more autonomous about their studies. This will lead to academic success.

The qualities that characterise the efficacious student include:

■ The ability to monitor oneself through a task through giving oneself feedback. Children will easily do this for themselves when they have been shown how to question themselves at each step.

■ Persistence and perseverance. Remember the old adage 'If at first you don't succeed, try, try and try again'.

■ Readiness to experiment. The student should try out new strategies and reflect on how useful/adaptable they may be. How much leeway is given to the student when tasks are set?

Developing self-efficacy, together with challenging false beliefs, are two important ways in which a strong, healthy sense of self is built up. If individuals are feeling powerless, talk by itself will not change behaviour. The encouraging word must be accompanied by some action that enables them to change their belief about themselves. With regard to dyslexia, it is good to reinforce and remind children of all their accomplishments and talents but all the nice words and encouragement will not raise their self-esteem about their academic ability unless they are helped to find strategies to read, spell and organise their learning.

Practical suggestions for developing self-esteem and self-efficacy
It may be useful to try to identify which area of the self is vulnerable. With dyslexia one would expect the skills of reading and writing to be a possible source of concern to children. In that case providing strategies that improve their learning capabilities will be effective. Included above in the profile of 'efficacious students' is the identifying

of the qualities that will help them to attain their goals. Good teachers will direct progress of students with carefully structured, cumulative tasks, moving step-by-step over the ground, discussing progress with child and parent at the appropriate level. But developing reading skills should not always be relegated to school. Reading with children, so that they can talk about the latest book their friends are reading may be one way of minimising their sense of isolation and keeping their self belief high.

The tasks and the way in which it is presented may be a key factor in developing confidence in one's own competency. It is wise to survey carefully the task so that what children are being asked to do is in part within their competence and in part a challenge to go beyond their present stage. Children with dyslexia need to be **walked through** the task by judicious prompting, explanation and demonstration, repeated as often as needed until such time as they know they can do it on their own. It has already been noted that children with dyslexia take considerably longer to become automatic in a task. By giving them the opportunity to become expert by multiple repetitions, self-confidence and self-esteem are being built up.

Establishing habits of self-reflection is integral to this process. The child needs to become as independent and self-directive as possible. Creating a learning checklist/diary in which they keep track of their own learning behaviour is one way of encouraging good habits. A checklist of items that helped during study-time might include statements such as:

■ Ignored noise around me;

■ Turned off the IPOD and mobile phone;

■ Cleared desk of clutter;

■ Quietened myself before starting;

■ Followed my homework plan;

■ Revised work.

Where the item cannot be ticked off as satisfactory on a particular occasion, this action is targeted for improvement at the next session. Thus actions are seen in context and failures are seen as possible to correct.

The child with dyslexia, however, may have other concerns as well. Bearing in mind that many children with dyslexia, may have co-occurring difficulties associated with Asperger's Syndrome, dyspraxia, dyscalculia, ADD, ADHD and language disorders, it may be necessary to identify other areas where they are unsure and lacking in self-belief. Whether these arise for poor social understanding or poor motor-co-ordination, the principles can be applied:

■ Identify and understand the baseline belief (I am clumsy);

■ Make the evaluation (being clumsy is a bad thing) with feeling (I do not like being clumsy) and the behaviour initiated by this evaluation (I don't want to go out because I cannot run with the others);

■ Challenge the evaluation (clumsy is neither good nor bad; it stops me running but there are other ways of playing with my friends);

■ Initiate some action by getting help to improve motor-co-ordination or to provide opportunities to engage in other fun activities which are acceptable to peers.

■ Develop other accomplishments and interests to which the child can introduce friends.

Similarly the child for whom social skills are difficult to learn, the steps could be:

■ Provide the cues;

■ Point out conventions;

■ In time, point out behaviours that may be keeping other children at a distance;

■ Model how it might be done.

Be careful with language! A recent study on the forms of language parents use found that in the group who were being studied 90% of the sentence forms used were directives. These would be orders such as 'You ought to do this' or 'Stop that noise'. Think about some of the following:

■ How is praise given? How often? Is there usually a *but* coming next? Has the praise been earned? Praise for insignificant actions may devalue it. Does the child value the praise?

■ Avoid negative comments or instructions such as 'Your clothes are still on the floor' instead of 'You haven't hung up your clothes yet';

■ Establish ground rules together. Negotiate exceptions;

- Discuss what went wrong, when it goes wrong and what to change the next time;
- Ask for opinions and treat these with respect;
- Teach ways of problem solving and a habit of self talk. This latter helps to focus attention and also to quieten the little inner voice which says 'You're going to make a mess of this as usual!';
- Set goals together for the day, the week. This is like the 'Positives' notebook. If the child can tick each off as accomplished at the end of the week, one experiences what it is to achieve. This gives one some sense of being in control of one's life. Being 'out of control' is usually associated with frustration and anger;
- 'Let not the sun go down on your anger'. The parent may forget about what has happened but children may still remember and internalise only the disappointment and anger displayed. They need to be assured that it hasn't changed the parent's love and respect for them. Later it can be discussed.

Summary

Children with dyslexia need to pass through the same stages of development as any other child and acquire the same life skills and problem-solving ability. The foundations for a healthy sense of self and self-esteem are laid by the messages children hear and interpret which are given to them by people who are significant in their lives.

An atmosphere at home and at school that is warm, accepting and understanding will help to bring the child through the difficulties of feeling they cannot accomplish the task of learning to read and write as quickly or effortlessly as many of their peers. Close co-operation between the teacher and parent will ensure maximum opportunity for learning.

References

1. Burden, R. (2005) *Dyslexia and Self Concept* London: Whurr
2. Coopersmith, S. (1959) *Method for Determining Types of Self-Esteem*
3. Journal of Abnormal and Social Psychology. Vol. 59, 1, 87-94

Useful Resources

1. O'Moore, M. (2010) *Understanding School Bullying – A Guide for Parents and Teachers* Dublin: Veritas
2. Plummer, D. M. *Helping Children to Build Self-Esteem* London: Jessica Kingsley
3. Rose, R. & Shevlin, M. (2010) *Count Me In – Ideas for Actively Engaging in Inclusive Classrooms* London: Jessica Kingsley

CHAPTER 7
COPING AT SECOND LEVEL – EDUCATIONAL CHOICES

This chapter will be of most use to parents and students with dyslexia in the last years of primary education and at second level. At the beginning of second level, students are still very young and parents have a key role in making educational decisions. As students mature, they should take an increasing responsibility for decisions so that by the time they are in senior cycle, they are deciding about their future with guidance from parents and teachers.

In this chapter you will read about the following educational choices:

- Choice of school;
- Subject choice;
- Choices in the state examination system;
- Choices after Junior Certificate.

These decisions should be based on the child's abilities and interests and on the opportunities available. If students enjoy the subjects/courses which they are studying, it increases motivation and helps them achieve. Education has become increasingly more flexible with new courses and new routes to qualifications. Students with dyslexia tend to have an ability profile with clearly defined strengths and weaknesses. The flexibility in the education system enables them to concentrate increasingly on their strengths as they progress through second level to third level and further education.

Choice of School

Deciding which second level school is the most suitable for a student with dyslexia is a key decision for parents. Some parents may not have a choice since there may be only one school for the area. Other parents have a choice, particularly in city areas. To make the best choice, the parents need to have as much information as possible.

There are many different factors to be considered when choosing a school. There is no perfect school that meets all criteria. Parents need to decide on what they consider to be the most important criteria that will best meet their child's needs.

Below are some points to consider when choosing a school.

Class Placement

How does the school place students in classes? Most schools have more than one class in each year group. Different ways to place students in classes include:

- *Mixed ability*: Students are randomly placed in class groups so each class has students with varying abilities;
- *Setting*: Students are assessed in an individual subject usually Irish, English and Maths. The students are placed in class according to their ability in that subject. Thus a student may be in a top Maths class and a weaker English class;
- *Streaming*: Students are placed in classes by their performance at assessment. The assessment could include standardised testing in general ability, literacy and numeracy. Thus there may be a top ability, middle ability and weakest class;
- *Banding*: This is an attempt to merge mixed ability and streaming. The year group may be divided into two halves, based on ability, and then classes are formed on a mixed ability basis inside each half.

What is the most appropriate class placement for an individual student with dyslexia who may have an uneven profile of ability? Mixed ability and setting both have advantages. Mixed ability allows the student to benefit from the range of ideas and stimuli in the class. Setting allows the student to specialise in subjects they are good at. Streaming is criticised for the effect it can have on morale and motivation in lower streams. Students may become disaffected with resulting discipline problems. For students with dyslexia this may be the worst scenario. They may be placed in a low stream because of weaker verbal skills but the class might not provide the challenge and stimulation to cater for their strengths.

The Post-primary Guidelines on the Inclusion of Students with Special Educational Needs (2007) discuss class placement at some length. They state that, in general, schools are advised to include all students in mainstream mixed-ability class groups to the greatest extent possible and in a manner that allows them to participate in a meaningful and beneficial way in classroom activities. Teachers often state in reports of research on mixed ability teaching that there are beneficial effects for both high-achieving and low-achieving students from placement in such classes. The benefits include not only academic progress but also social and personal development. Research by the ESRI shows an increase in the use of mixed ability since the 1990's. It notes that 70% of schools surveyed used mixed-ability in first year, 16% used banding and 14% used streaming.

The guidelines state that advocates of streaming often suggest that streaming of students is not only organisationally attractive, but it also enables teachers to concentrate on priority learning needs of students with low achievement. It allows for individualised attention for these students and the opportunity to make progress at their own pace. However recent research suggests that the outcomes for students in streamed classes fall far below these expectations. The negative efforts of streaming include the possibility the students may be segregated from their peers rather than included with them. Those in the low streams may make poor academic progress and may feel marginalised and isolated in the school community. The range of subjects available may be reduced for these students. *Moving Up* (2004), a report of a study carried out for the National Council for Curriculum and Assessment (NCCA) found where streaming is used it tends to result in the labelling of students as either 'smart' or 'stupid'. It also found that students in the higher streams took longer to settle in post-primary school. Many experienced difficulties in handling the increased pace of learning and volume of work.

Discipline
Students with dyslexia tend to be disorganised. They need a clearly organised classroom with clear instructions and a sense of order as they may need to concentrate quite hard to process their teacher's instructions. Some students learn much more from listening attentively than they do from reading from a textbook. They require a well-structured and disciplined atmosphere in which to do this.

Size of School
Large schools (schools of over 500 pupils) can provide a wider range of subjects. With more choice, students are more likely to find

subjects in which they can do well. Smaller schools have a reduced range of subjects, which may be a disadvantage. However, the smaller school provides an environment where each student is known by all the staff, which can have a beneficial effect on self-esteem and strengthen a feeling of being part of the school community. There may also be smaller classes and less streaming.

Class Size
It is very much to the student's advantage if class sizes are small. In a small class the teacher has more time to pay individual attention to students. However in most publicly funded schools classes are at the maximum class size. This is 30 students or 24 in classes where there is a practical element such as Science or Home Economics.

School Attitude to Learning Difficulties
Some schools can be very supportive of the needs of students with diverse learning difficulties, including dyslexia, and have structures in place to assist them. In meeting with the principal of a school for the first time to discuss the needs of the student, it will become apparent whether the school has a supportive attitude or not.

Unfortunately, it has been the experience of some parents that not all schools are supportive. Some schools are oversubscribed with many more applicants than places. Parents have spoken about the fact that some principals attempt to persuade them that the school would not be suitable for their child with a learning difficulty. They point to a lack of resources and argue that other schools might have more. They may even mention the *academic* ethos of their own school or point to the fact that all students must study one or even two foreign languages in first year. In some cases such persuasion occurs despite the fact that the student's siblings are already attending the school. It seems to be inequitable that a school is willing to enrol some children in a family but is unwilling to enrol the child with learning difficulties. Reluctance to enrol students with learning difficulties means that up to 10 per cent of the population may not be considered appropriate intake. Imagine if this was a physical disability and the schools could argue that a child with glasses or a limp could not be catered for adequately and that the appropriate placement was in other schools.

The reality is that under the Education Act all schools should provide equality of access and appropriate educational provision to meet the needs of the child. The school cannot discriminate on the grounds of disability. Also it is unfair on schools with inclusive policies if such schools are expected to enrol a disproportionate number of students with learning difficulties. With the media focusing on league tables based on student results, the true achievement of such schools may not be appreciated.

The Post-primary Guidelines on Inclusion discusses school enrolment policy. It states that there is evidence that some post-primary schools continue to have restrictive enrolment policies that lead to the effectual exclusion of children with SEN and those with other learning differences. It states that the Department of Education and Skills considers the practice of selecting certain students for enrolment and refusing others so as to ensure only a certain cohort of students is enrolled – for example those who are more able academically – is unacceptable and that where such practices exist they should be discontinued. It is also inappropriate for a school to include a clause in its admission policy to the effect that the enrolment of a student with SEN is dependent on the allocation of appropriate resources. It is good practice for a school to seek all relevant information on a student with SEN prior to entrance. This information should not be normally used in any way, implicitly or explicitly to determine whether or not the child is to be enrolled in the school.

If parents have decided to send their child to a particular school and have concerns about the possible school attitude, one strategy is that they do not tell the school about the needs of the student until they have first been offered a place in the school. At this stage discussions should then be centred on how the school can best meet the needs of the student. If parents meet difficulties, they should use their increased rights under the Education Act and ask to see the school policy on enrolment, particularly with reference to students with learning difficulties. If the principal makes a comment such as that the school does not cater for students with a learning difficulty, ask that this be put into writing.

One very immediate way to improve provision for students with dyslexia and other learning difficulties is to provide in-service training for teachers. Many teachers at second level have received no training on the topic of dyslexia either in pre-service or in-service courses. Schools are allowed one day for in-service training for the whole staff during the academic year. Parents could, either themselves or through the Parents' Association, request that the school consider holding an in-service day on the topic of dyslexia. The Special Education Support Service (SESS) provides training for teachers on the topic of dyslexia when requested by the school principal. The Dyslexia Association of Ireland also provides similar training. Such training is particularly relevant in view of recent legislation.

Learning Support/Resource Teaching
Students, on entrance to second level, may still need additional help. Such help may be provided by a learning support teacher or a resource teacher. Are such facilities available? Does the student meet the criteria to access them? The criteria are discussed in Chapter 3.

Friends
In some cases students with learning difficulties may have difficulty making new friends easily. This may be the result of past bullying or low self-esteem. Such students might have a small number of friends. It will help the transition to second level if they go to the same school as their friends.

Extra-curricular Activities
Self-esteem can be fragile in students with dyslexia. They may have experienced difficulty and failure with the academic part of the curriculum. However, they can achieve success and peer recognition in other areas such as the extra-curricular activities organised by the school. Some schools put on a wide range of activities which can include sports, debating, drama, a school bank, camera clubs and social activities such as Amnesty International. Parents should check the range of activities available.

Subject Choice
Subject choice is of critical importance to students with dyslexia. The average student may have individual preferences about subjects but is likely to do, on average, equally well in different subjects. Students with dyslexia may find some subjects at second level in which they will do exceptionally well and others where they face failure from first year. At primary level the main challenge for students is the development of literacy and numeracy. This may mean that for a major portion of

the school day, students with dyslexia may have been confronted by tasks which they found difficult and struggled to achieve in. Now at second level, while they must continue to develop literacy and numeracy, they may find subjects in which they can achieve well. If students can access the information in a subject and communicate such knowledge in an exam, they will achieve. This success helps with self-esteem and motivation. The NCCA website (www.ncca.ie) has twenty five junior cycle factsheets on the different subjects available for junior cycle. These useful sheets would be of benefit to parents and students when considering what options to choose.

There are no clear rules about subject choice as each child with dyslexia has a unique profile of strengths and weaknesses. However, here are some pointers to help with choice.

- Languages may prove to be a difficulty for some. Indicators that a student may have difficulties with languages are poor achievement in English and Irish, poor aural and oral ability, poor phonic skills and poor memory of sounds. A student who has good oral and aural skills may succeed well in languages, particularly as a large part of the marks in the state exams are awarded to the oral and aural elements of the exam. It is a widely-held belief that a student needs a foreign language for entry to third level. However, it is only in the National University of Ireland (NUI) colleges that this is an entry requirement and the student with dyslexia may apply for an exemption from this requirement. Other third level colleges do not require that students have a foreign language for entry to the college. However, a language is likely to be a course requirement on courses where students intend to study languages.

- Subjects that require answers containing factual information may be easier than subjects in which answers are in essay-type format, where the student has to analyse and sequence information to structure the answer. Therefore, science may be easier to achieve in rather than English or History.

- Some subjects such as Technical Graphics, Maths and Accounting rely on the student learning skills by doing several examples of the same task. For the student with short-term memory difficulties, this may help.

- Some students with dyslexia have excellent spatial/visual abilities and will do well in subjects such as Art, Construction Studies and Technical Graphics.

■ Continuous assessment may help the student with short-term memory difficulties. Some subjects such as Art, Home Economics, Construction Studies and Religion have a project or journal to be filled in prior to the terminal exam and marks are awarded for such work.

At senior cycle it is even more important that the subjects taken suit the student. Firstly, as in Junior Cycle, motivation and interest will be maintained if the student enjoys the subjects studied. Secondly, the Leaving Certificate is the gateway to higher and further education. This is a key moment in career choice for students. In Ireland, because students may take seven subjects or more for the Leaving Certificate, it is still possible to leave many paths open and not narrow one's options after the Junior Certificate. This is generally a good thing as it gives students time to mature before making critical career decisions. In the UK, this is the time when students specialise and take a narrow range of subjects for A levels.

However, in Ireland where such a wide range of subjects is offered, option structures may be restricted and students with dyslexia may be at a disadvantage. They may have to take subjects that are verbally based and they may not be able to specialise in their best subjects. As an example, take students with dyslexia who are very proficient in the Maths, Business and technical subjects. Such students may have to take English, Irish and a third language as three of their seven subjects. Unless the option structure is very open, it is possible they may have to take other verbally based subjects such as Economics or History. If the same student could choose subjects such as English, Maths, Physics, Chemistry, Accounting, Technical Graphics and Engineering, it would certainly improve their chances of maximising points for the CAO system as well as giving them subjects they may enjoy studying. In Chapter 3, the example is given of a student in 2004 who, by being able to take the subjects of Technical Graphics and Applied Maths outside school hours, increased his overall points by 110. This made a dramatic difference to the courses open to him.

Entry to the colleges in the Central Applications Office (CAO) system is based on the points system. Students need to be able to present their six best subjects in the Leaving Certificate if they are to achieve their best possible points score.

Table 8.1: The Points System*

Leaving Cert. grade	Higher level	Ordinary level	Bonus**
A1	100	60	40
A2	90	50	35
B1	85	45	30
B2	80	40	25
B3	75	35	20
C1	70	30	15
C2	65	25	10
C3	60	20	5
D1	55	15	
D2	50	10	
D3	45	5	

*The best six results are counted for points calculation.
**Bonus points for Higher Maths are awarded by the University of Limerick. Check current position with college due to the introduction of bonus points for higher level Maths in 2012.

In October 2010 it was decided by the universities that bonus points for Maths are to be introduced from 2012. Every student taking higher level Maths and gaining a grade D3 or higher will receive a bonus of 25 additional points. A student scoring a D3 will get the current 45 points and the 25 bonus points, a total of 70 points.

Another consideration in option choice at senior cycle is that colleges and courses may have specific entry requirements. It is necessary to know these requirements in order to ensure that students do not exclude themselves from any course in which they are interested by not having the necessary subjects. Senior students should keep a careers file which includes details of colleges and courses. All colleges have websites where such requirements can be accessed.

CAO colleges set minimum entry requirements. An example of this is the institutes of technology where there is an entry requirement of five D3s at ordinary level in the Leaving Certificate which must include a pass in Maths and English or Irish for many of their courses.

The four colleges of NUI (UCC, UCD, UCG and Maynooth) specify six subjects, two at higher level, with a pass in English, Irish and a third language. NUI recognises the Irish exemption granted by the Department of Education and Skills. It also grants an exemption in the third language requirement to students with serious dyslexia. Applications for this exemption should be made prior to the student entering senior cycle and forms are available from NUI, 49 Merrion Square, Dublin 2 and on the NUI website: www.nui.ie.

As previously discussed such exemptions are important for some students with dyslexia. In the competitive points race that exists for courses at CAO level, it is important for students to be able to maximise points by presenting their six best subjects. Some students with dyslexia may have poor achievement in languages. As a result it is possible that subjects such as English, Irish and the third language may be taken at ordinary level. They may have excellent abilities in other subjects. Without exemptions in the language requirements, a student may have to take nine subjects in the Leaving Certificate in order to have six higher level subjects. This imposes two additional burdens. Firstly, nine subjects is an excessive amount particularly when the fact that these are students who have a diagnosed learning difficulty is taken into account. Secondly, the students have to take language subjects in which they may have to work much harder than their peers to achieve a pass mark.

Certain courses have specific entry requirements. These are often related to what students will be studying. Some examples of subject requirements include:

- *Maths*   Higher level Maths is essential for Engineering honours degrees and Actuarial Studies.
  Ordinary level Maths is a minimum requirement for many courses in the Institutes of Technology.
- *English*   Higher level English is essential for Clinical Speech in TCD, Journalism in DCU and Communications in DCU.
  Ordinary level English is required for a wide range of institute of technology courses.
- *Science*   Science/medical/paramedical courses require a science subject. TCD requires two sciences for some medical/paramedical courses. DIT requires higher level Chemistry for Dietetics.

Complete information on course requirements is available in the college brochures. These are available from the Admissions Office in each college. Each college also has a website that can be found through the CAO website at www.cao.ie.

In conclusion the criteria for choosing subjects for Leaving Certificate include:

- Students should have the essential subjects needed for the courses they may consider doing after Leaving Certificate;
- They should choose subjects which will be of interest to them and that they will enjoy. This helps with motivation. Logically these subjects would tally with the strengths shown in their profile of abilities;
- If they are interested in applying for courses in the CAO system, they should choose subjects that will give them the best examination grades to maximise points.

Choices in the State Examinations System

Levels of Examination of Subjects

In the Junior Certificate, students take the core subjects of Irish (unless exempt), English, Maths, History, Geography, CSPE (Civic, Social and Political Education) and SPHE (Social, Personal and Health Education). They then take either three or four other subjects from option lines.

In the case of Irish, English and Maths, subjects are offered at three levels: Higher, Ordinary and Foundation. CSPE is offered at one common level. The other subjects are offered at two levels: Higher and Ordinary.

The grade structure at second level is as follows:

Grade	%
A	85+
B	70–84
C	55–69
D	40–54
E	25–39
F	10–24
NG	<10

In the Leaving Certificate examination, there is a further breakdown of grades into A1, A2, B1, B2, B3, C1, etc. At both Leaving and Junior

Certificate, students have to achieve a 'C' or above grade on a **higher** level paper to obtain an Honour result. Any grade below a 'D' is a fail grade.

It is generally the case that, if students wish to take a subject at higher level in the Leaving Certificate, they should take the subject at higher level in the Junior Certificate. At Leaving Certificate six subjects count for points. There are more points given for higher level subjects, so for a student who may wish to apply to the CAO system at a later stage, it is advisable to take as many higher level subjects as possible in the Junior Certificate.

There is no foundation level English available at Leaving Certificate. There is foundation level Maths and Irish. Students who take Foundation Level English at Junior Certificate level and then go on to do the established Leaving Certificate will face a huge jump in standard of English. If a student's English skills are so poor that foundation level at Junior Certificate is the appropriate level, it might be advisable to consider the Leaving Certificate Applied (LCA) as a route to Leaving Certificate.

Foundation level Maths at Junior Certificate is likely to lead on to foundation level Maths at Leaving Certificate. Foundation level Maths is not acceptable for entry to many courses and careers. The entry requirement for the vast majority of level six and seven courses in the institutes of technology is that the student should have five subjects in the Leaving Certificate including a 'D' in ordinary level English or Irish and in Maths. A decision that a student should take foundation level Maths might be made as early as second year. The student and parents often may not realise that the consequence of this decision means that the student is not eligible for entry to courses in the institutes of technology after Leaving Certificate. There may be some students who, with additional work and perhaps some extra help, could manage to do ordinary level and therefore keep more options open for themselves. However, it is possible for a student to do a Post Leaving Certificate Course (PLC) course and then apply to CAO colleges for entry based on the results of the PLC course.

Junior Certificate Programmes
The Junior Certificate examination is the exam taken by the vast majority of second level students.

The Junior Certificate Schools Programme (JCSP) was introduced in 1996 for students whose particular needs were not adequately addressed in the broadly-based Junior Certificate. The programme reaches out to young people who leave school early without obtaining any qualifications. The programme involves greater student activity and specific goals are set for literacy and numeracy. It is based on the concept that all young people are capable of achieving real success in school. It is a way of working within the Junior Certificate programme which is specially designed to help young people who have had a difficult experience of school. Instead of examination grades, a student-profiling system is used to measure achievement.

Leaving Certificate Programmes

There are three types of Leaving Certificates programmes: the Leaving Certificate Applied Programme (LCA), the Leaving Certificate Vocational Programme (LCV) and the established Leaving Certificate Programme.

Leaving Certificate Applied (LCA) is a two-year self-contained programme. Its objective is to prepare participants for adult and working life. It has three main elements:

- Vocational preparation, which focuses on preparation for work, work experience, enterprise and communications;
- Vocational education, which gives students general life skills, including the arts, social education, leisure and languages;
- General education, which is concerned with the development of mathematical, information technology and practical skills necessary for specialist areas such as tourism, business, horticulture, engineering or technology.

Students are assessed continuously throughout the two years. They receive credit for completing modules of the course and there are examinations at the end of the two years. After finishing the course, the students go on to employment or to PLC courses. They are not able to apply for CAO courses directly as the points system does not apply to the LCA. However, a student may proceed to a PLC course and then, on the basis of the PLC qualification, apply to the CAO colleges. The LCA was offered for the first time in 1996 in about 60 schools. It is now offered in over 300 hundred schools as a route to Leaving Certificate. The Department of Education and Skills website: www.education.ie has details of schools where it is offered.

The Leaving Certificate Vocational Programme (LCV) is a two year Leaving Certificate where the student takes the established Leaving Certificate with additional modules. Its objective is to strengthen the vocational dimension of the Leaving Certificate through relating and integrating specific pairings of subjects. The student takes a minimum of five subjects. These include Irish and a foreign language. Subjects, which complement one another, are grouped together and the student takes a particular group of subjects such as Engineering and Technical Drawing or Home Economics and Biology. There are link modules covering preparation for work, work experience and enterprise education to increase the vocational focus on the LCV. As students sit the established Leaving Certificate examination they can apply to CAO at the end of the LCV.

The established Leaving Certificate is one where students do a two-year course of study and there is an examination at the end of the two years. There are thirty four subjects available. In some subjects such as Home Economics, Construction Studies and Geography, there is a project or journal element. In most schools the timetable allows that students take seven subjects inside the school day. Students can take extra subjects outside school such as Music. Subjects are offered at two levels, higher and ordinary. In Irish and Maths, foundation level is also offered.

The National Council for Curriculum and Assessment (NCCA), website: www.ncca.ie is engaged in the review and revision of Leaving Certificate subjects, and their assessment, on an ongoing basis. Since September 2000 revised syllabi in Biology, Chemistry, Physics, Home Economics, History and Geography, and Religious Education, have been introduced, as well as a non-examination course in Religious Education. Revised syllabi in Art, Physical Science, Economics, Architectural and Construction Technology, Art, Design and Communication Graphics, Engineering Technology, and Technology, will be introduced on a phased basis, having due regard to the implementation issues in schools. Subjects currently under review include Mathematics, Applied Mathematics, Agricultural Science, Latin, Ancient Greek and Classical Studies. New courses are currently being developed in Physical Education and Social, Personal and Health Education.

In 2003 the NCCA published a document called *Developing Senior Cycle Education*. It was based on an extensive consultation process and discussed the direction developments in senior cycle should take. It was felt the current examination puts too much stress on rote learning and places too much pressure on students. The proposals contained in the document looked towards a more adult learning culture, with a greater stress on self-directed learning. The NCCA stated the case for reform was clear. The current system was failing some 40% of teenagers. 20% perform poorly in the exam and a further 20% drop out of the school system after Junior Certificate.

The NCCA have identified five key skills so that learners are prepared for life, learning and work in the 21st century. Things have changed in the world in recent years and continue to change every day. As well as learning knowledge, learners need to develop skills to create new knowledge and to deal with and navigate their way through this new world. There are five skills identified as central to teaching and learning across the curriculum at senior cycle. These are critical and creative thinking, communicating, information processing, being personally effective and working with others. Much of the work on the revision of syllabi is informed by these identified skills.

Choices after the Junior Certificate

The majority of students decide to continue in education after the Junior Certificate and proceed to one of the Leaving Certificate programmes. However, some students leave education after Junior Certificate. While they may enter into the workforce, it will generally be into low pay, low skill and frequently temporary employment. Many of these young people do not have the skills or resources to maintain any long-term position in the labour market. For those early school-leavers who do obtain employment there are significant pay differentials in rates of pay between those who leave school with a Leaving Certificate and those who do not. Leaving school early will affect the life chances of students. This has become more evident as unemployment has grown from 2008 onwards.

Options available to early school-leavers include:

Apprenticeships
Apprenticeship is the route to becoming a skilled craftsperson. The apprentice works for an employer in a chosen occupation and learns the necessary skills and knowledge. Apprenticeships are standard-

based. This means apprentices must pass specific tests and assessments to ensure they meet certain pre-set standards of competency and skill. Apprenticeships comprise on-the-job training with the employer and off-the-job training in a FAS training centre or in an educational college.

The entry requirements for apprenticeships are that the applicant has reached sixteen years of age and has obtained a D grade in five subjects at Junior Certificate level. Although Junior Certificate is the minimum requirement for entry, most apprentices have a Leaving Certificate. Students with weaker literacy or numeracy skills may find it difficult to pass these tests/assessments and may require tutorial assistance from their college or training agency. Failure in these tests/assessments means that the apprenticeship cannot continue.

Apprenticeship places have become scarce since the downturn from 2008 onwards.

Youthreach

Young people who leave school without any qualification or with a Junior Certificate are the most vulnerable in the job market. Statistics show the highest unemployment and lowest wages are amongst this group. Youthreach is a special programme sponsored by the Department of Education and Skills and the Department of Enterprise, Trade and Innovation to give early school-leavers a second chance.

Youthreach offers young people an opportunity to gain qualifications and build self-confidence so they can move on into further education, training or work. It offers a range of qualifications including the Further Education and Training Awards Council (FETAC), City and Guilds and Junior and Leaving Certificates.

Employment

Most employment for early school leavers will be poorly paid, much of it part-time or temporary, with poor prospects of training or promotion.

The National Learning Network

The National Learning Network (website: www.nln.ie), is Ireland's largest non-Government training organisation with 46 centres throughout Ireland catering for over 2,000 students annually. There are no formal entry qualifications to any NLN course. Applicants must be over sixteen, be eligible for European Social Fund funding and be approved by the National Disability Authority. Applications from dyslexic students are considered for these courses. For the severely affected dyslexic student who is having enormous difficulty coping with the demands of second level school, these courses provide a route to qualifications and skills. Courses are certified by outside examination bodies such as FETAC.

CHAPTER 8
COPING AT SECOND LEVEL
– STUDY SKILLS

This chapter is primarily addressed to students with dyslexia. It also should be of help to parents. At the beginning of second level, students may need help and guidance from parents in setting up study routines and establishing study methods. This chapter gives parents guidelines on how to help the student. As students mature, they should take increasing responsibility for their work, so that they become independent self-motivated learners by senior cycle. This is why the chapter is first and foremost directed to them.

In it you will read about:

- The transition to second level;
- Organisation of time, study and work area;
- Accessing help;
- Study skills;
- Communicating information learnt;
- Examination strategies.

The Transition to Second Level

The change to second level is a big transition point for all students. Students go from having one teacher all day to having several teachers in the course of a day. There is the introduction of new subjects. There is more emphasis on examinations, both state and school-based. The school building is larger and there is far more movement as students move from class to class. Students may feel disorientated and lost as they try to find their way around. From being the biggest and oldest students at primary, they are now the smallest and youngest. The timetable for subjects each day differs and students need to be organised to have the correct books and/or homework ready on the right day.

The majority of students cope well, are very positive about the move and have settled in well by mid-term of first year. However, this transition may bring more pressures for students with dyslexia. The most obvious change is that at primary level students had one teacher who knew them and their difficulties well. Now they may face up to nine different teachers during the course of a single day. The pace at which information is passed on becomes faster as subject teachers have to complete courses in time for exams.

Parental support is critical at the start of second level so students make a successful transition from primary school. There is a major challenge in coping with all the new subjects, new teachers and the new structure of the school week. If they do not achieve some level of success, there is a risk that, as a defence mechanism, they may turn off the idea of school. Parents can help by communicating with each teacher the profile of the student's strengths and weaknesses and in asking the teacher about how they can best support the student at home. Parents can help with the organisation of homework, setting up routines for students that, over time, will become part of their study habits.

The following sections give guidelines on study skills for students or for parents who are helping them.

Organisation of Time, Work and Workplace

- Have a legible copy of the timetable in the front of the homework notebook so it can be referred to easily. It is useful if this is colour coded for the different subjects.

- Do homework at a regular time each day, preferably as early as possible. Again, at the weekend, try to do homework on Friday night or Saturday morning leaving the rest of the weekend free.

- Schools give guidelines for the amount of time to be spent on homework. Students in first year, on average, would be expected to do about an hour and half to two hours a night. This includes written homework, learning homework and revision. This increases as students proceed through second level. Short breaks of about five minutes during the study time help with concentration.

- Alternate subjects, beginning with a subject which is liked, followed by one subject which is disliked.

- Have clear targets. Often the teacher will set such goals in homework assignments. However, students may need to organise their own revision work for exams. Targets should be specific and quantified. An example of such targets would be:
  - Learn five causes of coastal erosion;
  - Learn three examples of imagery in a poem with a quotation to illustrate each.
- It may be more difficult for students with dyslexia to cram before an exam. It can lead to confusion and the feeling of being overwhelmed. Therefore it is recommended that you work consistently throughout the term.
- Have one homework notebook in which to enter all homework assignments, project dates, examination schedules and deadlines. It should be used to check that all homework is done and to pack the school-bag for the following day.
- If you do not understand the homework set, ask the teacher for clarification at the end of class.
- Study/homework should be done at a desk, in a quiet and comfortable environment. Mobile phones should be switched off as they can be a major source of distraction and can lead to time-wasting. Equipment and books should be easily accessible. Good lighting should be in place. Keep a calendar close to the desk.
- Having a locker in school can lead to problems with books/equipment being left in school or at home. You need to develop a good checking procedure to see this does not happen. Having two sets of basic equipment such as pens, rulers, etc. will minimise such difficulties. Colour coding can be used by putting stickers on subject text books and copies, for example, red for Maths. Coloured folders could be used for the notes in different subjects.
- At the beginning of a lesson, get everything ready on the desk so that you do not waste time.

Accessing Help

- In the early years of secondary school, it is likely to be your parents who ensure that teachers are aware of the learning difficulties. Schools are very busy places. Teachers deal with several hundred students in a week. It is easy to overlook the needs of an individual student. Parents should send in a summary of the assessment to each teacher at the beginning of the school year. They should not assume that if they inform the principal or another teacher that this information will be passed on to the other staff automatically.

■ As you mature and understand more about how you learn, you can provide information to teachers on techniques that help you learn. The CD ROM/DVD *Understanding Dyslexia* has a self-help section. It helps students understand dyslexia and how it affects them. It assists in analysing individual learning profiles. It also includes a form for asking for help. Students can use it to inform teachers about what they could do to help the individual student. The form gets students to analyse what teachers do that the students find helpful and what teachers could do to help them learn better. This provides a format for such information to be given to teachers diplomatically. See Appendix C for the checklist.

■ Sometimes students may encounter a teacher who is not aware of the range of difficulties that a student with dyslexia may have. Be prepared. Have information on the topic to hand out and then be ready to explain how you are affected. This is good preparation for third level and working life, where you may have to explain dyslexia to others.

Study Skills

■ Successful learning does take effort. It becomes easier the more the techniques are practised. Material must be gone over several times to ensure it is remembered. Rewriting notes, taping and reading aloud are all ways to help memory. There are websites that may help develop study skills such as www.skoool.ie.

■ It is easier to learn material that is understood. Ask for help if you do not understand what has been taught in class.

■ Keep a vocabulary notebook in each subject for the new words and their specific meanings in that subject.

■ If you learn more effectively by listening in class, sit near the front of the classroom and close to students who want to learn. The more you learn in class, the less that needs to be done at home.

■ Students who miss a lot of school tend to be low achievers. Students with dyslexia usually have more difficulty catching up on missed classes and so it is important to attend school regularly.

- Do homework as thoroughly as possible. This is part of the learning process.

- It is relatively easy for a teacher to check on written homework and so students often make written homework a priority. However, it is the learning homework that is important for success in exams. Many students believe that if they read over a text several times, they know it. Unfortunately this is not the case. They need to actively learn the material and then have a checking process to make sure it is learnt. Techniques such as note-taking help with active learning.

- Some students with dyslexia may find it very difficult to summarise material in textbooks and make their own notes. This can be due to poor or slow reading, where they may have to reread a piece several times to see the points the writer is making, difficulties in summarising and organising material or difficulties in the presentation of legible and clearly laid-out notes. The essential task is to learn the information. Having to make their own notes from the text can place additional barriers in their way. These students can therefore benefit hugely from getting precise and concise notes.

- Revision handbooks are a useful way to access the key points in the different subjects and could be used from first year on. They are available from a number of educational publishers in a range of subjects at Junior and Leaving Certificate level. Some factors to consider when choosing which version of a revision book to buy are as follows; clear large print, bullet points, definitions to be learnt by heart in bold print, use of colour and numbering. The website www.skoool.ie contains study notes on some subjects in the Junior Certificate and Leaving Certificate.

- If teachers dictate their own notes to the class, it can be a problem for students with dyslexia because difficulties in processing language and in spelling and handwriting, make it challenging to listen and write at the same time. If necessary, the teacher should arrange for photocopies of notes to be given to students. These could be photocopies of teacher notes or the notes of a student who makes well-organised, legible notes.

- Some students feel that once the notes are made and filed that the work is done. Notes must be learnt. This learning can be checked by an oral recital or writing them out again. Memory techniques such as chunking information together and mnemonics may help with learning. Mnemonics are techniques to help memory. An example is that to remember the four factors of production – capital, enterprise, land and labour – the student makes up a word, *CELL*, which comprises the first letter of each word. Another well known mnemonic is FATDAD for the six counties of Northern Ireland; Fermanagh, Antrim, Tyrone, Derry, Armagh and Down.

■ If you are an aural rather than visual learner, tapes of notes and/or texts can be helpful. You may benefit from repeating material to be learnt aloud or reading drafts of essays aloud to see if they make sense. Co-operative learning might help if a small group of friends study together and test each other.

■ You may have a strong visual memory. This can be used when learning. You may be able to recall the look of a page of notes. This assists in the recall of the content of the page. Make use of colour, numbering of points, margins, headings and diagrams when making notes. Mindmaps are a technique that helps students organise and summarise information. They can be used for note-taking or for planning essays. The Video/CD/ROM *Understanding Dyslexia* has a section on mindmaps.

■ At the end of the study period, check that you have learned the key points by a quick test.

■ You may have difficulty in deciphering the meaning of complex texts, having to reread pages several times to make sense of the material. It can be helpful to make notes showing the development of the points in the text.

■ Ask a teacher prior to a class for the notes or a copy of the overhead slides that will be used. It means less writing and you can listen and concentrate on what is said. The structure and sequence of the lecture is clearly laid out. It is also possible to include additional notes or points where relevant.

■ If you find you cannot read the textbooks quickly or well enough to understand the content, ask someone such as a parent or sister/brother to read the text aloud so you can concentrate on listening. Certain computer programmes scan and read text aloud as the words appear on the screen.

■ When reading, use a highlighter to mark important parts of the text.

Communicating Information Learnt

- Before beginning an assignment, check you understand what you are being asked to do.

- Presentation and layout can help teachers understand written assignments, so try to improve the legibility of handwriting and ensure that headings and question numbers are clearly indicated. In maths, numbers should be aligned correctly so mistakes will not be made.

- If you have great difficulties with written homework, ask teachers if they would accept alternatives such as taped or typed homework.

- If you will be using reasonable accommodations in state examinations, you should be able to use similar accommodation in house examinations. You need to become familiar with the relevant type of accommodation and practise it.

- Become computer literate as soon as possible, preferably early at second level. Computers are of enormous help to students with dyslexia. They help with presentation, spelling, grammar and editing.

- Some students with dyslexia have difficulty seeing and organising patterns. Good notes are an effective way to see the structure of what you are learning. The notes are a useful device in organising material and are helpful in formatting your own answers. Because the notes are structured, you can use that structure when answering questions.

Examination Strategies

- As you proceed through second level, organising course material for revision becomes increasingly important. Make out a master sheet showing all the topics to be covered in each subject. Have a timetable where each subject is revised twice or three times a week. When a topic has been revised, mark it off on the master sheet. Monitoring the progress made when revising the subjects will help with exam anxiety.

- A revision plan sets out a timetable where the subject is revised on a frequent basis. Such a plan could entail learning the material on the night of the lecture, a weekly revision of all new material learnt and a monthly revision of the month's work. Each revision should take a shorter time.

- Have copies of the exam timetable in prominent places showing the date, time and place of the examination.

- Check you have the correct equipment for each examination. Ensure you have spares for essential equipment, for example, spare batteries for the calculator.

- Prior to the exam, make sure you are familiar with the examination format and how marks are allocated. Also make sure you understand the words used in examinations. Words such as *describe, analyse, classify, contrast, evaluate* and *define* describe very precise tasks. Use past examination papers to help you. These and marking schemes for the Leaving and Junior Certificate are available from the website www.examinations.ie.

- Allocate a time for each question. If you find yourself running out of time, use bullet points to show the information that you have not had time to complete. Leave space between the points, so that if you have time at the end to return to the question, you can add in extra information.

- Make sure you have a watch so you can watch your timing. Be careful not to make the classic mistake of spending more than your allotted time on one or two questions to the neglect of others. If you only do two out of five questions that have equal marks, no matter how well you have answered, you can only obtain a maximum of 40 per cent.

- Take time to read the paper thoroughly, making sure you understand each part of the question. Mark the questions you intend to answer. Start with a question to which you are fairly confident you know the answer.

- Underline the key words in a question and answer that question. Marks are not given for writing down all you know about a subject. The information needs to be relevant to the question asked. This is a very common mistake. An example from English at Leaving Certificate could be when asked in a question to discuss MacBeth's motives for murder, the student ends up telling the story of the whole play.

- Plan your answers by doing mindmap or bullets points. The answer will be clearer and more logical. It also helps keep the answer to the point.

- Remember to number questions and parts of questions clearly. Drawings should be labelled precisely.

- Do every step of a question. Do not take shortcuts. In subjects such as Maths and Business Studies, you get marks for the correct method, even if the final answer is wrong. If you skip some steps, it is easier to go wrong. Also, some marking schemes give marks for showing the workings of the answer.

- Make sure you answer all parts of a question. If the question asks for three points to be made, the answer needs to make three points. Otherwise you lose marks.

- Proofread the whole paper once it is completed, if you have time. Double-check calculations.

- It can be very useful to analyse returned examination papers to see where you lost marks. Make out an analysis grid where the marks allocated for each part of each question are set out and then enter the mark you obtained and work out what percentage you obtained. This allows you to see the questions in which you did well and where you lost marks.

CHAPTER 9
DYSLEXIA AND MATHEMATICS

This chapter will be of use to parents and teachers. In it you will read about:

- Maths difficulties that may affect students with dyslexia;
- How parents can help the student in Mathematics;
- Project Maths at second level;
- A brief guide for teachers including sources of information on teaching Mathematics to students with dyslexia.

Difficulties with Mathematics

Many people believe that dyslexia affects spelling, reading and handwriting. It may take parents by surprise when achievement in Maths is also affected. These mathematical difficulties may vary considerably from the child who verges on dyscalculia (having extreme difficulty with Maths concepts and calculations) to students who have good or superior ability in Maths but whose dyslexia may hold them back in some way.

The types of difficulty that may affect the mathematical achievement of students include:

- Students may not be able to read the English in the question and therefore may not know what task they are being asked to do.
- Confusion about the vocabulary used in Maths and the exact meaning of words. Words such as *equal, product* and *add* have exact meanings in Maths that may not be the same as their everyday meaning. The words *write* and *right* can be particularly confusing with all the varied meanings the same sound can convey. These varied meanings include:
  - The opposite of wrong;
  - The opposite of left;
  - Correct;
  - To write down;
  - A right angle of 90 degrees.

- The use of different words to describe the same mathematical action. An example is the instruction for adding. The words *add*, *increase*, *plus* and *total* may be used. It is no wonder some students get confused.

- Students may not understand the instructions given by the teacher. This may be because the teacher uses different words to those in the text. It could also result from students having difficulty following the sequence of instructions given verbally due to short-term memory difficulties. Lack of confidence may compound this difficulty, as students may be hesitant in asking questions.

- In textbooks some questions are phrased such that information is put in a different sequence to the actions the student is required to take. For example, 'John has 46 cents. He wants to buy a bar that costs €1. How much more does he need'? A more straightforward way of putting this question is to ask, 'A bar costs €1. John has 46 cents. How much more does he need'? This follows the sequence of the task and the student understands it more easily.

- Students may not be clear on the meaning of the symbols used in Maths. Many students with dyslexia show a weakness in the coding subtest in the psycho-educational assessment. This means they may find symbols confusing. Students with spatial or directional confusion may even find it difficult to distinguish between the symbol + and x.

- Sequencing and short-term memory difficulties may mean that learning tables becomes a marathon task. Frequently, students would be able to do complicated Maths tasks if they could remember their tables.

- Poor organisation and layout on the page may result in numbers not being aligned correctly, with figures squashed together so that it is difficult to read them or lines which have not been drawn with a ruler so the page looks untidy.

- Poor writing skills, so that numbers are not clear and are misread, thus leading to the wrong answer. Other students, due to poor hand-eye co-ordination, find it difficult to draw lines, measure angles and even to use a ruler competently. Some may still reverse numbers.

- There may be confusion about place value, so the student may confuse tens, hundreds and thousands. This confusion is increased when decimal points are involved.

- Sequential memory difficulties can mean some students may remember fewer numbers in their heads than the average student. This slows down the speed of processing. In questions with a number of steps the student may lose focus and feel lost.

- Some students need to decipher mental arithmetic sums in order to visualise the question and then process the answer. This slows down answering.

- Left/right difficulties. In Maths the student usually works from right to left, which is opposite to the way words are read. For students with spatial/directional difficulties this adds to the confusion.

- Different learning styles. Some students do not show the workings of problems, but often appear to have the right answer without knowing how they got there. Others are so methodical in doing each stage of a calculation that they lose sight of the overall goal of the question.

These difficulties result in students underperforming in Maths and possibly, as a result, disliking the subject. Maths is a sequential subject, where each lesson is based on previous learning. If students have not acquired the earlier skills for some reason such as absenteeism, they may have difficulty in understanding the current work in class.

As students proceed through the school system, the verbal content of the subject lessens. At the same time reading stamina and skills are developing. This may mean that students, who had difficulty with understanding the language of Maths or deciphering questions, may find more success at the second level. Therefore it is important to have an accurate assessment of the child's potential to ensure informed decisions are made about the appropriate level at which the student will study Maths.

At second level, Maths is taught at three levels for the Junior and Leaving Certificate. These levels are higher, ordinary and foundation. If students are capable of taking the higher level paper, they need to be studying it from first year. Dropping to ordinary level may have career implications later on. From 2012 there will be 25 bonus points for students who achieve a D3 grade or higher in higher level Maths in the Leaving Certificate. A C grade in higher level Maths at Leaving Certificate is a requirement for Engineering honours degrees at third level. In a school where classes are streamed, it might be the case that a student with dyslexia with good Maths skills, may be placed in one of the weaker classes on account of poorer verbal skills and higher level Maths is not taught in that class. Higher level Maths is a long and extensive course both for Junior Certificate and Leaving Certificate and the pace in these classes is very fast. A student who has not been in the higher level class in the early years of second level will find it very difficult, if not impossible, to catch up at a later stage.

Taking foundation level Maths may have major implications when a student is applying for courses after second level as it is not accepted as an entry requirement for direct entry to the Institutes of Technology. More detailed information about entry requirements is in Chapter 7.

The difficulties listed at the beginning of this chapter may mean that the entrance assessment for second level may not give a realistic indication of the student's potential in Maths. If there are questions expressed as problems in English and the child cannot read the question, it is more a test of the child's English than Maths. Some assistance at entrance assessment should be part of the support services provided by schools. This could include the reading of the questions and the provision of a calculator or tables square.

How Parents can Help

There are many ways parents can help the child develop number skills from an early age. Many of the ideas below can be incorporated in play and everyday activities. They could become part of everyday routine such as each time children brush their teeth they count the strokes or each time a cake is cut it is divided into halves, then quarters and eighths. A word of caution, however, parents only have so much energy so it is important that such activities are relaxed and fun, that the effort expended does not exhaust the parent and that the child does not perceive the activities as more work. The most important contribution parents can make is a stable loving relationship. Many of the activities below build on this relationship but if parents are exhausted and tired, patience can be one of the casualties. Therefore, choose activities that seem most relevant at a particular stage for the child. Be consistent and build them into the daily or weekly routine. Do not try to do everything.

Possible activities to encourage numeracy include:

■ Encourage the development of hand skills through drawing and colouring tasks. This is a natural stage of development when the child is very young. It may help if it is encouraged to continue through middle childhood. Using rulers and other drawing games, such as Spirographs, helps develop better hand control.

■ Play family games that help develop an understanding of number. Many card games help develop number skills. Games such as *Ludo* and *Snakes and Ladders* may help develop counting skills and an understanding of concepts such as up/down and counting backwards.

■ Songs and nursery rhymes help with the memorising numbers and days of the week, while making the activity fun.

■ Ask the child to read the bus, train or ferry timetables when travelling.

■ Simple household tasks can be used to provide examples of mathematical concepts. Cut a pizza into halves and then quarters and eighths, and use the terminology of fractions when giving out slices.

■ Use car journeys to help them work out a sense of distance. Get them to watch the speedometer and ask them to estimate how long the journey will take. Keep a record of the distance travelled and how long it took.

■ The younger child could count the steps in the stairs.

■ When shopping, ask the child to pick items from the shelves and check the weight or volume.

■ Parents can help develop a sense of time that can include the hours, months and seasons. Put up cards showing the important times during the day and then ask children to read the clock to confirm the time. Suggest children read the TV guide to pick out programmes to watch and then use the clock to identify the time. Enter future events in a calendar on the wall. Get them to work out how long it is until a birthday or other celebration. Help the older child use the homework notebook as an aid to see the routine of the week and term, and to check that the right books and homework for the different school days are in the school bag.

■ Play games with young children that involve counting using items such as buttons or dolls. This means that they have a multi-sensory approach, which helps give them a concrete concept of number.

■ If there are particular symbols or words causing problems, put them on cards so the child sees them regularly. The cards could be used as a bookmark, or put up on the fridge.

■ Do not help them so much with homework that it becomes mainly your own work. The teacher needs to know if they have difficulty doing the tasks set. If the homework is presented with the right answers, it means the teacher may overestimate their ability in the subject. However, there are practical ideas for helping:

- If the child does not understand the question, read it aloud, maybe putting the question in simpler language, so that the mathematical task is understood.

- Provide them with number squares or calculators so their lack of knowledge of tables does not hold them back.

- Use direction arrows and colour coding for the different mathematical operations.

- Make sure they have the proper equipment. Maths copies with pages made out in squares help presentation and they should use a square for every number. When doing fractions they should not try to squash the fraction into one square but use a square for each number, even if it appears to use a lot of space. Pens with padded grips can help if their grip on the pencil is very tight. Rulers should be used for anything that requires the drawing of a straight line. Show them how to lay their work out with plenty of space so it does not end up squashed up in the corner of the page.

- Listen to them and try to identify their difficulty. Could it be the English in the questions, the inability to remember tables or the inability to hold a series of numbers in their head? The latter makes mental arithmetic difficult. As parents, you are with the child on a one-to-one basis more often than anyone else and you are more likely to observe such problems. Pass any observations on to the school.

- Give students time to rest. They make more mistakes when tired and may find it more difficult to understand a concept. A change to another subject or a short break for something to eat may boost energy.

- Help them develop the technique of estimating answers. Use concrete examples such as, 'If you have €20.00 and buy a CD for €9.99, roughly how much change will you have?' Encourage them to round it to €10 for a rough answer.

- If they write numbers backwards, have a card close to their working area with the numbers clearly shown so they can refer to it.

- Some children may look at a Maths question and work out the answer in their heads. Writing down the interim steps in reaching that answer seems like too much hard work. However, it is necessary to develop the step-by-step approach for several reasons. Firstly, Maths will become more difficult and they need to be accustomed to writing down each stage. This teaches them a methodical approach, which will benefit their maths and also have a knock-on effect in other subjects. Secondly, marks in examinations are allocated to the stages of working out answers. If a child follows the correct procedure and gets the answer wrong, they still get marks for the correct method. The child, who does not show the working out of problems, will get zero for a wrong answer.

- Many children understand the concept when taught in class and are able to do the homework that night. However, over time, they can lose that understanding. Regular revision of work done can help ensure the concepts remain understood.

- Computer programmes can reinforce mathematical concepts while making such activities fun. The websites in Chapter 10 are a useful source of information on such software.

Project Maths

Project Maths involves the introduction of revised syllabuses for both Junior and Leaving Certificate Mathematics. It involves changes to what students learn in mathematics, how they learn it and how they will be assessed. It has been introduced on a phased basis for all students from 2010. Much greater emphasis will be placed on student understanding of mathematical concepts, with increased use of contexts and applications that will enable students to relate mathematics to everyday experience.

The initiative will also focus on developing students' problem-solving skills.

The Mathematics syllabuses will be introduced by strand as follows:

- 1. Statistics and Probability
- 2. Geometry and Trigonometry
- 3. Number
- 4. Algebra
- 5. Functions

The first two strands which have been worked on in the 24 pilot schools were introduced nationally for incoming first year and fifth year students in September 2010.

According as the revised strands are introduced, students will experience mathematics in a new way, using examples and applications that are meaningful for them. These will also allow students to appreciate how mathematics relates to daily life and to the world of work. Students will develop skills in analysing, interpreting and presenting mathematical information; in logical reasoning and argument, and in applying their mathematical knowledge and skills to solve familiar and unfamiliar problems.

However one concern about Project Maths is that many of the questions/problems are expressed in words. For some students with dyslexia who have excellent Maths skills but weaker literacy skills, this could pose difficulties in the examination. They might find it hard to decipher the English which explains the mathematical task they have to complete but would be well capable of accomplishing the task once they know what they have to do.

Project Maths in Junior Cycle

In the junior cycle, a more investigative approach will be used which will build on and extend students' experience of mathematics in the primary school. To provide better continuity with primary school mathematics, a bridging framework is being developed that links the various strands of mathematics in the primary school to topics in the Junior Certificate mathematics syllabuses.

A common introductory course in mathematics at the start of the junior cycle will make it possible for students to delay their choice of syllabus level until a later stage. Two revised syllabus levels will be implemented at Junior Certificate, Ordinary level and Higher level, with a targeted uptake of 60% of the student cohort for Higher-level mathematics. This is expected to facilitate increased uptake of Leaving Certificate Higher level mathematics.

Initially, a Foundation level examination, based on the revised Ordinary level syllabus, will also be provided. As the revised syllabuses and the targeted uptake become established, the necessity for the Foundation level examination will be kept under review.

Project Maths at Leaving Certificate

In the senior cycle, students' experience of mathematics will enable them to develop the knowledge and skills necessary for their future lives as well as for further study in areas that rely on mathematics. Leaving Certificate Mathematics will be provided at three syllabus levels, Foundation, Ordinary and Higher, with corresponding levels of examination papers. An uptake of 30% at Higher level is targeted. The issue of the status of the Foundation level course and the examination grades achieved by candidates in terms of acceptability for some courses at third level is to be explored.

How Teachers can Help

It is important that teachers understand how dyslexia can affect the progress of a student in Maths and that there are teaching strategies and techniques that have been successfully used in teaching Maths to students with dyslexia. Some of these include:

- Multi-sensory teaching so that the student will use concrete objects to establish abstract concepts;
- Ensuring the students understand the language and symbols used in Maths;
- Having appropriate aids available if the student has difficulty and ensuring the student knows how to use them;
- Use of computers to consolidate knowledge.

Teaching Maths is an extensive topic, as the difficulties the child has at age four are very different to those at age eight, age twelve or age sixteen. Therefore, outside the general principles above, the teaching strategies vary as the child develops.

There are many books and other aids that give specific advice to teachers at the different stages and these should be consulted when a teacher has difficulties teaching a particular child Maths. In the library section of the CD ROM *Understanding Dyslexia* there are lists of books dealing with teaching Maths. The Resources section of this book lists a number of relevant books as well.

CHAPTER 10
COMPUTERS AND INFORMATION TECHNOLOGY

This chapter you will read about the following:

- How computers can help students with dyslexia;
- Keyboarding skills;
- Screening programmes;
- Assistive technology;
- Programmes that support learning;
- Sources of information;
- Irish suppliers.

Computers and information technology are of enormous help for all students but, in particular, provide essential and significant help to students with dyslexia. Such help is invaluable and this generation is very fortunate in having information and communications technology available to it. While there is no substitute for individual tuition from a trained teacher, computer programmes provide valuable reinforcement, variety and can increase motivation. There are also many assistive technology programmes which enable learners to access material while others support writing and learning.

How Computers can Help Students with Dyslexia

Computers can provide assistance in the following ways:

- Increased motivation, as computers may be fun to use;
- Programmes that adapt to proceed at the student's own pace so boredom and frustration do not set in. There can also be immediate feedback rather than waiting for the teacher's corrections;
- Assistive technology, where the computer may help students carry out tasks that they find difficult such as spelling, reading or writing;
- Programmes that help diagnose dyslexic characteristics;

- Word processors allow students to present work clearly and legibly. This can help achievement and self-esteem. It also helps students to complete work faster and allows for editing. Spelling and grammar checks are available;
- Programmes to help students gain literacy and numeracy skills. Students with dyslexia benefit from multi-sensory teaching and repetition, both of which computers provide;
- Programmes to help develop study skills or organisation skills;
- Speech recognition software so the student can dictate to the computer and obtain a typed copy;
- Access to websites on the topic of study skills or that provide study notes for subjects in the Leaving or Junior Certificate.

With so many programmes and products available, it is easy to become confused with the choice. Computer software is often expensive and comes packaged, so it is difficult to find out prior to purchase if a product will meet the specific needs of the student. Ways of obtaining practical experience of the software include advice from teachers, demonstrations of software at conferences or exhibitions, or demonstration disks provided by suppliers or downloaded from the Internet. Students may use a particular software package in school or in a Dyslexia Association of Ireland workshop and find it of benefit. The websites listed at the end of this chapter also provide a means of obtaining current information.

VAT can be claimed back on the purchase of computers/assistive technology for home/personal use via Form VAT 61A from the VAT Repayments Section. The form can be downloaded online from the website: www.revenue.ie. Currently for primary or second level students with significant dyslexia, whose literacy skills are at the 2nd percentile or lower, the school may apply to the SENO for a computer/ laptop and any specialist software needed by an individual student.

Here are some low cost technology items which may help:

- It can be very helpful if teachers provide students with typed or word processed notes rather than handwritten ones. Type should be clear and well separated, using line and half or double line spacing. Type should be a minimum size of 12 or 14. Sans serif fonts are best such as Arial, Comic Sans, Verdana, Helvetica and Tahoma. Use of lower case or sentence case helps as material written in all capitals can make it harder to read.

- Photocopying information or printing onto coloured paper. Some people find they get less glare or experience less visual stress when using colours. Some individuals use coloured overlays, which they place over the textbook.

- Colour coding key information can aid memory. Use of different coloured highlighters, or colour coding documents or files may be beneficial.

- An electronic dictionary, such as a Franklin Spellmaster, is an inexpensive portable tool for checking spelling. As long as the individual can make a reasonable phonetic attempt, there is a good chance that the correct spelling can be identified. Some of these dictionaries came with a thesaurus feature.

- Some texts are available on tape/CD/DVD, particularly English novels, drama, or even some poetry. All make good interactive tools.

- Some students, who learn best through hearing, benefit from taping/recording lectures, or their own study notes. They can build up an audio library which they can use for revision. A MP3 player can be used so they can listen to the notes while travelling.

Keyboarding Skills

At the present time, the main method of inputting information into the computer is keyboarding. To be able to use a word processor effectively, touch-typing skills or at least keyboard familiarity using eight fingers is needed. It takes the investment of time and effort to persevere to learn to touch-type but it is well worth the effort, particularly for the student with dyslexia who is likely to benefit so much from using word processors. It is very difficult for a person who uses the two-finger approach and looks at the keys to change over to touch-typing, so developing these skills as early as possible is recommended. Some students are well motivated and can learn by themselves. Others may need the discipline that comes from a course of structured learning with a teacher. Like all skills, keyboarding needs to be practised regularly if it is to develop and be maintained. There is a wide range of typing tutors available for all ages such as *Touch Type Read Spell, Mavis Beacon,* the *IDL System* and *Learn to Type.*

The reasonable accommodations allowed in state examinations include the use of a word processor for a small number of students.

If the school is to assess whether a student would benefit from using a word processor in examinations, the student needs to be proficient in its use. This means that, in the case of a Junior Certificate student, good keyboarding skills should be in place by the end of second year.

If the use of a word processor helps students, it should be possible to produce projects, homework and house exams in this way.

Screening Programmes

In l996 the Computer Resource Centre at the University of Hull developed a diagnostic screening system called Cognitive Profiling System (CoPS) to be used in the four to six age group. It measured a child's reaction to various challenges on the computer screen. This has been developed into four programmes for different ages which can be used by teachers:

- CoPS baseline for children between four years and five years and six months.
- Lucid CoPS for children between four and eight years.
- LASS Junior for individuals between eight and eleven years.
- LASS Secondary for individuals between eleven and fifteen years.

All four programmes use standardised norms researched in the UK. Such screening programmes will confirm if there are indicators of dyslexia present, but a psycho-educational assessment is always needed for a diagnosis of dyslexia.

Assistive Technology

Assistive technology provides the student with help in doing tasks they find difficult. In the case of dyslexia, computer technology provides very real help for the student.

The main forms of assistive technology are:

- *Word processors with spelling and grammar checks*. These enable the student to provide written material of good quality. This is particularly useful if handwriting is poor and takes a lot of effort. It can be faster and easier than writing by hand provided the student has good keyboarding skills. It is also good for self-esteem to see one's work look well. Editing and rearranging text is easy, so students do not have to rewrite laboriously to produce a final copy. This facility also helps students who have sequencing difficulties, as it is easy to edit the text so as to rearrange the sequence of points. Mistakes are easy to correct as spelling and grammar checks are provided. Because the word processor minimises spelling and handwriting difficulties, students are free to concentrate on ideas and the way they want to express them. It encourages them to be more adventurous and creative. It helps the student organise work as it can be saved and filed on the computer. *Alphasmart* is an example of a machine that does word processing only. It can hold 64 pages of material in eight separate files in its memory that can be downloaded to a printer or to a computer for filing. It has a small screen displaying four lines at a time. It is robust and relatively inexpensive. It can be used in school and downloaded to a computer at home.

- *Speech recognition software*. This allows the student dictate to the computer, which produces a typed copy on the screen. More and more of these systems are coming on the market. The programmes need to learn the voice of the user so it takes time to train a system to an individual's voice. The user also needs training in being consistent in giving commands and punctuation instructions. Accuracy does improve over time as the programme learns more about the user's voice, speech patterns and vocabulary. Developing dictation accuracy is important for students with dyslexia, as they may have more difficulty identifying mistakes made on the screen and correcting them. *Dragon Naturally Speaking* is one such programme. While this type of software has improved greatly in recent years, it will be rarely 100% accurate.

- *Programmes that scan text and read it aloud. Kurzweil* is such a programme. It scans written material, displays it on-screen and reads it aloud. It can be used on texts suitable for young children all the way to college students. It is easy to see how such a system can benefit the student who is learning to read, but it is also of huge benefit to second and third level students who may have to read complicated text a number of times to extract the main points. By hearing as well as reading the text, this task can become much easier. The programme also displays and reads aloud Internet documents. It is possible to scan coloured documents although there is a cheaper version of Kurzweil that only uses black and white. Text sections can be highlighted in different colours and users can note or extract text to produce a study outline. Users are able to read along, take notes and highlight relevant text on-screen. Language tools such as a dictionary, thesaurus and phonetic spelling capability provide additional support. The student can add notes to the text, either written or by voice.

- *Read and Write Gold* allows text to be read back and spoken as it is typed. Words can be highlighted as they are typed. *Claroread* and *Texthelp* are similar screen reading programmes. There is a phonic spell checker that can speak the words aloud. There is a context-based word prediction facility. As the user types the first letter of a word, suggestions are made in the word prediction list. This reduces the number of keystrokes used, helping with speed and sentence construction.

- Reading pens such as the *Quicktionary*. These hand-held reading pens can scan a word or line from any printed text, display the word(s) in large letters, read the word(s) aloud and define the word(s). It is possible to use a headset for private listening.

- *QuickLink* Pen is a 'Digital highlighter' for scanning information when away from the computer. It scans and stores the information and then downloads it to the PC. It is very useful for taking notes and quotes.

- *Electronic personal organisers* can include a diary, spreadsheet, database, word-processing facility, calculator, alarm and e-mail facility. Some students with dyslexia can tend to be disorganised. Structuring their life with the use of such an organiser helps in recall of important facts and deadlines.

- *Textease* is a talking word processing package, with many of the facilities of desktop publishing. The speech options allow the user to listen to letters, words, sentences or all the text. In the multimedia version, video, animations and sound files can be added to pages.

Programmes that Support Learning

There are hundreds of excellent programmes available which support the development of basic skills in reading, phonics, spelling and maths. However, it must be remembered that no computer programme is a substitute for individualised specialist teaching.

Examples of some of the software available are detailed below. Again the websites listed at the end of this chapter have comprehensive information on such programmes. Many programmes come in a range of levels. It is important to choose the right level.

■ *Wordshark* combines the excitement of computer games with learning to spell and read. It offers 26 different games that use sound, graphics and text to teach and reinforce word recognition and spelling. It is based on the *Alpha to Omega* programme which teaches reading through a phonetic approach.

■ *Starspell* helps develop spelling skills from the young child to teenagers. It uses the Look-Cover-Write-Check strategy. Every word is spoken and many have pictures. It is possible to create personal lists of words.

■ *Lexia* is a reading series that helps students to strengthen skills through interactive exercises working on areas such as phonemic awareness and decoding skills.

■ *Numbershark* is a programme to help anyone improve basic numeracy. It uses a wide range of computer games to develop number skills. It offers 30 totally different games covering addition, subtraction, multiplication and division in ways that add meaning and understanding to these operations. It is suitable for ages six to adult.

■ *Nessy* is designed to reinforce spelling, reading and listening skills in a multi-sensory way. It includes printable card games, activity sheets, mnemonics and computer games.

■ *My Reading Coach* offers a comprehensive reading programme aimed at phonetic awareness, pronunciation, word building skills, grammar and reading comprehension. After an initial test, it sets out an individual programme for a child, focussing on the areas that need development. It builds in lots of repetition and reinforcement and monitors progress.

■ *Inspiration* and *Kidspiration* are programmes to help students in structuring written work. People with dyslexia often prefer to think in pictures than in words. They like to use idea mapping – to build a visual map of ideas using pictures, colours, shapes and relationships. They use the technique for note-taking, remembering information and organising ideas for written work. *Inspiration* allows the student build pictures on screen and then convert the image to a linear outline. The outline can be copied into the word processor and used as a basis for writing.

- *Wordswork* is a multi-sensory programme on study skills. It was designed primarily for undergraduates with dyslexia but is very relevant for students at second level and for adults who want to improve their skills before going back to formal education. It uses graphics, voice-overs, colour and humour to develop a variety of language skills which students with dyslexia (and others) need to address. Topics covered include essay writing, exam revision and time management. It also included sections on reading, spelling and grammar.

- *Mastering Memory* is an example of programmes to enhance memory. It presents sequences of pictures, words and symbols to be remembered and gradually increases the difficulty level

Useful websites with information on the use of technology in education

www.bdadyslexia.org.uk British Dyslexia Association (BDA)

www.dyslexic.com   IANSYST Ltd. Website on technology for dyslexia

www.ncte.ie   National Centre for Technology in Education

Irish Suppliers of ICT

Andrews Award Systems, 38 Pine Valley Park, Dublin 16.
Tel: 01 4930011; Web: www.awardsys.net

Ash Technologies, Naas, Co. Kildare. Tel: 045 882212; Web: www.ashtech.ie

Carroll Educational Supplies, Unit 5 Western Industrial Estate, Naas Road, Dublin 12. Tel: 01 4567279; Web: www.carrolleducation.ie

Computerspeak, Guinness Enterprise Centre, Taylor's Lane, Dublin 8 Tel: 01 6777620; Web: www.computerspeak.ie

Diskovery Educational Software, Unit 2, Waveney, Howth Harbour, Co. Dublin. Tel: 01 8063910; Web: www.diskovery.ie

Edtech Software Ltd., Murrisk, Westport, Co. Mayo. Tel/Fax: 1850 923459; Web: www.edtech.ie

Jackson Technology, 24 Kiltipper Ave, Aylesbury, Dublin 24.
Tel: 01 4518508/01 4624793; Web: www.jacksontechnology.com

Learning Horizons, 44 Laurel Park, Clondalkin, Dublin 22. Tel: 01 3111537: Web: www.learninghorizons.ie

Learning Software Ireland Ltd., 17 Dromsally Woods, Cappamore, Limerick. Tel: 086 3490886: Web: www.learningsoftwareireland.ie

Texthelp Systems Ltd., Enkalon Business Centre, 25 Randalstown Road, Antrim, N. Ireland BT41 4JL. Tel: 028 9442 8105: Web: www.texthelp.com

CHAPTER 11
CONTINUING EDUCATION

This chapter will be of most use to students with dyslexia in the last years of second level and in third level education. It is also targeted at adults who are considering returning to education. At a time of high unemployment, it is well recognised that those without qualifications are more vulnerable in the job market. It is recommended that students gain additional qualifications after the Leaving Certificate in order to compete in a very competitive labour market.

In this chapter you will read about the following;

- College and course choice;
- National Framework of Qualifications;
- The main applications systems after Leaving Certificate;
- Accessing support;
- Adult learners;
- Study skills.

Career and course choice

Students are better equipped for the job market if they have further training or education after the Leaving Certificate. This is why the major decision for students in their last year at second level is the courses they should apply for to continue their education.

There is rapid change and development in the courses provided after the Leaving Certificate. To be properly informed, prospective students need to make themselves aware of the major changes. Some of these changes include:

■ The major contribution made by the institutes of technology. In some cases employers would look first to these colleges rather than the traditional universities because of the strength of the reputation of certain courses.

■ The National Framework of Qualifications and the progression routes available for students.

- The growth in Post Leaving Certificate courses.
- The increasing flexibility and adaptability of the system so students can move from Post Leaving Certificate courses (level 5) to levels 6, 7 and 8. This provides alternative routes to qualifications.
- Systems such as ACCS (Accumulation of Credits and Certification of Subjects scheme) to aid the part-time student acquire qualifications. Subjects can be completed and certified individually and the student can accumulate credits to attain a level 6, 7 or 8 qualification.

Because of the number of courses and alternative routes to qualifications, students need to research courses. It is not something that should be left to sixth year. It can be difficult to make students realise the urgency to become informed about courses and to begin research in 5th year or earlier. The first place to start the research is with the guidance counsellor in the school, who will be able to provide information about colleges, courses, open days and application procedures. The level of provision of a careers service can vary from school to school depending on whether there is a guidance counsellor and the number of hours that are allocated to guidance counselling. Since the guidance counsellor works within the school, he/she will have a good knowledge of the student's abilities, interests and possible results.

The development of the internet has made access to information much easier. The website: www.qualifax.ie is the national learners database. It is the 'one stop shop' for learners. It provides comprehensive information on further and higher education and training courses. It has developed services to ensure all learners have all the information needed to make informed choices about education, training and career paths. It provides a search facility when looking for specific courses. Included are links to college and other education/training websites in Ireland and abroad. Detailed information on an extensive selection of careers is supplied, also the definitive calendar of career events, an interest assessment to assist students to make career choices, help for students when choosing subjects for senior cycle and a plethora of other useful information for students of all ages. It has a section for adult learners.

Further information can be gained from newspapers particularly around mid-August and mid-January. However there can be an element of hyped-up information and headlines can tend to focus on courses where points have risen or the handful of courses that require 500 plus points. Outside the louder headlines, the papers do contain excellent information and sometimes information that is not available elsewhere. This is because of the rapid change in the nature of courses provided and in the job market itself. These articles are often accompanied by large advertisements about colleges and courses. Remember that the colleges in highest demand do not need to advertise heavily!

Open days are held from September on. Some schools organise trips to visit colleges. It is possible to get a list of the main open days on the website: www.qualifax.ie. The major career information event is the Higher Options Conference in September organised by the Irish Times and the Institute of Guidance Counsellors. Over 180 institutions from Ireland and abroad attend. There are talks on topics such as how to apply to CAO and UCAS (the U.K. university application system), alternative routes to third level, how to choose a course and how to cope at third level. There are also talks on the working in different sectors such as law, science, green energy, nursing, social services and hospitality.

If the students are interested in a particular college, they should ring the college and ask if there is to be an open day. Even if there is not, the staff in the various colleges often make the time available to talk to individual interested students.

Work experience can be another invaluable way to obtain information about careers. Students could look for work experience during transition year or the summers following transition year or fifth year. It can help them choose a career direction and be of positive benefit if there is an interview for the course.

The key questions are: what career is of interest to an individual? and what courses help them achieve that career? The answer to these questions lie in a process of information gathering. Some of the constituent factors in making the decision are:

- Ability. Each student has a different profile of ability. A test used in many Irish Schools is DATS (Differential Aptitude Testing) which gives a percentile score based on national norms of a student's ability in Verbal Reasoning, Numeric Reasoning, Abstract Reasoning, Spatial Relations, Mechanical Reasoning, Clerical

Speed and Accuracy, Spelling and Grammar. In the case of students with dyslexia, psycho-educational assessments provide much more detailed information on the student's ability. These assessments could be even more relevant than the DATS. If the student's profile either from DATS or a psycho-educational assessment has particular strengths and weaknesses, career choices should be centred on the strengths. The student with difficulties in spelling and verbal expression would be wise to avoid careers where verbal skills are important such as office work or journalism. It appears to be a pattern that some students with dyslexia have a strength in spatial relations. This may lead into art, architecture, engineering or design.

■ Achievement. Achievement is different from ability. Some students with seemingly low levels of ability can achieve very good results because they have the perseverance and motivation to focus on their studies. Other students with excellent ability can do quite badly if they do not do the necessary work. A pattern of achievement will be built up by monitoring school reports. Expectations of results in state exams can be based on this. It is highly unlikely that a student who is achieving the grades of 'E' and 'D' during fifth and sixth year will jump to grades of 'A' and 'B' in the Leaving Certificate examination. For most students their grades will be close to their level of achievement in school. This makes it possible to predict the probable range of results in state examinations that a student may achieve. This information can form part of the career decision and helps to make the choice realistic. If a student's results in house exams are around 250 points, the estimated range of the Leaving Certificate results could be between 200 points to 350 points. It is realistic for the student to ensure courses in this range are included on the CAO application. In the CAO system where there are twenty choices, students may still use some of those choices for their dream courses that may go for 400 plus points but they should also ensure they include courses in the range of 200 points.

■ Interest Testing. These are tests which ask the students questions about careers and indicate their level of interest in different careers groups. These tests are often used at the stage of option choice for senior cycle. In recent years computerised interest tests have become more common. The websites: www.qualifax.ie and www.careerdirections.ie have such tests available. Included in some of the interest testing can be questions about the students' interests and personality such as: What do they like to do with their spare time? Do they like to work as part of a team? Do they enjoy organising events? Would they prefer to spend their time mending machines or playing sports or board games? Do they like activities that help care for people such as First Aid or visiting elderly relatives?

■ Other achievements outside the academic: Have they been involved in sports, Scouts, First Aid, drama, life-saving, sailing or music? How proficient are they in these activities? Do they want this activity to continue as part of their career? Do they have a driving licence? Sometimes leisure interests and achievements provide a route to a career choice.

■ Work experience will also give students ideas about the type of work they would like to pursue or avoid in the future. It will also provide them with a reference which may be useful at interviews later on.

All these threads; achievement, ability, interests, personality, work experience and other non-academic achievement, form a realistic basis to the process of career decision. It should also provide a list of possible career directions that the student would like to research further. Once students begin to research the courses available and different routes to qualifications, their ideas will be further refined. It is a process that will take time and should be ongoing during all of senior cycle.

Occasionally students may say they have no idea as to what career interests them. This can provide a serious obstacle to a discussion. However, if presented with a list of broad career groupings, many of these students have very clear ideas about careers they do **not** want to pursue and it is possible to reduce the list to maybe six broad career headings which they might consider. This provides a good starting point for research.

The above discussion on career choice focuses on the individual's aptitudes, interests and achievements. Another factor to consider is the employment trends. These are notoriously unpredictable. This is because of the changing nature of jobs due to technology and the global market. There are many jobs being advertised now which were not in existence ten years ago. The Irish economy since 2000 reflects how volatile the job market is.

However there are some patterns discernible:

- The more qualifications/skills a person has, the more positive the work opportunities open to them are.
- The Government has set up the Expert Group on Future Skills Needs, website: www.skillsireland.ie. The Group is intended to be the most comprehensive source of all research on labour and skills issues in Ireland. It has identified a number of key occupation/skills areas which are expected to experience skills shortages over the coming years. It produces bulletins at regular intervals. In the bulletin in July 2010 these key occupation areas included:
  - Computer and software developers.
  - Science such as physicists, biochemists, etc.
  - Food science and technology.
  - Mechanical design engineers.
  - Actuaries, risk managers, fund specialists.
  - Manufacturing technology.
  - Telecommunications.
  - Power generation and management of energy.
  - Multi-lingual telesales staff
- There is going to be more contract work and fewer permanent appointments.
- Because of the developments in technology and resulting changes in job practices, there is a great need for adaptability and flexibility. Workers will need to constantly up-date their skills and information. This is evident by the development of the concepts of continuous professional development and lifelong learning.

Up-to-date information on career trends appears in the newspapers usually in August and January, both critical times for course choices. It makes sense that information on employment trends would be part of a decision on career direction.

National Framework of Qualifications

The National Framework of Qualifications (NFQ) was introduced in 2003. It is a system of ten levels of qualifications that incorporate awards made for all types of learning, wherever it is gained. The NFQ, through its ten levels, provides a means of comparing and contrasting national and international education and training qualifications. It helps learners explain what qualifications they hold at home and abroad. It is based on standards of knowledge, skills and competence. It includes all types of learning such as the awards from the State Examinations Commission in the Junior and Leaving Certificates, awards for further education and training and awards from the universities and institutes of technology.

All qualifications in the NFQ are recognised at home or abroad. The NFQ is used to compare Irish qualifications with foreign qualifications. Thus, Irish citizens working abroad can have their Irish qualifications recognised. Learners or workers with qualifications earned abroad can have these qualifications recognised in Ireland.

A full explanation of the ten levels are on the NFQ website: www.nfq.ie. Some key qualifications are as follows:

- Junior Certificate   Level 3
- Leaving Certificate   Spans levels 4 & 5
- PLCs   Most level 5, but some at level 6
- Higher Certificate   Level 6
- Ordinary Degree   Level 7
- Honours Degree   Level 8
- Master's Degree   Level 9
- Doctoral Degree   Level 10

The Further Education and Training Award Council (FETAC) is the national awarding body for all further education and training qualifications. The Higher Education and Training Award Council (HETAC) is the qualification awarding body for third level education and training. The Government has announced plans to amalgamate these bodies. The new organisation will be called the Qualifications and Quality Assurance Ireland.

The Main Application Systems after the Leaving Certificate

The choices after Leaving Certificate have improved for all students including those with dyslexia. There are more courses, more places on courses, new routes to qualifications and increased support services for students with dyslexia at third level. The two key application systems are the CAO and Post Leaving Certificate courses. These two systems account for approximately 50,000 places. There are 60,000 students approximately in the Leaving Certificate cohort. Outside of these two systems, routes to qualifications include:

- Direct entry to the Gardai, website: www.garda.ie, Army, Air Corps and Navy website: www.military.ie.
- Failte Ireland, website: www.failteireland.ie, courses in the hospitality industry.
- FAS, website: www.fas.ie, training courses or apprenticeships.
- UCAS, website: www.ucas.ac.uk, the U.K. application system for university.
- Teagasc, website: www.teagasc.ie, agriculture, horticulture, equine, and forestry courses.

Central Applications Office (CAO)

This is the application system for courses at honours degree, ordinary degree and higher certificate level in the universities, institutes of technology, nursing colleges and some other colleges. The closing date for applications is 1 February. Offers of places are determined by points, provided the student has satisfied the entry requirements of the college and any specific course requirements. The points from the previous year can be used as a rough guide but the points in any year are set by the number of applicants for a course and the number of places available. The CAO handbook sets out the rules and procedures for the CAO system. This handbook is available in audio format as a download on the CAO website: www.cao.ie.

In 2005 the classification of courses in the CAO system was changed. In the past, courses were called National Certificate, National Diploma and Degree. This has changed as follows:

Previous designation	New designation
National Certificate	Higher Certificate/level 6
National Diploma	Ordinary Degree/level 7
Degree	Honours Degree/level 8

On the application form students may list ten level eight courses and ten courses from levels seven and six, a total of twenty courses in all. It is essential that these are listed in order of preference.

Some points relevant to students with dyslexia:

- It is essential to research the colleges and courses thoroughly. It is necessary to acquire college brochures, attend open days and talk to the staff and students in the college.

- Consider the structure of the course. Continuous assessment is when assessments are graded throughout the year and the marks form part of the final grade for the year's work. Semesters mean that the year's work is divided into two semesters and examinations take place at the end of each semester. Both continuous assessment and semesters can help the student with dyslexia by spreading the academic demands throughout the year and reducing the amount to be memorised. Some courses in certain disciplines are taught through lectures and practicals in which the student applies the knowledge learnt. This hands-on experience provides multi-sensory learning which suits many students with dyslexia. Other courses may be taught through reading lists and lectures. This may pose greater difficulty for such students.

- Use the CAO system fully. Do not restrict the choice to honours degrees/level eight. Use the level six and seven route as well. The CAO system is very flexible. Students may do a two-year higher certificate, transfer to an ordinary degree and then transfer to an honours degree if they obtain the necessary results.

- It is possible to apply for up to twenty courses. The courses *must* be listed in order of preference. Do not try to guess what the points may be. This leads to mistakes on the form.

- Consider courses outside the major cities. Frequently the same course has lower points in an institute of technology outside the major cities of Dublin, Cork, Limerick and Galway.

Support Services for Students applying to the CAO

The Association for Higher Education Access and Disability (AHEAD) is the organisation working to promote full access to and participation in third-level education for students with disabilities in Ireland and the website www.ahead.ie is a very useful source of information.

The first point of support for students may be the reduction of the points required for chosen courses. This is operated through the Disability Access Route to Education (DARE). Further information on DARE is available at the website: www.accesscollege.ie. DARE is a supplementary admissions scheme for school-leavers with disabilities which operates on a reduced points basis. This means, for students who are considered eligible, they can be admitted to their course of choice on lower points than those set by the CAO process. DARE was established by a number of Higher Education Institutions because there is clear evidence to show that disability can have a negative impact on educational attainment at school and as a result progression to higher education.

School-leavers (under 23 years of age in the January of the application) who have the ability to benefit from and succeed in higher education but who may not meet the points for their preferred course due to the impact of a disability should apply to DARE. There are other admission routes for mature students (those over 23).

DARE covers a wide range of disabilities including specific learning disability (including dyslexia). 60% of the students with a disability attending college in 2008 were diagnosed with a specific learning disability.

The colleges participating in DARE in 2011 are as follows:
- Athlone Institute of Technology
- Dublin City University
- Dublin Institute of Technology
- Mater Dei Institute of Education
- National College of Ireland
- NUI Galway
- NUI Maynooth
- Trinity College
- University College Cork
- University College Dublin
- University of Limerick

Each of these colleges has a reserved number of places to offer eligible DARE students at lower Leaving Certificate points. Students must meet the minimum entry requirements for the college to be considered for one of the reduced points places. If a student has exemptions for Irish or a third language, it is their responsibility to ensure the CAO and the college are aware of such exemptions.

Students are asked when completing the CAO form if they wish to be considered for DARE. They are then asked to complete a supplementary information form (SIF). There are three parts to this form.

Section A is completed online by the student by February 1st. It asks for information on the disability and the supports received at second level. The student has to complete a personal statement which outlines the impact of the disability on their education. It gives the student the opportunity to give information on their experience in school and the challenges encountered. These could include difficulties in some of the following: access to texts/materials, memory and concentration, meeting deadlines, attendance, ability to participate fully in classes and examination performance. This can be up to 300 words long. **It is important that students take their time to plan and compose this statement.** The decision from DARE will be based solely on the SIF Section A, B and C, so the student should make the best case possible in this statement.

Section B is to be completed by the school principal, and guidance counsellor or teacher. This provides background information on the student's educational experience and helps to determine appropriate supports at third level. This section must be returned to CAO by 1st April. The student prints the form from the CAO website and asks for it to be filled in by the school and stamped with the school stamp. It is important that the person completing the form is familiar with the impact of the disability on the academic performance of the student.

Section C is to be completed by a medical consultant. However, in the case of applicants with specific learning difficulties, a full psycho-educational assessment completed by an appropriately qualified psychologist is the document to be provided. This must be less than three years old. (In 2011 the assessment must be dated after 1st February 2008). The student should go to www.cao.ie for guidelines on the information required in the assessment.

The use of criteria as cut-off points for Disability Access Route to Education (DARE) makes access to such support more problematic. The criteria state that for students with dyslexia the general ability should be at or above a standard score of 90 and that standard scores in two literacy areas should be at or below a standard score of 81 which is the 10th percentile. These criteria can be accessed on home page of the CAO website: www.cao.ie. There is an item on the menu called Downloads. One of the downloads is Disability Route to Education – Eligibility criteria.

These criteria rely on scores in two literacy areas. It does not take into account other difficulties such as processing speed that a student with dyslexia may have. A processing speed difficulty will cause the student to be much slower in the exam and run into time difficulties completing it fully and therefore have poorer exam performance. This is not taken into account.

The maximum number of points in the CAO system is potentially 600 based on having 6 A1 grades at higher level. Students hoping to gain a place on a course where there is a high demand for places and therefore high points will take six higher level subjects. There are many students with dyslexia who, due to their poorer language skills, may be taking Irish, English and possibly a third language at ordinary level. The general ability scores of these students could be above the 70th percentile and spelling/reading scores around the 30th, a potential discrepancy of 40 to 60 in percentile terms. Indeed this is the most likely profile of students with dyslexia who are applying to the CAO as the CAO is the system which attracts the best and most able students. They have not been able to access support in RACE, an exemption for Irish or additional teaching support because their scores were not low enough to fall within the very low levels set for criteria for these. They have struggled at second level. Their potential points are reduced to 520 as they are not taking six higher level subjects. The criteria mean they will not be considered for help through DARE.

The use of such criteria facilitates the system in making decisions quickly and all that needs to be checked are the criteria. It does not take into account the individual difficulties of students and multi-faceted ways dyslexia affects the students. Also students and teachers are involved in time-consuming form filling. Is this information used or are the decisions based on the criteria alone?

It is the student's responsibility to ensure all sections of the form are returned by the given dates. Students should keep a copy for their personal records.

All applicants will be informed in writing by the end of June of the outcome of their DARE application. Applicants who are not eligible for consideration will be informed of the reasons of their ineligibility. An applicant can request a review of the application if they have reason to believe an error occurred during the screening process.

If the student is ineligible for DARE, they will get a college place through the CAO if they qualify under the entry and course requirements and points for their chosen course.

Disability/Access Support while at college

All students with a disability, irrespective of whether they come through DARE or not, can avail of a variety of academic, personal and social supports while studying at college. Therefore it is important for a student with a disability to inform the disability/access officers in the college they are attending of any difficulties.

The role of the disability/access officer is to work with students with disabilities in arranging supports that they may need while in college. Such supports may include assistive technology, examination arrangements, organising additional tuition or support during lectures. The level of support may vary from institution to institution. For example the National College of Art and Design and Dun Laoghaire Institute of Art, Design and Technology both offer a writing and research skills course. Check the websites of the different institutions to see what they offer.

In December AHEAD and Disability Advisors Working Network (DAWN) organise the Better Options College Fair. DARE and supports and services in the universities and institutes of technology are discussed. Students and graduates with disabilities talk about college life. Students, parents, teachers, guidance counsellors and psychologists are all welcome. Details are on the AHEAD website: www.ahead.ie.

To register with the Disability/Access service, students will need to make an appointment with the Disability/Access Officer. In order to register, most services will require written confirmation of disability. In the case of dyslexia, this is the psychological assessment. The disability or access officer carries out a needs assessment and then submits an application to the Fund for Students with Disabilities on the student's behalf, which is used to pay for equipment and or supports that have been identified as necessary. The types of supports available include assistive technology, alternative examination arrangements and learning support.

Students attending third level have to deal with considerably higher academic demands. Unfortunately, some students with disabilities realise that they could have availed of supports when it is too late. For example, there is no use looking for alternative examination arrangements on the morning of the examination as these must be agreed and arranged with faculty staff and the examinations board well in advance.

It is also important to remember that while the Disability/Access Service will liaise with other college staff (e.g. lecturers) to ensure that supports are implemented, it is always important for the student to take a certain level of responsibility for their own learning and support. Students should introduce themselves to lecturers at the start of term and discuss their needs with them independently. They are the best person to clarify their own needs and to explain their disability to those who may be unfamiliar with it.

If a student chooses not to disclose their disability, it is almost impossible for the college to make the adjustments that could help meet their educational support needs.

Support for graduates

AHEAD also runs two programmes relevant to students and graduates with disabilities

GET AHEAD provides a national forum for graduates with disabilities on the AHEAD website: www.ahead.ie. It also provides in-depth career training through the *Get Ready 4 Work* programme. This is a unique two day skills development programme for graduates with disabilities/specific learning difficulties. Topics to be covered include: career decision making, job-seeking/interview skills, CV preparation, recruitment and selection processes. There will also be training and discussion on the issue of disclosure. Job preparation skills will be imparted in a hands-on approach, including lively interactive workshops, mock interviews given by HR staff from different companies and seminars by professional recruitment specialists

WAM (Willing Able Mentoring) provides mentored work placements for graduates with disabilities. The mentored work placements offer real life work setting to identify the issues facing both employers and graduates in the recruitment and retention of people with disabilities

Post Leaving Certificate Courses (PLCs)

These courses are offered in colleges of further education. They are primarily designed to prepare students for the world of work and to develop vocational skills. While the vast majority are aimed at the ordinary level Leaving Certificate student who is unlikely to obtain a place in the CAO, some are in such specialised subjects that they could be a student's first choice regardless of CAO offers. Most courses last one year, but some may be two or three years.

There is no central application process. Students apply directly to individual colleges. Many of the colleges have open days in February/March. Applications should be sent in from January on. Selection procedures differ and may include interviews, portfolios or aptitude tests.

There are increasing links between PLC courses and the colleges in the CAO system. This means that a student who achieves a good grade point average on a PLC course may apply and be considered for a course in the CAO system. Certification for PLC courses is provided by FETAC. There are two schemes linking FETAC awards with entry to CAO. Details are on the website: www.fetac.ie.

The Higher Education Links Scheme (HELS) links PLC courses to places in the universities mainly. There is a quota of places set aside for applicants. Allocation of places is decided on the basis of a grade point average on the eight modules of the PLC course. The PLC course must include modules which are linked to the course being applied for. The FETAC website: www.fetac.ie has a document called Progression from FETAC level 5 Certificate and level 6 Advance Certificate to Higher Education courses 2011. This document gives details of these links.

A scheme was introduced in 2005 for applicants to the institutes of technology and some other higher education institutions. Applicants for level 6 and 7 courses may present results from any PLC course. Points are awarded for the 8 modules of the PLC course: 50 points for a distinction, 35 for a merit grade and 20 for a pass grade. This means that a student with 8 distinction grades gains 400 points and competes with the cohort of Leaving Certificate students applying to the CAO on the basis of these points.

Disability support services are not as developed in the PLC sector as in CAO. However, there is a partnership between the National Learning Network and City of Dublin Vocational Educational Committee (VEC), which offers a wide range of supports to students with disabilities in eight VEC colleges of further education in Dublin. These are Ballyfermot College of Further Education, Pearse College of Further Education, Inchicore College of Further Education, Colaiste Dhulaigh College of Further Education, Colaiste Ide College of Further Education, Plunkett College, Whitehall College of Further Education and Killester College of Further Education. When students initially approach the service, the Disability Support Officer carries out a needs identification process with them to ensure they get the support they need in areas such as transport, assistive technology, benefits, study support and one to one tuition.

Adult learners

There are many adults with dyslexia who, for a wide variety of reasons, did not succeed in education the first time around. It might be that they were not diagnosed until later in life and found school difficult or that even with an assessment, they still faced significant challenges at school. Later in life, they want to re-engage with education. While a great deal of the general information in this chapter is still relevant to them, there are specific courses or supports available to adults who wish to return to education. The national learner's website, www.qualifax.ie has a section for adult learners as well as being a comprehensive database for further education, third level and training courses. Below are the main initiatives and courses for adults planning to return to education.

Career Paths for Dyslexia

FAS, in conjunction with DAI, runs a course called *Career Paths for Dyslexia;* website: www.Careerpathsfordyslexia.com. The FAS course code is AT58F. It is the only course in Ireland catering for the specific needs of unemployed adults with dyslexia. It is run in Celbridge, Co. Kildare. The duration of the course is six months. The course content includes Information Technology, Literacy Development, Career Planning and a work placement. It aims to improve the skills knowledge and experience of adults with dyslexia to a standard to enable them enter the labour market or return to education or college. This course has been run since 1999. There has been a recent development in that an evening course is being offered at the Career Paths Centre which runs two nights a week for five weeks. It focuses on literacy and basic computer skills. Again the main aim of the course is to encourage unemployed adults with dyslexia to re-enter the workforce or undertake further education.

AONTAS

AONTAS, The National Adult Learning Organisation, website: www.aontas.com, provides information on opportunities and courses for adult learners. There is a very comprehensive booklet on the website which is full of information This booklet is essential for any adult who is interested in returning to some form of education. Topics covered include:

- Adult learning initiatives
- Second chance and further education
- Community education
- Apprenticeships
- Access and foundation courses
- Higher/third level courses
- Distance education
- Workplace learning
- Financial support, grants, scholarships, tax relief.

AONTAS host an Adult Learners Festival in February each year. There are events throughout the country. In 2010 three hundred and fifty events were held nationwide. Since 2008 *Which Course Expo* has been in held in the RDS in Dublin at the end of August. It is Dublin's largest adult learning Expo and in 2010 Aontas was represented at it.

Adult Education Guidance Initiative

The Adult Education Guidance Initiative aims to provide a guidance service to adults wishing to re-enter education. There are 38 guidance projects throughout the country which provide a service to participants in VTOS and other adult and community education programmes. It looks at the choices of the adult learner and matches skills and experience to possible learning options. The service is free of charge.

Adult Basic Education

Courses, organised by the Adult Literacy Service in each county, are offered to adults who wish to improve their reading, writing, spelling, basic maths, and computers. Courses can be on a one-to-one basis or as part of a small group. The courses are free of charge and are very accessible as the majority of them are delivered in local outreach centres. This type of learning is 100% focused on the needs of the learner and allows learners get advice on their education.

Back to Education Initiative (BTEI)

This initiative provides part-time further education programmes for young people and adults. The aim is to give people an opportunity to combine a return to learning with family, work and other responsibilities. The aim of the initiative is to increase the participation of young people and adults with less than upper secondary education, and to target the individuals and groups that experience specific barriers to participation in education. BTEI offers a wide range of subjects. These range from Junior Certificate and Leaving Certificate subjects. Basic adult education courses can be taken in a range of subjects such as catering, tourism, arts& crafts and sport & leisure which are certified by FETAC.

Vocational Training Opportunities Scheme VTOS

These courses give unemployed adults the opportunity of returning to full-time education without losing their social welfare benefits. Applicants have to be 21 years of age, unemployed for six months and in receipt of social welfare benefits. They attend the centre for six hours for five days of the week. The courses may last up to two years. The courses are run by 33 VECs in over 100 colleges throughout the country. Certification is at a range of levels including Junior Certificate, Leaving Certificate and FETAC level 1, 2, and 3. Full details are on the website www.vtos.ie.

Foundation/Access courses

Foundation/Access courses have been established in many third level institutions to prepare mature students for the challenges of third level. The courses are primarily aimed at adults who have been away from formal education for a number of years and would like to improve their skills, confidence and knowledge in order to access a third level course. Depending on the learner's requirements courses can be full-time or part-time, usually over a year. Some prepare the learners for specific courses such as engineering or science while others are more general.

Distance Education

Distance Education is learning which is not linked to a physical location or specific times throughout the academic year. It involves learning at a distance from the teacher with the help of a package of materials. Students may receive telephone or web-based guidance or may meet occasionally at week-ends. Open learning, on-line learning and distance learning are all types of distance learning. There is a wide range of courses with different levels of qualification available.

It facilitates the learner allowing them work at their own pace and it means that study can be combined with home and work commitments. There is no time wasted on travelling to a venue. However students need to be very disciplined. Fees may be charged and the free fees scheme does not apply. There may be entry requirements so this needs to be checked.

Some examples of distance education

■ The Open University, which is based in the U.K., is one of the biggest providers of distance education. It offers more than 360 undergraduate and post graduate courses in arts, modern languages, social sciences, health and social care, science, maths, computing, technology, business and management, education and law. The average time to attain a degree qualification is six years. Website: www.open.ac.uk

■ Oscail is the national distance education centre of Ireland. It is based on the DCU campus. It offers an opportunity to receive an Irish university qualification. It offers one-to-one tutorial support and support through email and telephone. No previous qualifications are required for undergraduate programmes for those over 23. Website: www.oscail.ie.

■ The institutes of technology provide a range of courses through distance learning. However many of the course require some attendance for practicals so that the programmes mix attendance with online learning modules. The institutes of technology have developed many flexible courses in terms of how they are delivered. ACCS (Accumulation of Credits and Certification of Subjects Scheme) allows for the accumulation of credits over time and the student can attain a level 6, 7, or 8 qualification.

- FAS Net College provides a range of E-Learning courses, aimed at employers, employees and unemployed people. Courses categories include business, office applications, web design/programming and technical support. Website: www.ecollege.ie.

- On-line learning is where the programme is delivered over the internet. NALA, the National Adult Literacy Agency, provides a number of Distance Education supports so that learners have the opportunity to brush up on their English or Maths in the privacy of their own home. This involves a series of TV programmes which are accompanied by a free workbook. DVDs of the TV series and workbooks are available from the freephone support line at 1800 202065. The website, www.literacytools.ie , provides help for adults who would like to improve their spelling, reading and number skills using the internet.

Applying to the CAO as a mature applicant.
Individuals, who are under the age of 23 years old and interested in applying to the CAO, apply in the same way as school leavers and places are allocated under the points system.

Generally mature applicants should be over the age of 23 before the start of the January for admission the following autumn and they must apply by Feb. 1st. However each college in the CAO sets its own procedures for mature applicants. Certain restrictions may apply for mature applicants. Therefore these applicants must contact the Admissions Office or the Mature Students Office in the college they are interested in applying to well in advance of the closing date for applications.

The procedure in Trinity College Dublin is outlined below as an example. 10% of students in Trinity are classified as mature. Leaving Certificate is not a necessary requirement, but specific courses may have specific entry requirements. Applicants fill in the CAO form and a separate form to be submitted to the Admissions Office by Feb. 1st. Not all applicants achieve a place as there are more applicants than places. An interview will be held to decide on the allocation of places. Applicants should have a keen interest in the subjects chosen and, if possible, relevant work experience or study.

Study skills at third level/further education
At this level students need to have independent learning skills in place with an understanding of their learning strengths. For the

student with dyslexia this means they should have an understanding of the psycho-educational assessment. From listening to many groups of students talk at courses run by the Dyslexia Association it is evident that many of them do not know exactly how dyslexia affected them and what were the most appropriate learning strategies. Some of this confusion is explained by the fact that dyslexia affects each student differently. The psycho-educational assessment can be used to help students understand how dyslexia affects them personally and what are their own particular strengths and weaknesses. The most appropriate learning strategies will depend on these. It is up to students to test out the possible strategies and decide what works best for them. They also need to understand their dyslexia if they are to seek support from the disability support services or from individual lecturers. They need to be able to explain how dyslexia affects them individually and what supports work best for them.

Below is a list of suggestions on how to learn and cope with the demands of college for students to consider.

Organisation of time, work and workplace

- Timetable. Have a structured timetable for study from the first day of a course, so steady progress is made. It is more difficult for the student with dyslexia to cram before an exam. It can lead to confusion and feeling of being overwhelmed.

- Regular time of day. Check which part of the day suits best for study. Some students find morning the most beneficial, some the evening. Consider the foods and drinks that might affect concentration such as coffee. Lack of food can also do this.

- Decide on a given period of time, not too long. Students with dyslexia often have to concentrate harder than other students. Working for too long can mean that learning and/or concentration may deteriorate and mistakes multiply. For the same reason, try to avoid study when rushed, under pressure or tired.

- Set out realistic study goals and priorities.

- Keep only one diary for all appointments, dates, exams, assignments, projects, social life, and work commitments. A personal organiser may be useful.

- Study at a desk, in a comfortable chair and comfortable clothes with a quiet environment.

Finding help

■ Talk to the academic staff and disability support staff in the institution about the support services. Do this early in the academic year so that the supports are in place to help.

■ Seek assistance from a counsellor, tutor or mentor who could help developing strategies for learning more effectively. Do this when the course begins and don't wait until demands of the course are overwhelming.

■ Ask the following be given in writing:
  • Booklists, course outlines and schedules of assignment dates.
  • Timetables, late changes in the timetable and exam timetable.
  • Guidelines on how to present assignments, bibliographies, footnotes, etc.
  • Feedback on completed assignments.
  • Practice exam questions that demonstrate exam format.

■ Join or form a co-operative learning group.

■ Ask someone to proofread essays or projects before handing them up. It would be useful if such work was discussed with a tutor prior to preliminary drafting and that the early assignments are checked by a tutor prior to submission. Such supports are available in some colleges.

■ Sometimes the student may encounter a lecturer who is not aware of the range of difficulties that a student with dyslexia may have. Be prepared and have information on the topic ready to hand out and then be ready to explain personal difficulties.

Study Methods

■ Become computer literate as soon as possible, preferably early on at second level. By third level, computer skills need to be excellent. Many colleges now expect students to be using computers and laptops as a necessary tool. For some courses lecturers put lecture notes on the college website for students to download. This is very good news for students with dyslexia. Students will be expected to hand up assignments done on a laptop. Where lecture notes are not downloadable, and the student is expected to take notes during the lecture, it is easier to study lecture notes that have been entered on a computer, the print being more legible than handwriting. Will lecturers give students permission to use a laptop? If not, enter the notes on the computer the same evening as the lecture, when the notes are still fresh in the mind.

■ Check if assistive technology can help. Read the chapter on computers to check out what is available. Talk to the disability support service in the college about what is available.

■ Do prescribed reading in advance and so be prepared for lectures. It will make students familiar with main topics and key words and will help with spelling new vocabulary.

■ Sit in the front of the room where visual and auditory cues are clearer and it is easier to concentrate on the content of the lecture.

■ Attend every class, tutorial, and laboratory session. Much of the learning will result from the lecture presentation where learning can be facilitated by the visual, aural and written elements. Students with dyslexia usually have more difficulty catching up on missed lectures from other students' notes that are only in written form.

■ If taking notes by hand, take down the main points and structure of what a lecturer is saying. Use mindmaps or headings, sub headings and points. Leave plenty of space, so points can be expanded on later. If a lecturer uses a word that is difficult to spell, write it phonically and circle or mark it. This means time will not be wasted wondering how to spell it and the thread of the lecture lost. Listen carefully to the opening remarks of the lecturer. Good lecturers will state the purpose of the lecture and will sum up at the end. They may also give clear guidelines that help with notes such as enumerating the number of points to be made. If handwriting is a difficulty, perhaps ask a fellow-student to take a carbon copy or photocopy his/her notes. Don't miss the lecture while doing this.

■ Ask lecturers prior to the lecture for the notes or powerpoint presentation they will be using. It means less writing and it is possible to listen and concentrate on what is said. The structure and sequence of the lecture will be clearly laid out. It is also possible to include additional notes or points where relevant.

■ Tape lectures (with prior permission). It is possible to concentrate on listening to the lecture in order to understand it and use the tape to make notes that evening. A good mike is needed to cut out background noise and sit at the front of the room. Label the tape clearly. It may provide a welcome break from reading to listen to such work.

- Transcribe or refine notes as soon as possible after a lecture to ensure they are legible and structured and that you understand the points in them.
- Write down questions or points not understood for discussion later with the tutor or lecturer.
- Develop a shorthand for keywords which help to minimise writing such as 'envr' for environment.
- Ask lecturers to shorten booklists so that the essential texts are clearly marked.
- Make sure to understand the essay, project, or assessment requirements before starting.
- Use a reader service or ask to have essential texts audio-taped if you find this helpful.

Specific strategies

Students who learn aurally
If the student learns more through aural than from written information, think of using tapes of lectures, taping notes and find out if any of the texts are available on tape. Get involved in discussions of topics with lecturers and fellow students. Repeat material to be learnt aloud. Read drafts of essays aloud to see if they make sense.

Students who learn visually
Some students have a strong visual memory. This can be used when learning. Such students are able to recall the look of a page of notes. This assists in the recall of the content of the page. Make use of colour, numbering of points, margins, headings and diagrams when making notes. Mindmaps will be very useful here.

Difficulty with text
Some students may have difficulty in deciphering the meaning of complex texts. They may have to reread pages several times. This may be as a result of the number of clauses in each sentence or new vocabulary. Ask for help and direction. Ask that reading lists highlight the essential texts to be read. Always know the purpose in reading a

text. Make notes showing the development of the points in the text. Reading the text aloud may help in comprehension. If the type is very small, have it enlarged. Do reading early in the day, because tiredness can make it more difficult to concentrate. Assistive Technology can be of great help with programmes such as the *Kurzweil* or *Read and Write Gold.*

Spelling

If spelling difficulties remain, develop strategies to cope. Ask others to proofread documents. Use the spell check on the computer or a Franklin Spellmaster. Keep a list of new words and learn them off by heart. Inform the academic staff of the difficulties and give examples of your spelling. Ask that examiners be informed of the difficulties. In a number of courses spelling might be critical to success such as medical or paramedical courses where the correct spelling of drugs or conditions is essential or teaching where the teacher will be expected to be able to spell correctly before a class. In these cases it will be necessary to develop spelling strategies for accuracy. Gilroy & Miles in *Dyslexia at College* have a useful chapter on this topic.

Memory Difficulties

Some students find it difficult to retain information over time. Strategies that might help include:

- Good note-taking skills so the notes are clear and comprehensible.
- Learning the notes. Some students feel that once the notes are made and filed, that the work is done. Notes must be learnt. This learning can be checked by an oral recital or writing them out again. Mnemonics may help with learning.
- A revision plan where the topic is revised on a frequent basis. Such a plan could entail learning the material on the night of the lecture, a weekly revision of all new material learnt and a monthly revision of the month's work. Each time you revise it will take a shorter time.
- Make sure you understand what you are learning, as this makes it easier to memorise.

Quest for Learning

Quest for Learning, website: www.questforlearning.org, is an excellent website targeted at students, teachers and employers around disability issues and has been developed by AHEAD, FAS, DIT and NLN. It includes topics on study skills, disability awareness and employability skills.

The Quest for Learning website provides a virtual learning support network designed to support all students making the move into third level courses. It recognises that the academic demands of a third level course are very different from those at second level and this website has very useful tips on how to deal with those demands and quickly improve one's study skills in third level, guiding the student on how to set up an effective study system, how to take effective lecture notes and retain that key information. QFL has information on how to do all of the following:

- Planning study programmes.
- Finding out learning preferences.
- Making most use of time.
- Organising writing.
- Taking notes.
- Planning and writing an academic paper.
- Writing bibliographies.
- Writing summaries.
- Improving writing techniques.
- Answering examination questions.
- Memorising vast amounts of information.
- Supports available for students with disabilities.

Students with disabilities or specific learning difficulties such as dyslexia may need additional study skills tuition due to the disadvantage of their disability or learning difficulty in a new learning situation. For example a student with dyslexia may need additional tuition in learning how to lay out an academic paper and may benefit from additional hours with a study skills tutor.

Useful Websites

www.aontas.ie   National Adult Learning
                                       Organisation

www.ahead.ie   Association for Higher
                                       Education Access and Disability

www.careerdirections.ie	Career information and interest testing
www.careerpathsfordyslexia.com	FAS course for adults with dyslexia
www.cao.ie	Central Applications Office
www.ecollege.ie	FAS E-learning courses
www.failteireland.ie	Courses in the hospitality industry
www.garda.ie	Gardai website
www.literacytools.ie	Help for spelling, reading and number skills
www.military.ie	Army, Air Corps and Navy
www.nfq.ie	National Framework of Qualifications
www.open.ac.uk	The Open University
www.oscail.ie	National Distance Education Centre of Ireland
www.qualifax.ie	National database for all third and further education courses
www.questforlearning.org	Study skills, disability awareness, & employability skills
www.skillsireland.ie	The Expert Group on Future Skills Needs
www.ucas.ac.uk	The U.K. University Application System
www.vtos.ie	Vocational Training Opportunities Scheme

CHAPTER 12
ADULTS WITH DYSLEXIA

This chapter will be of most use to adults with dyslexia and to employers. In it you will read about:

- Dyslexia in adulthood;
- Psycho-educational assessment for adults;
- Practical help for adults with severe literacy difficulties;
- How dyslexia affects adult life;
- Understanding dyslexia in the workplace;
- How employers can help;
- How adults with dyslexia can help themselves (See also Chapter 11).

Dyslexia in Adulthood

A common misconception is that dyslexia, like measles or mumps, is a hazard of childhood. Sadly, this is not the case. And while it is acceptable, perhaps even amusing, when a child misreads a word or makes a basic spelling error, it is anything but funny when it happens to an adult. Dyslexia causes great embarrassment, anxiety and even humiliation to many adults who live in fear of being asked to read unfamiliar text aloud, to take detailed notes or to summarise the main points of a meeting.

Adults with dyslexia are found in all areas, from the board room to the box factory, and from the operating theatre to the performance stage. Anyone, at any time of life, or in any occupation may have dyslexia.

Anyone who works in an organisation employing twenty or more people is likely to have one or two colleagues with dyslexia. Some of these people may be highly qualified graduates working at very high levels. Dyslexia does not prevent high achievement provided the job suits the person. Many people with dyslexia find career success and fulfilment working for themselves or by choosing work areas which highlight their strengths and skills.

In an article in Fortune Magazine (May 2002), Betsy Morris profiles some very successful business people, bankers, lawyers and entrepreneurs, all millionaires or billionaires, who succeeded in spite of major dyslexic difficulties. The best known, on this side of the Atlantic is tycoon Richard Branson, who left school at sixteen and went on to build an aviation empire. The author, Thomas G. West[1] has written in detail about the achievements of engineers, scientists and information technology innovators who have dyslexia. In Harvard, he reports, dyslexia is known as the M.I.T. (Massachusetts Institute of Technology) disease because so many of the students at this prestigious institute have the condition.

Sadly, for the majority of adults with dyslexia the story is not so positive. Many do not even know that they have a specific learning disability. They may have struggled for years to overcome difficulties, whose origins they do not suspect. A common feature is fear: fear of being found out, fear they will not be able to cope with the next challenge, fear that someone will discover the strategies they use to cover up or fear that they may just be stupid and ineffective.

We have already seen that dyslexia is not merely a difficulty with literacy and language learning. It affects all aspects of information processing, short and long-term memory and organisational skills. It may also affect mathematical processing and physical co-ordination. Going hand-in-hand with these difficulties, and often more damaging, is the lack of confidence and self-esteem caused by years of academic struggle or failure.

How is dyslexia identified in a grown man or woman? How is it seen beneath the layers of strategies and coping mechanisms that have been developed by resourceful and inventive people to hide, what they consider to be, their own inadequacies. The list of indicators for adults is included in Chapter 1.

Also remember that despite the difficulties an individual may have, there can be strengths which include:

- Having a skill at visualising, i.e. thinking in pictures.
- Having good practical, problem-solving abilities.
- Being creative and innovative.
- Ability to think 'outside the box'.
- Having good spatial ability.

■ Possibly having excellent computer skills.

■ Being patient and determined in spite of difficulties.

The check-list in Chapter 1 is not comprehensive. Many people experience some of the difficulties listed and may also have some of the skills listed above. However, if the difficulties are numerous and they are causing a problem in the person's life, then further investigation would be wise. Perhaps the strongest indicator of a dyslexic-type difficulty is a deep-seated feeling by the individual that something is amiss. Many adults, when diagnosed with dyslexia, reported that they always knew they were somehow different but they did not know why. Many believed, as one woman put it, that they had a 'lazy brain' or that they were simply not very smart.

The Psycho-Educational Assessment for Adults

The only way in which dyslexia can be positively identified in an adult is by carrying out a thorough psycho-educational assessment. There are four stages in the identification of dyslexia according to McLoughlin, Fitzgibbon and Young (1994).[2] These are:

■ Information gathering.

■ Psychological testing and diagnosis.

■ Developing an understanding of dyslexia.

■ Taking action.

Information Gathering

This can be more difficult than one would imagine. Obviously it is necessary to have information on a condition in order to detect its existence. So many adults who have dyslexia have never even heard the word and have no idea of how it affects learning. They are, therefore, unlikely to seek assessment unless encouraged by someone who knows about the condition. Anecdotal evidence records that parents are often identified following psychological assessment of their children. They find that the difficulties experienced by their children are so similar to their own that they are prompted to explore the possibility that they, too, are affected.

Psychological Testing and Diagnosis

The second step, psychological testing, is a more contentious issue. It is costly, difficult to access and not everyone believes that it is essential. Psycho-educational assessment is carried out by a psychologist and can range in cost from €400 to €700. There is no state provision for adults, even for those who are unemployed or who have a medical card. It can also be hard to locate a suitably qualified psychologist and waiting lists tend to be long. The Dyslexia Association of Ireland carries out a great number of subsidised assessments for adults who would otherwise be unable to access assessment. This facility depends on funding from the Department of Education and Skills but this funding is not guaranteed. A list of psychologists in private practice may be obtained by telephoning the Psychological Society of Ireland.

Is Assessment Necessary?

It is important to discover just why a learning difficulty exists, because unless you know the precise nature of the problem, it is not going to be possible to deal with it effectively. Psycho-educational assessment for adults is about pinpointing the difficulty and advising on remediation. It is not about putting a label on the person. A diagnosis of lung cancer does not create a stigmatising label. Instead it gives medical experts the information they need to prescribe suitable treatment. Likewise, a diagnosis of dyslexia enables a person to begin the process of dealing with the condition. It is often an enormous relief for adults, who have felt stupid and inadequate all through life, to realise that they have an identifiable difficulty. In all fairness, adults with dyslexia are entitled to this knowledge about themselves. Knowledge empowers and knowing about a condition is the first step towards managing it.

The argument is sometimes made that, as some adults have been upset by their psycho-educational assessment, the procedure is unhelpful. This is not logical. The problem may not have been with the assessment in itself, but with the issues it raised. Appropriate assessment with a competent and sensitive professional can be a very therapeutic experience. The cognitive testing which is carried out by a psychologist, the personal observation and the dialogue between client and professional, are central to the assessment process and are necessary to devise a strategy for dealing with the difficulties caused by dyslexia.

The technology now exists to carry out screening and certain assessment procedures on computer. Screening tests, whether paper or computer based, can be a valuable starting point, but they do not provide comprehensive information and a basis for future action. Computer based assessments, however sophisticated, lack the human element. There are many issues for the newly diagnosed adult to deal with; regret for wasted years, anger at past treatment in school or at work or fear of the future. These are best handled in a professional way by a trained psychologist.

Only a psychologist may carry out the necessary psychometric testing. McLoughlin et al (1994) say:

> The accurate diagnosis of dyslexia requires the measurement of general ability and working memory. Any procedure that fails to incorporate appropriate cognitive tests is likely to produce both false positives and false negatives.

The authors add that the appropriate assessment of intelligence is one of the most crucial factors in diagnosis. This stands to reason. There are many reasons why adults have literacy difficulties and dyslexia is only one of them. While the effects of literacy difficulties are similar, the causes are very different. The results of the International Adult Literacy Survey, published in 1997, indicated that twenty-five per cent of Irish adults had pronounced literacy problems. The reasons for these difficulties may have been early school leaving, irregular school attendance, overcrowded classrooms, lack of family support for learning, low academic ability **or** dyslexia. These latter two factors were often confused in the schoolrooms of the past, resulting in inappropriate educational placement or neglect of the actual problem.

The Assessment Process

The purpose of a psycho-educational assessment for adults is to determine whether they have a dyslexic-type difficulty, the nature and extent of the problem and how the person can be helped to cope. The focus of the assessment, therefore, is on finding out how these adults learn and helping them to use their best learning channels. Its aim is positive – to put the person in the driving seat in relation to their own lives, but the process can be daunting.

The psycho-educational assessment begins with a review of the person's family and school history. Areas of difficulty encountered are listed and family incidence of dyslexia is noted. Cognitive assessment is carried out using appropriate tests. The tester is interested in how the person tackles different items in the test and in the relative strengths they show. Reading, writing and spelling skills are also looked at, with a view to identifying problem areas and suggesting strategies to overcome difficulties. The procedure may last from two to three hours and will probably include discussion on the results of the assessment and advice on future action.

The most positive result of a psycho-educational assessment for an adult is often the validation which it provides. Self-esteem and self-confidence are likely to be very badly affected by adverse school experiences and failure to reach potential in the workplace. A positive assessment often provides the encouragement necessary to go for job promotion or to take on further study. Knowing about dyslexia and the support which now exists at third level can be the key to a new future.

Practical help for adults with severe literacy difficulties

Many adults who opt for psycho-educational assessment do so because of frustration with reading and spelling difficulties which continue to cause distress. If the assessment reveals dyslexia, then they will want some practical help with literacy. Ideally, an adult with dyslexia should work with a specifically trained teacher who utilises the information provided by a thorough psycho-educational assessment to devise an effective teaching programme. As quoted in the Moser Report [3], American research found that 'between 550 and 600 hours of instruction are needed to become fully literate and numerate'. While this level of tuition may not be possible outside of a full-time course, best results are obtained when teaching is provided on an intensive and consistent basis. Tutoring adults with dyslexia successfully requires considerable skill and training. The Dyslexia Association of Ireland maintains a list of such teachers and this is available to members. Tuition may also be obtained through the adult literacy services which now have some tutors experienced in working with adults with dyslexia. Information can be obtained from the National Adult Literacy Agency, or from local Vocational Education Committees.

Dyslexia and How it Affects Adult Life

Once a positive diagnosis has been reached, the adult with dyslexia must then begin to gain an understanding of the condition in order to come to terms with it. Dyslexia affects people's lives. It affects all aspects of their lives, not just their school years. When a person learns differently and takes longer to develop skills to an automatic level, this has an impact on a wide variety of areas such as learning to drive a car, use a computer, acquire a second language, handle tax affairs or secure a house mortgage. All of these everyday tasks can be complicated by the information processing styles of a person with dyslexia.

How much dyslexia affects a person's life depends on many factors: the age at which the condition was diagnosed, the degree of severity, the ability of the individual, the type and quality of support received – both educational and social, and even the personality of the individual. Some people are lucky enough to have had their dyslexia identified as children and to have received support through their school years. They have had an opportunity to understand their own learning difficulties and to take them into account when planning further education or choosing a career. The fact that they have overcome basic literacy difficulties and even secured satisfactory results in examinations does not mean that they have been 'cured' of their dyslexia. Information processing difficulties, poor short term memory, auditory processing deficits or hand-eye co-ordination difficulties do not go away. A person who chose a work area where literacy was not of vital importance could find that promotion or changing work practices require them to read and write a great deal more. Another could discover that dealing with clients abroad demands second language skills which were not acquired at school. Updating computer skills, learning to use new technology or new equipment, re-training which has to be undertaken in certain sectors of industry, can all be difficult for a person who thought that dyslexia was left behind with schooldays. If the difficulties encountered at school were severe, then the adult may well have a reluctance to re-enter a learning situation.

To tell or not to tell

Adults, particularly young adults who have recently completed their education, may find that the working environment is not as supportive of people with dyslexia as third-level institutions. A great deal of help and support is now provided at third level and it is very acceptable to declare one's dyslexia. In the working world the situation is very different. A major dilemma facing young people about to enter the workforce is whether to inform prospective employers that they have dyslexia. Despite the passing of the Employment Equality Act in 1998 and the Equal Status Act in 2000, the position of workers with dyslexia is still not clear. If a person is dismissed or not hired because of dyslexia then there may be a case for the employer to answer. But it is most unlikely that any employer is going to lay themselves open to such question. However, if a job candidate declares on an application form or at interview that they have dyslexia, even if they also have impressive qualifications, will they get the job? If they do not get the job, they will never know whether stating their dyslexia had anything to do with it.

Late Diagnosis

Adults, who reach the age of forty or fifty before being identified as dyslexic often experience great anger and frustration because of their learning difficulties. This can make them uncomfortable people to live or work with and can have implications for personal and family relationships. The tensions and stresses caused by trying to cover up learning difficulties or to cope in a world which thinks and functions differently to oneself may cause people with dyslexia to seek release in alcohol or other addictive behaviours. Scott in *Dyslexia and Counselling* (2004)[4] says:

> I have certainly encountered a remarkable degree of alcohol and drug-related anxiety conditions in both dyslexic men and women. In this respect, I would estimate that, as a group, they are significantly more likely to use drink and drugs to cope with their anxiety than non-dyslexics are.

Much publicity is given to famous people with dyslexia such as Albert Einstein, W.B. Yeats, Richard Branson and others, but less attention is paid to those who fail to cope. Adults, who dropped out of school or under-achieved because of dyslexia, are more likely to find themselves in low-paying jobs or unemployed. This, in turn, affects the life chances of their children as the link between literacy difficulties and poverty is well established.

In extreme cases, young men (and it is almost invariably young men) get into trouble with the law and end up in prison. A British study reported that the young offenders surveyed first got into trouble while truanting from school. They dropped out of school because of learning difficulties which had not been addressed. Is there any reason to believe that the same situation does not apply in this country?

Understanding Dyslexia in the Workplace

The consequences of having dyslexia depend very much on the time and the culture. When literacy was neither vital to daily life nor very valued, having dyslexia was not a problem. In the future, it may well be that developments in information technology will make literacy, as we know it, irrelevant. Reading and writing may be as outdated as the horse and cart. Then, the person with dyslexia will not be at a disadvantage at all. Possibly, with good creative, visual and problem solving skills, they will have a distinct advantage. However, in today's society people with dyslexia are in an unenviable position. Not only is work, travel and leisure dominated by the written word, but skill in planning, organisation and time management are more important than ever before. Completing tasks to a time schedule, absorbing new information quickly and working under pressure are requirements of every workplace. None of these come easily to the person with dyslexia.

Organisation and Time Management

If one word were to be applied to the adult with dyslexia who is having problems in the workplace, it would probably be **disorganised**. Where the words 'could try harder' are often used in school reports, the adult equivalent very often is 'can't get his act together'. Planning and organising, setting out timetables, distinguishing between the important and the urgent, remembering appointments, passing on telephone messages and meeting deadlines can be exceptionally difficult for many people with dyslexia. Many complain of a tendency to get bogged down, overwhelmed by the workload and very stressed.

Initial Job Training

The initial training may be insufficient, in that a dyslexic person may not have the same learning style as other employees. Skilled and well-qualified workers have reported an absence of flexibility in the approach to training in many firms. Research has indicated that it can take a person with dyslexia considerably longer to acquire a skill to an automatic level. Once the skill is acquired, performance may be similar or better but in pressured work situations this extra time may not be given. Awareness of the skills, as well as the difficulties, of people with dyslexia would help greatly in this area.

Information Processing

So many office workers today suffer from information overload that the pressure on people with dyslexia can be almost unbearable. Most adults with dyslexia who work in professional or white-collar jobs have good reading skills. They may read quite fluently and have excellent comprehension but their reading speed may be slower. They may also need to exercise more care not to misread a word or phrase. Letters, emails, reports, journals, magazine articles, newspaper reports – the amount of reading required to keep abreast of developments is a major burden and the time it takes often eats into leisure and family time.

Similarly, when it comes to letter or report writing, editing, checking spelling and grammar, double checking figures for reversals and placement errors, managing appointment diaries and recording telephone messages, extra time is also needed. Many people with dyslexia have problems with clerical speed and accuracy, so care is essential. While the advent of the word processor has made life easier, it has also meant that very few people indeed now have personal secretaries. Most people must produce their own written work. It is no longer sufficient to be a good engineer, one must also be able to write a clear and properly spelt report and perform tasks at high speed. A worker at a call centre must be able not only to do the job but also must complete each task within a stated time and meet hourly targets of calls answered.

Positive Aspects of Dyslexia in the workplace

It may sometimes sound as if adults with dyslexia experience nothing but difficulties. This is certainly not the case. While certain administrative tasks may take a person with dyslexia longer to complete, there are many areas where specific skills more than compensate. Many people with dyslexia have made successful careers in medicine, business, architecture, engineering, and of course in the creative arts as writers, actors, artists and sculptors.

One of the compensatory aspects of having a different learning style is that it often enables very fresh and innovative thinking, an ability to see solutions where others see problems and the diligence and perseverance to put these into effect. Learning to cope with a school system which does not understand you, overcoming obstacles, keeping going in spite of failures and having to work harder than others to achieve the same results or less, build up strength and a determination which is worth having in any work situation. Scott (2004) cites four authorities to back up her claim that 'dyslexic people do work much harder than others and are more persistent'. Employers who are too narrowly focused on accredited qualifications, or whose work practices allow for no variation, may miss out badly on possible employees. An example is the man who set up and successfully ran a company while on a training scheme. When the company became viable and the job was advertised, his application was rejected because he had no formal qualifications. If neat handwriting and good spelling is the criteria, neither Albert Einstein nor W.B. Yeats would get past the Human Resources desk, Richard Branson would not make it to interview stage and Steve Redgrave (five Olympic gold medals to his credit) might not even complete the application form.

Employer Awareness

A major issue for adults with dyslexia in the workplace is whether to disclose the fact that they have dyslexia to an employer or prospective employer. Dyslexia is a hidden disability. When a person attends for interview on a wheelchair or with a guide dog, it is quite obvious that this person has a disability. If an employer hires such a person, they do so in full knowledge of the disability.

Dyslexia is an unknown entity to many employers. The assumption is often made that if a person has dyslexia then they cannot read at all. Regrettably many people still assume that dyslexia means illiteracy or possibly impaired mental functioning. Things have not changed so much since Albert Einstein lost two lecturing posts because of his erratic spelling and poor handwriting.

Equality legislation in Ireland prohibits discrimination against people with disabilities but proving that someone has been discriminated against in employment is extremely difficult. Anecdotal evidence suggests that it is happening and that employees are being bullied because of dyslexia but the facts are hard to establish. It would be a great pity if employers did not take full advantage of the particular skills which people with dyslexia have to offer. The creativity and problem solving skills, the ability to think differently and to devise coping strategies are all talents which need to be fostered in the working environment. Diversity needs to be cherished. If working practices demand only square pegs for square holes, what happens when a round hole appears?

How Employers can Help

Employers are in an enormously powerful situation in relation to workers with dyslexia. They can determine whether the person becomes a productive and happy member of staff or whether their employee becomes nervous, stressed-out and anxious. Some relatively simple procedures would make life easier and work more productive, not only for employees with dyslexia, but perhaps for all staff.

- Become aware of dyslexia. It is a fact of working life. Perhaps 6% to 8% of the workforce may be affected by dyslexia to some extent. A literacy difficulty may explain why some workers are reluctant to keep records, write reports or even to seek promotion. It may also explain difficulties with time-management and even reactions to perceived authority figures. Many adults with dyslexia, who have unhappy memories of school days, carry over the fear and resentment felt as children to their work situation.

- Create an open environment in which employees have no fear that declaring a difficulty will result in dismissal or sidelining. Trade unions can be helpful here in setting up mechanisms to manage access to information and support. If a dyslexic problem is identified it can be taken into account. A difficulty which is being covered up is much more likely to result in mistakes than one which is recognised. Colleagues can be encouraged to help each other out. The good reader may proof-read written work in return for help with a technical matter. Work can be allocated to suit the talents of the individual and the employer gets the best from every worker.

- Look at the whole person. Reading may not be a strength, but there may be many other skills and abilities which are untapped. Many people with dyslexia have great interpersonal skills and are very vocal. Others have exceptional facility with information technology. Adults with dyslexia have usually learned patience and tolerance and so make understanding trainers and instructors.

- Remember that staff with high-level qualifications can still have dyslexia and that it may affect their work, particularly if they are trying to cover up the condition.

- Use the many support systems which exist. Outside specialists can provide screening and psycho-educational assessment if necessary. Individual tuition and support for employees is available and studies in the U.K. have found that productivity increases when areas of difficulty are targeted.

- Consider how technology can help. Word processing packages with spell and grammar check can work wonders. Voice operated software, screen readers, scanners, mobile phones with recording memory, electronic dictionaries, talking calculators, reading pens, electronic organisers, one or more of these may solve the problem. (See Chapter 10).

- Consider low-tech solutions. People with dyslexia often find that increasing print size to l4 points, using a plain font, or changing the background colour on a computer makes a huge improvement in legibility. Photo-copying information on coloured paper, use of colour coding, or coloured hi-lighters, use of coloured transparent sheets to cover reading material may also help. Instructions do not always have to be given in densely printed form. Short clear sentences, in plain English and well spaced on the paper are more accessible for all workers. A picture is worth a thousand words to a person with dyslexia. Illustrations, diagrams, flow charts and mind maps can be enormously helpful. Visual literacy is a skill not to be underestimated. Some day we may all need to have it!

- Be flexible. A key factor in dyslexia is **difference**. Employers can view this difference as a positive or a negative. If a worker with dyslexia does not find a particular system, or training practice suits their learning style, ask them what would suit. There may be another way and it may even be better.

How Adults with Dyslexia can Help Themselves

Adults with dyslexia must remember that they are a minority of the population. Minorities, while they have rights, must adapt to living in a world which does not see things the same way as they do. For the person with dyslexia, the question of how they adapt to their condition is of crucial importance. In the end success will depend on the action which they take to manage their own lives and fulfil their own potential.

Adults whose dyslexia was identified in childhood are relatively lucky. At best, they may have had remedial support and been enabled to make a smooth transition from school to third level and so to the workplace. At worst, they knew the reason for any learning difficulties which they encountered. The following points are directed to those identified in adulthood and also to those people who feel they have not fully come to terms with their dyslexia.

- Find out as much as possible about your own particular situation. Dyslexia can be mild or severe. It can affect the academically gifted, the average learner or the less able. It can be accompanied by attention and concentration problems, dyspraxia, speech and language processing difficulties and by anxiety conditions. It is very important to be aware of your own profile. The person who can tell you this is the psychologist who carries out the psycho-educational assessment. Don't be afraid to ask. It's your life. If you were assessed as a child and did not receive this information then consider having a new assessment and asking questions.

- Learn about dyslexia. There are numerous sources of information from books and web sites, to talks and conferences. The more you understand about the condition, the more you will understand yourself. You will also learn that it is a two edged sword. It carries advantages as well as disadvantages. Learn to capitalise on your strengths. Concentrate on what you can do, rather than on what you can't.

- Take positive action. If you were advised by the assessing psychologist to seek professional help to improve your literacy, or to support you in further study, then go ahead. The Dyslexia Association of Ireland maintains a list of qualified teachers who offer individual tuition to adults with dyslexia. The Dyslexia Association also sponsors a full-time course for adults which is administered by FAS. This course called *Career Paths for People with Dyslexia* is a very useful means for adults who have been unemployed or working in the home to upgrade their literacy skills and acquire computer training. Both day and evening courses are offered.

■ If you left school without achieving formal qualifications, consider the possibility of going back into education. There is a wide variety of choices – from night classes at your local college of further education to access courses for university. As an adult, with life experience and maturity, you may be surprised at your success.

■ The National Adult Literacy Agency (NALA) now offers support to adults whose literacy difficulties are caused by Dyslexia. A document published by NALA *Keys for Learning* provides information on services available. NALA can be contacted at 76 Lr. Gardiner Street, Dublin 1, Tel. 01 8554332. email: literacy@nala.ie, website: www.nala.ie. Information can also be obtained from local Vocational Educational Committees.

■ The Adult Education Guidance Initiative offers information, advice and guidance on a one-to-one basis for adults who wish to return to education. This valuable service is provided by the Department of Education and Skills and can be accessed through the National Centre for Guidance in Education, 42-43 Prussia Street, Dublin 7. Phone: 01 8690715. email: info@ncge.ie, Website: www.ncge.ie.

■ Third-level colleges, institutes of technology, colleges of further education and training centres are all now much more aware of dyslexia and some excellent support services are in place. Many provide specialist tuition, facilitate note taking in class, allow extra time or use of technology in exams.

■ Employers are increasingly becoming aware of dyslexia. There is still a lot of improvement needed in this area but if you have an understanding employer you may be able to make adjustments in your work situation to minimise your particular difficulties and improve your own productivity.

■ You may find that the attitude of family and friends towards you changes when it is discovered that you are a capable person with dyslexia who has been hampered by the difficulty. You may also find that your own self-esteem rises and you become more confident. This is, perhaps, the most common side effect of receiving a diagnosis of dyslexia. When your confidence reaches the level of being able to say, "I have dyslexia, so what"? then you have made a major leap forward.

■ Investigate what modern technology can offer. Computers, with their spelling and grammar checking facilities are a boon and a blessing to people with dyslexia. Scanners which can be used to put printed text on computer and screen readers which can read it back are very useful. Software packages such as *Texthelp Read and Write* and *Dreamwriter* make it easier to put ideas on paper. Voice operated software lets you talk to your computer and it writes your information and spells it properly. The *Quicktionary* pen can be used to read unknown words and also give you a definition. Even your mobile phone can be used to record information and your organiser can help keep track of appointments and addresses.

■ Be aware that not all of your difficulties may be the result of dyslexia. There are other hidden learning difficulties such as attention deficit hyperactivity disorder, dyspraxia and Asperger syndrome. Like dyslexia, these are life long conditions and so may continue into adulthood. It is now widely understood that it is quite common to have more than one of these conditions. It is important to understand what other factors affect your learning and your work life. Information on these co-occurring conditions is available in chapter 1. It may be necessary to seek professional help from experts in other areas if you suspect that you may be affected by one or more such condition.

■ It is now recognised also that people who suffer from more than one hidden learning difficulty are more likely to suffer from depression and low self-esteem. This is hardly surprising given how hard it can be to cope with one learning problem.

■ Some people, particularly those whose learning difficulties caused distress in childhood, may find that they need professional counselling before beginning to tackle the practical task of getting help with reading and writing. You need a clear head and no other side-issues which might hamper learning.

■ Finally, your own attitude towards your dyslexia will be the most significant factor. If you believe that fate has treated you unfairly and that the world owes you a living, you are going to compound your problems. If, on the other hand, you decide that dyslexia is not going to stand in the way of your achieving your goals and you are prepared to put in the hard work and use every strategy you know to get round, through and over the obstacles in your path, you will get there, as many others have before you.

Useful Resources for Adults with Dyslexia

Living with Dyslexia, an information booklet for adults available from the Dyslexia Association of Ireland

www.careerpathsfordyslexia.com. This website contains information on day and evening courses for adults with dyslexia.

Technology Advice Service provided by Dyslexia Association of Ireland. This service helps people to make informed choices about suitable assistive technology.

References

1. West, T.G. (1991) *In the Mind's Eye* Buffalo, New York: Prometheus Books.

2. McLoughlin, D., Fitzgibbon, G. & Young, V. (1994) *Adult Dyslexia* London: Whurr.

3. Moser, C. (1999) *Improving Literacy and Numeracy: A Fresh Start.* The report of the Working Group chaired by Sir Claus Moser: Department of Education and Employment, UK.

4. Scott, R. (2004) *Dyslexia and Counselling* London: Whurr.

CHAPTER 13
FREQUENTLY ASKED QUESTIONS

In this chapter you will find some very brief answers to common questions. This chapter may also be used as a quick reference. More detailed information on all topics is provided in the foregoing chapters.

What is dyslexia?

This simple question is one of the hardest to answer. Dyslexia is, literally, a difficulty with language, coming from the Greek words *dys/dus* meaning *bad* or *hard* and *lexis* meaning *language.* So dyslexia is a difficulty with language, specifically written language. It makes it hard for people to read, write and spell correctly. It is a genetic condition, not related to overall intelligence and not caused by laziness on the part of the individual. It occurs in 6% to 8% of the population.

What's the difference between dyslexia and specific learning disability?

Specific learning disability (SLD) is an umbrella term for a number of learning difficulties including dyslexia. While dyslexia is often used as a synonym for SLD, there are other conditions which are also classed as specific learning disabilities. ADHD, Dyspraxia and Asperger's syndrome are probably the most common. A person with dyslexia may well have one or more of these conditions also.

What are co-occurring conditions?

The conditions mentioned above, ADHD, Dyspraxia, Asperger's Syndrome, as well as Specific Language Impairment often occur along with dyslexia. Recent research would suggest that it is extremely common for a child to have more than one such condition. When more than one specific learning disability is present, it appears that problems are more severe and that there is a greater risk of behavioural problems such as aggression or withdrawal, due to frustration and low self-esteem. There may also be a higher risk of childhood depression and anxiety. It is important, therefore, that all difficulties are identified and appropriate support provided.

Why does my child have dyslexia?
Dyslexia is a genetic condition, so it is very likely that your child inherited it from a parent or grandparent. There is no way that a parent or teacher can cause a child to have dyslexia and no way to prevent it. There is no reason for any parent to feel guilty about a child's dyslexia or to be ashamed of the condition.

Why does my child have to be assessed?
In order to deal with any problem it is necessary to have a great deal of information about it. Dyslexia can be mild, moderate or severe. The child affected may be very bright, of average ability or may be of less than average academic ability. This information can only be gleaned from the results of tests administered by a qualified psychologist. Learning difficulties may result in behaviour problems and these may be seen as the cause, not the result, of the difficulty. A child with dyslexia may also have attention deficits or speech and language difficulties. The diagnosis and remediation of a specific learning difficulty is a complex process, so assessment by an educational specialist is necessary if a comprehensive education plan is to be put into effect.

How can I get an assessment?
A school may request psycho-educational assessment through the National Educational Psychological Service. This service is free but it can take a long time for such an assessment to be obtained as there is limited access to the service and schools must prioritise the students with the greatest need. Many parents, therefore, are forced to seek private assessments. Such assessments may be obtained privately from the Dyslexia Association of Ireland or from psychologists in private practice. The Psychological Society of Ireland, website: www.psihq.ie; Phone: 01 4749160 may be contacted at info@psihq.ie with queries. Assessments cost from €400 to €700 in 2010, and may take several weeks or months to arrange.

Will my child be labelled?
The word **label** is the problem here. Identifying a problem, making a diagnosis and giving a name to a condition, all of these are a necessary

part of dealing with it. Making sure that a diagnosis of dyslexia is not used as an excuse by a child for not trying to learn, or as a stigmatising label by an uninformed person, is a matter for the parent.

How often do I need to have my child assessed?

In general, a full re-assessment should be necessary only at critical points in the child's academic career. It may be advisable before transferring from primary to secondary school, particularly if the first assessment was carried out when the child was in first or second class. A full assessment should not be carried out within a year of the original. A recent assessment (one less than three years old) must be available when applying for reasonable accommodations in the Leaving Certificate or for accessing disability services at third level. Other than on these occasions a full assessment should only be considered in the light of individual cases. A review of progress, which does not involve a full psycho-educational assessment, may be carried out whenever necessary.

Do children grow out of dyslexia?

No. Dyslexia is a life-long condition. Though a child may learn to read, write and spell adequately, the underlying difficulty will always be present. It may cause difficulties in learning a foreign language, in learning to drive a car or in acquiring other skills.

Do children with dyslexia ever learn to read?

The vast majority of people with dyslexia do learn to read if given the appropriate help and particularly if this help is received at an early age. Becoming a confident speller is rather more difficult and some people experience this problem all through their lives. However, these problems can now be overcome to a large extent through the use of information technology.

Will my child have to go a special school?

Only children who have a severe reading delay, as indicated by the fact they are performing at or below the second percentile, are entitled to attend special reading schools. There are three reading schools in Dublin, one in Cork and a number of special reading units in national schools around the country. These cater for a relatively small number of children, who attend for a maximum of two years. The vast majority of children with dyslexia attend regular schools.

What kind of secondary school should I choose?

The choice of school is a very personal thing and the individual needs of the child must be taken into account. While there is no ideal school for children with dyslexia, a dyslexia-friendly school may be identified by reading its policy on admission and participation by students with disabilities. (See Chapter 7)

Can I do home schooling?

In theory you can, but few parents feel equal to this challenge. Advocates of home schooling argue that it allows children to work at their own pace and learn in their own individual style. Critics of the system say that children need the company of peers and the social, sporting and cultural aspects of school are just as important as the learning.

Will my child be able to go to college?

This depends on the overall academic ability of the child, the severity of the dyslexia and the amount of help the child receives. Statistics from the third-level sector in Ireland record ever-increasing numbers of students with dyslexia and colleges now offer great support. It is important for students with dyslexia, when completing CAO forms, to apply through the Disability Access Route to Education (DARE) and to ensure the three sections, the personal statement, the school reference and the psycho-educational assessment are completed and returned by the due dates. It is also important to note that education has become much more flexible and students can progress from PLC to Higher Certificate and to degree level courses.

How can I teach my child at home?

Teaching and parenting are both highly important and demanding occupations. While many teachers are also parents, the roles are not similar. Teachers are trained to be objective and unemotional. Few parents can remain uninvolved when trying to teach a child with a learning difficulty. In general, the teaching done by parents is best done informally and by providing support as requested by the child. Formal teaching is best carried out in the classroom or by the specialist teacher.

What can I do to help?

There is no one better placed to help a child with dyslexia than a willing and informed parent. Parents can help by understanding the difficulty, explaining it to the child, acting as an advocate for the child, informing teachers and other relevant people about the difficulty, maintaining the child's self-esteem, setting the difficulty in perspective and in providing support for the child socially and educationally.

Are there special glasses for dyslexia?

No. Some people with dyslexia find it hard to read printed material when there is a glare from the page. Tinted or coloured lenses or tinted overlays have been found to reduce this glare and make reading easier.

What is the difference between learning support, resource, remedial and special needs teachers?

Learning support teaching is provided to children with low achievement. It was formerly called remedial teaching. It does not need an individual application. Assessment for access to such help is done in school through the use of standardised testing. The *Learning Support Guidelines* state that when selecting pupils for such help, priority should be given to those who achieve scores that are at or below the 10th percentile on a standardised test of English reading or mathematics.

Resource teaching is granted based on an individual application for a child with special educational needs to the SENO for the school. Such applications have to be accompanied by an assessment. At primary level children with dyslexia are considered higher incidence and so do not qualify for resource teaching. At second level the student has to be at or below the 2nd percentile in numeracy or literacy as well as having a specific learning difficulty.

Increasingly the term special needs teacher is being used which describes both learning support and resource teaching.

What is the difference between an IEP and IPLP?

Under the *Education of Persons with Special Educational Needs Act*, an individual education plan (IEP) should be drawn up for the child who has been assessed as having special educational needs. For the child who falls within the criteria for learning support, an individual profile and learning programme (IPLP) is drawn up.

These plans are similar and record information about learning attainments and learning strengths of the student. Both contain an outline of the learning programme which sets out learning targets and activities. There should be parental involvement in planning both.

Should my child continue in the Gael Scoil?

Research indicates that children with severe phonological deficits find it hard to cope with learning more than one language at a time. This applies much more to written than spoken language. Many children with dyslexia successfully complete their entire education within the all-Irish system. However, every decision must be made with the individual child in mind and the advice of an appropriate educational specialist would be invaluable in such cases.

How does my child get an exemption from studying Irish?

Children, who have a specific learning difficulty and severe reading and spelling difficulties that place them at or below the 10th percentile on a recognised standardised test, may be exempted from the study of Irish. Parents must write to the school principal, enclosing a report from a psychologist which is less than two years old. This report must specify the child's reading score and recommend the exemption. (See Chapter 3)

If my child gives up Irish, will this limit choice of jobs or universities?

Formal certificates of exemption are recognised by the National University of Ireland and so students holding such certificates will be exempt from college matriculation requirements in relation to Irish. The other universities and colleges do not have a compulsory Irish requirement. Irish is still required for training as a national teacher and for some Civil Service occupations. Garda recruits do not require Irish at entry level but must have achieved passes in two languages at Leaving Certificate.

If children are exempt from studying Irish will they be able to study another language at second level?

This will depend on the individual situation. Some children with severe dyslexia may find it almost impossible to master the written element of a second language. Others who have received specific help at an early age may have sufficient competence in literacy to take on a new language at second level. Some languages are easier for students with dyslexia. Those languages which are pronounced and spelled as they look such as Italian and Spanish, may be easier to master than those with what is called 'deep orthography such as French. However, given the constraints on school timetables it may not always be possible to choose the desired language. The best advice may be to allow a student to take on a new language, in the knowledge that once an Irish exemption has been granted, a second or third language will not be required for entry at third level. Thus, if a language proves just too difficult for the students, they do not have to continue to study it.

What help is available for students in exams?

The Department of Education and Skills offers reasonable accommodations in Junior and Leaving Certificate exams to students whose performance is impaired by their dyslexia. Students may be allowed the use of a reader to read questions correctly and/or a tape recorder on which to record answers, the use of word processor or may be given a waiver from having marks deducted for spelling and grammar errors. Specific extra time for students with dyslexia is not normally awarded. (See Chapter 3).

Students who are granted special accommodation in state exams will have their certificates annotated to that effect.

Universities and third-level colleges offer a wide variety of supports in examinations and are very receptive to applications for such help from students.

Are there special computers for dyslexia?

No, but there are many software packages which make organising and producing written work very much easier. (See Chapter 10)

Can I get any help with expenses?

There is no doubt that providing support for students with dyslexia can be very costly. Parents are not entitled to any allowances, though schools may apply for grants for assistive technology for specific students. The cost of psycho-educational assessment is a valid claim on the Med 1 Form for tax-payers. VAT can be claimed back on the purchase of computers/assistive technology for home/personal use, via Form VAT 61A.

Why don't children get more help in school?

Unfortunately it is not possible for all children with dyslexia to get all of the help they need within the school system. Many parents find themselves looking for extra help outside of school. This may be because of limited resources within the school or it may be that the child's problem is not seen as severe enough to warrant learning support. At present, dyslexia is regarded by the Department of Education and Skills as a high incidence special educational need. This means that it is a difficulty shared by many pupils. Pupils with high incidence difficulties are not eligible for individual resource teaching at primary level. Schools must allocate learning resource hours to the students most in need of such support.

CHAPTER 14
CONCLUSION

Dyslexia is a complex condition. It is as old as mankind, but it presents as a problem only at a particular point in time. In pre-literate societies it would have gone unnoticed. While writing first appeared over 5,000 years ago, it was the preserve of a few. In any case, as early scripts were ideograms or picture scripts, people with dyslexia would not have had much difficulty either in reading or writing them. It is only within the last one hundred years that universal literacy has been the objective in the developed world. Interestingly, dyslexia as a phenomenon did not arouse much attention before the turn of the 19th century. In the future, information technology may well make reading and spelling less necessary. Being born in the 20th century was really bad luck for many people with dyslexia, because literacy has never been so necessary for education and for the workplace.

Many people with dyslexia say, and many experts in the area would agree, that dyslexia is not so much a learning difficulty as a teaching disability. Because people with dyslexia learn differently, and because it is a minority way of learning, it is not well understood by teachers and is not catered for within mainstream schools. Many older people will remember when writing with the left hand was strictly forbidden in Irish schools – it was a minority activity and severely discouraged. Luckily this era has passed and hopefully in the future pupils with dyslexia will be accommodated as comfortably within schools as are left-handed pupils now.

What is needed to bring this transformation about? Greater awareness, greater acceptance and greater adaptability are required. Parents, teachers and education authorities need to acknowledge that dyslexia is a common condition affecting up to 10 per cent of the population and that even at the milder end of the condition the child with dyslexia has special educational needs. Increased awareness resulting in early identification and appropriate intervention is likely to yield significant results. The existence of dyslexia much be accepted and this means that dyslexia-friendly teaching must be provided and dyslexia-friendly schools must be promoted as an intrinsic part of the education system, not an optional extra when funds permit. The necessity of adapting to social and cultural differences is becoming apparent in our schools. Pupils with dyslexia may well benefit from this acceptance of diversity. Insisting that there is only one way of thinking, one way of perceiving the world, one answer to every question is a luxury that the Irish education system can no longer afford.

A growing economy needs all the help it can get. The talents and abilities of people with dyslexia can be harnessed. Their creative visuo-spatial, problem-solving and inter-personal skills are assets too valuable to ignore. Literacy is the foundation stone on which education, academic success and qualifications are built. Society has little room for those who do not acquire written knowledge and the certification to prove it. As we do not yet have the means to bypass the literacy requirement, there is no choice but to alter our education system to meet the needs of learners with dyslexia, so that they also can access the knowledge that is acquired through the written word.

It is hoped that this book will help to bring that change about and that readers will find in it some of the information and encouragement they need. The authors wish all people with dyslexia and their families, success in overcoming the obstacles that learning differently puts in their path, and the strength and determination to pursue that path and achieve their goals.

THE DYSLEXIA ASSOCIATION OF IRELAND

The Dyslexia Association of Ireland (D.A.I.) is a company, limited by guarantee which has charity status. It was founded in 1972 by two women who had observed similar learning difficulties in their children. They had discovered that, though the children were bright and interested in learning, neither could read nor spell properly. Nobody seemed to know why this was, so they did some research. Having discovered that dyslexia was the cause of their children's difficulties they set up an organisation to promote awareness of dyslexia and to lobby for the provision of state services for those affected by it. However, they also realised that children with dyslexia needed specific help and they needed it right away. Therefore, the Dyslexia Association set about providing the information, psycho-educational assessment and specialist teaching which was needed. It is still doing so today, with more demand than ever for its services.

Information
The first, and often the most crucial, need of parents whose children are having learning difficulties is for information. The Dyslexia Association provides a public information service through a telephone helpline, a number of useful publications, and a website: www.dyslexia.ie. Members of the association are kept up to date with developments through newsletters, public meetings and conferences. Courses for parents, talks to parent/teacher groups and in-service courses for teachers are also offered.

Psycho-educational Assessment
Many parents, who are unable to secure assessment for their children through the National Educational Psychological Service, come to the Dyslexia Association. The D.A.I. has been carrying out such assessments for over thirty years and provides a service for children and adults. Funding from the Further Education Section of the Department of Education and Skills allows the association to offer

subsidised assessment to adults with limited means. The cost of psycho-educational assessment is €400 (2010). Waiting lists tend to be long for both children and adults.

Branches – Almost Nationwide

The Dyslexia Association now has branches all around the country. Branches are run by voluntary committees of parents and teachers. They act as local parent support groups and lobbyists, raise awareness and provide information. They also facilitate the running of workshops which provide supplementary teaching for children with dyslexia by trained local teachers.

Group Tuition

One of the earliest innovations of the association, and one of the most successful, is the provision of group tuition for children between the ages of seven and seventeen, outside of school hours. Special classes are offered for students at Junior Certificate and Leaving Certificate level. The teaching is done by specifically trained teachers and the pupil teacher ratio is kept very low. Children must have been assessed as having dyslexia before enrolment. Classes are usually held for two hours each week, in a local school. These classes, called workshops, organised by voluntary branch committees, are available in almost 40 locations around the country. Details of workshops can be found on the association's website.

Individual Tuition

The association maintains a list of teachers who have taken a course on dyslexia and who are willing to offer one-to-one tuition. Parents and/or individuals with dyslexia may access names on this list by becoming members of the association. Individuals must have been assessed by a psychologist as having dyslexia and a copy of a written report must be available before tuition can commence. Tuition is usually carried out in the tutor's home. Teachers are available in most parts of the country.

Course for Adults

A full-time course for unemployed adults with dyslexia is sponsored by the Dyslexia Association and administered by FAS. This course, which is the only one of its kind in the country, is called Career Paths for People with Dyslexia. Evening classes are also available for those unable to attend full time. Details are available on the DAI website: www.dyslexia.ie.

Technology Advice Service

A technology advice service is available at the DAI office in Dublin to students at second and third level, adults with dyslexia, teachers, tutors, trainers and HR personnel who wish to learn more about how technology can assist people with dyslexia. Details from 01 6790276 or email info@dyslexia.ie.

In-service Courses for Teachers

In-service courses for qualified teachers are offered at weekends, evenings and during summer holidays. Full information is available on the website.

Parents' Courses and Talks

Short courses for parents on how to help and support their children are organised and speakers are available to give talks to parent/teacher groups, employers and others.

For further information on DAI, contact 01 6790276, email info@dyslexia.ie or on the website www.dyslexia.ie.

APPENDIX B:
USEFUL RESOURCES

Government Publications

The Education Act (1998)

The Education of Persons with Special Educational Needs Act (2004)

Understanding Dyslexia (2005) video/CD ROM/DVD

Learning Support Guidelines (2000)

Inclusion of Students with Special Educational Needs, Post Primary Guidelines (2007)

Dyslexia Association of Ireland Information Books

All Children Learn Differently: A Parent's Guide to Dyslexia

Living with Dyslexia: Information for Adults on Dyslexia

Useful Books for Parents

Cogan, J. & Flecker, M. (2004) *Dyslexia in Secondary School, a Practical Handbook for Teachers, Parents & Students* London: Whurr

Cottrell, S. (1999) *The Study Skills Handbook* London: MacMillan

Frank, R. (2002) *The Secret Life of the Dyslexic Child* London: Rodale

Gaynor, K. (2009) *Tom's Special Talent*, Dublin Special Stories Publishing

Mackay, N. & Tresman, S. (2005) *Achieving Dyslexia Friendly Schools*, 5th Ed. Oxford: Information Press and BDA.

McCormack, W. (2007) *Lost for Words, Dyslexia at Second Level*, 3rd Ed. Dublin: Tower Press

Miles, T.R. and Westcombe, J. (Edits) (2001) *Music and Dyslexia: Opening New Doors.* London: Whurr

Miles, T.R., Westcombe, J. & Ditchfield, D. (Edits.) (2008) *Music and Dyslexia: A Positive Approach.* Wiley

Moore-Mallinos, J. (2010) *It's Called Dyslexia.* Dublin: O'Brien Press.

O'Moore, M. (2010) *Understanding School Bullying – A Guide for Parents and Teachers* Dublin: Veritas

Ostler, C. *Dyslexia: A Parent's Guide* Ammite Books.

Ott, P. (1997) *How to Detect and Manage Dyslexia* Oxford: Heinemann.

Ott, P. (2006) *Teaching Children with Dyslexia, a Practical Guide* Routledge

Payne, T & Turner, E. (1998) *Dyslexia: A Parents' and Teachers' Guide* Multilingual Matters Ltd.

Peer, L. (2000) *Winning with Dyslexia, a Guide for Secondary Schools* London: BDA

Peer, L & Reid. G. (Eds) (2001) *Successful Inclusion in the Secondary School* London: BDA

Reid, G. & Fawcett. A. (2004) *Dyslexia in Context* London: Whurr.

Books for Adults with Dyslexia

Bartlett, D. & Moody, S. (2000) *Dyslexia in the Workplace* London: Whurr.

Dyslexia Association of Ireland (2009) *Living with Dyslexia: Information for Adults on Dyslexia*

Goodwin, V. & Thomson, B. (2004) *Making Dyslexia Work for You – A Self-help Guide* London: David Fulton

Heaton, P. & Mitchell, G. (2002) *Dyslexia, Students in Need* London: Whurr.

McLoughlin et al. (1993) *Adult Dyslexia: Assessment, Counselling and Training* London, Whurr

Miles, T.R. & Gilroy, D. (2008) *Dyslexia at College 3rd Ed.* London: Methuen

Mullan, D. (2010) *The Boy Who Wanted to Fly.* Legend Press.

Reid, G. & Kirk, J. (2001) *Dyslexia in Adults: Education and Employment* New York: Wiley.

Books for Teachers

Cogan, J & Flecker, M. (2004) *Dyslexia in Secondary School, a Practical Handbook for Teachers, Parents & Students* London: Whurr

Crombie, M. (1992) *Specific Learning Difficulties: A Teachers' Guide* Glasgow: Jordanhill Publications.

Gathercole,S.E. & Packiam Alloway, Tracy. (2008) *Working Memory and Learning.* Sage Publications

McCormack, W. (2007) *Lost for Words, Dyslexia at Second Level 3rd Ed.* Dublin: Tower Press

Malone, G. & Smith, D. (1996) *Learning to Learn* NASEN Publications

Michelson, C. *Adult Dyslexia: A Guide for Basic Skills Tutors* Available from the Adult Dyslexia Organisation, 336 Brixton Rd., London SW9 7AA.

Miles, T.R., Westcombe, J. & Ditchfield, D. (Edits.) (2008) *Music and Dyslexia: A Positive Approach.* Wiley.

Ott, P. (2007) *Teaching Children with Dyslexia, a Practical Guide* London: Routledge

Pavlidis, G.I. (1990) *Perspectives On Dyslexia,* Volumes 1 and 2 Wiley.

Payne, T. & Turner, E. (1998) *Dyslexia: A Parent's and Teachers' Guide* Multilingual Matters Ltd.

Peer, L. & Reid, G. (2001) *Successful Inclusion in the Secondary School.* London: David Fulton.

Reason, R. & Boote, R. (1986) *Learning Difficulties in Reading and Writing: A Teachers' Manual* NFER Nelson

Reid, G. (1998) *Dyslexia: A Practitioner's Handbook.* Wiley

Rose, R. & Shevlin, M. (2010) *Count Me In!* Jessica Kingsley Publishers

Schneider, E. & Crombie, M. (2003) *Dyslexia and Foreign Language Learning* London: David Fulton

Snowling, M. & Hulme, C. (Edit.) (2005) *The Science of Reading – A Handbook.* Blackwell

Snowling, M. & Thomson, M.E. (1991) *Dyslexia: Integrating Theory and Practice.* London: Whurr.

Books on Maths and Dyslexia

Clayton, P. (2003) *How to develop Numeracy in Children with Dyslexia.* LDA Books

Ronit Bird, (2007) *The Dyscalculia Toolkit,* Sage Publications

Ronit Bird, (2009) *Overcoming Difficulties with Numbers,* Sage Publications

Chinn, S.J. (2007) *Dealing with Dyscalculia, Sum Hope* Souvenir Press

Chinn, S.J. & Ashcroft, J.R. (2007) *Maths for Dyslexics including Dyscalculia* Wiley

Emerson, J. & Babtie, P. (2010) *The Dyscalculia Assessment.* Continuum International Publishing Group

Henderson A. (2000) *Maths for the Dyslexic: A Practical Guide* London: David Fulton

Kay, J. & Yeo, D. (2003) *Dyslexia and Maths* London: David Fulton

Miles, T.R. & Miles, E. (1992) *Dyslexia and Mathematics* Routledge

Yeo, D. (2003) *Dyslexia, Dyspraxia and Mathematics* London: Whurr.

Websites

www.ahead.ie	Association for Higher Education Access and Disability
www.aspireireland.ie	Aspire (Asperger's Syndrome Association)
www.bdadyslexia.org.uk	British Dyslexia Association
www.cao.ie	Central Applications Office with links to the Higher Education Institutions websites.
www.dyslexia.ie	Dyslexia Association of Ireland
www.dyslexia.eu.com/	European Dyslexia Association
www.dyspraxiaireland.com	Dyspraxia Association
www.education.ie	Department of Education & Skills
www.hadd.ie	Hyperactivity Attention Deficit Disorder
www.nala.ie	National Adult Literacy Agency
www.ncge.ie	National Centre for Guidance in Education
www.ncte.ie	National Council for Technology in Education
www.nida.org.uk	Northern Ireland Dyslexia Association
www.nln.ie	National Learning Network

www.psihq.ie	Psychological Society of Ireland
www.schoooldays.ie	Online Resource for Parents and Teachers
www.scoilnet.ie	Site for primary and post-primary schools
www.sess.ie	Special Education Support Service
www.spectrumalliance.com	Spectrum Alliance

Educational suppliers for learning materials:

The Early Learning Centre: Branches currently in Dublin, Galway, Limerick and Waterford

ETC Consult, 17 Leeson Park, Dublin 6. Phone: 01 4972067

LDA, Duke Street, Wisbech, Cambridgeshire PE13 2AE, England. www.ldalearning.com

Outside the Box Learning Resources Ltd., Tougher's Business Park, Newhall, Naas, Co. Kildare. Tel. 045 409322 www.otb.ie

Prim-Ed, Bosheen, New Ross, Co. Wexford. Phone 051 440075 Web: www.prim-ed.com

Surgisales Teaching Aids, 252 Harold's Cross Road, Dublin 6W.

ASKING FOR HELP FORM

Asking for Help Form

To _____(teacher's name)

From _____(pupil's name)

1. I think I could do better in your class if you
    *   Let me work with a 'support buddy'.
    *   Let me sit in the front nearer to your desk.
    *   Gave me more time to answer questions and do my work.
    *   Gave me more help in the classroom when I don't know what to do.
    *   Showed me how to do things rather than just telling me.
    *   Let me photocopy the overheads or lecture notes.
    *   Gave more information on handouts.
    *   Used more visual information like illustrations, graphs, maps charts, videos, photographs and posters.
    *   Used simpler words when explaining things.
    *   Spoke slower.
    *   Would give instructions one at a time and repeat them.
    *   Let me use a coloured overlay in class when I read.
    *   Told me I didn't have to read out aloud in front of the class.
    *   Gave me more time to read.
    *   Let me tape record the class lesson.
    *   Let me use a computer to help me do my work.
    *   Let me use a dictaphone or tape recorder.

2. I think I could do better if, when you made worksheets, you
    *   Used a bigger and clearer font like Arial, Comic Sans MS or Sassoon Primary in size 12 -16 with double spacing.
    *   Used words that were easier for me to read.
    *   Printed on light coloured paper.

3. I think I could do better if, when you use the board or overhead
    projector, you
    *   Printed rather than used joined/cursive writing.
    *   Used colour chalk or markers.
    *   Read slowly or repeated whatever you write.
    *   Wrote less for me to copy.

4. I think I could do better with your homework if you
    *   Let me hand in work as mindmaps.
    *   Let me write less than the others.
    *   Let me just write the answers and not the questions.
    *   Let me memorise less.
    *   Let me check with you to see if I wrote down the homework
        right.
    *   Let me do my homework on my computer.
    *   Let me do my homework on my tape recorder.

5. I think I could do better in your tests if you
    *   Read the test questions aloud before the test.
    *   Gave me more time to do tests.
    *   Let me do the test orally.

Taken from *Understanding Dyslexia* CD
(Department of Education and Science) 2005

APPENDIX D
ACRONYMS

ADD	Attention Deficit Disorder.
ADHD	Attention Deficit Hyperactivity Disorder.
AHEAD	Association for Higher Education Access and Disability.
CAO	Central Applications Office.
DAI	Dyslexia Association of Ireland.
DCD	Developmental Co-ordination Disorder.
DEST	Dyslexia Early Screening Test.
DST	Dyslexia Screening Test.
FAS	Foras Aiseanna Saothair
FETAC	Further Educational and Training Awards Council.
IEP	Individual Education Plan.
IPLP	Individual Pupil Learning Profile.
LCA	Leaving Certificate Applied.
LCV	Leaving Certificate Vocational Programme.
NALA	National Adult Literacy Agency.
NCCA	National Council for Curriculum and Assessment.
NCGE	National Centre for Guidance in Education.
NCSE	National Council for Special Education.
NEPS	National Educational Psychological Service.
NLN	National Learning Network.
NUI	National University of Ireland.
PLC	Post Leaving Certificate course.
RACE	Reasonable Accommodation in Examinations.
SENO	Special Educational Needs Organiser.
SESS	Special Education Support Service.
SLD	Specific Learning Difficulties.
SLI	Specific Language Impairment.
WISC	Wechsler Intelligence Scale for Children.

GLOSSARY OF TERMS

Accommodations: Procedures and materials that allow individuals with dyslexia to complete school or work tasks with greater ease and effectiveness given their specific learning difficulties. Examples include providing a tape recorder, a reader or extra time in a written examination.

Alphabetic principle: Understanding that spoken words consist of sequential sounds and that letters in written words represent those phonemes.

Asperger's Syndrome: Often referred to as *High Functioning Autism*, Asperger's Syndrome is characterised by low ability to empathise and form reciprocal relationships, repetitive patterns of behaviour and intense absorption in special interests. Persons with Asperger's Syndrome often have extraordinary memories for facts. No delay in language or intellectual development occurs.

Assistive technology: Any device or system that helps to improve the functional capacity of people with disabilities. Examples include voice recognition and screen reading software.

Attainment test: A standardised measure of achievement in a particular skill or subject.

Attention deficit: Abnormal difficulty in concentrating or applying one's mind to a task for an acceptable length of time. The cause may be emotional or physiological. It may also be referred to as *short attention span*.

Attention Deficit Disorder (ADD): A condition thought to be neurobiological and genetic, whereby the person has more than usual difficulty maintaining attention for any length of time, is highly distractible, disorganised, forgetful and has difficulty taking in instructions.

Attention Deficit Hyperactivity Disorder (ADHD): A condition similar to ADD with the additional features of restlessness, overactivity and impulsivity.

Auditory discrimination in reading (sound discrimination): The ability to hear similarities and differences and process the individual sounds in words. Difficulty can lead to errors in auditory word attack, spelling by sound and in receiving orally given information like directions or dictation.

Auditory processing: In reading and spelling, this entails receiving, examining, weighing, understanding, ordering and remembering the constituent sounds of phonemes or syllables in words. A basic deficiency may involve a difficulty in retaining accurately in memory the order in which phonemes are perceived, i.e. auditory sequential memory. It may also apply to deficiencies in the speech process.

Dyspraxia/Developmental Co-ordination Disorder (DCD): A condition whereby the individual has more than usual difficulty with co-ordination, with organising movement and also has significant visual perceptual difficulties.

Blending (auditory or sound blending, auditory or sound synthesis): The process of combining or blending together two or more sounds or phonemes represented by letters to pronounce or spell words. In blending, each phoneme (sound) is represented by a corresponding grapheme (letter).

British Ability Scales (BAS): An intelligence test, consisting of a range of subtests which measure intellectual ability. It is sometimes used by psychologists as an alternative to the WISC or parts of it may be used to measure specific functions such as memory.

Cognition: The process or processes by which an organism gains knowledge or becomes aware of events or objects in its environment and uses that knowledge for comprehension and problem-solving.

Cognitive deficit: A perceptual/conceptual difficulty that affects intellectual functioning.

Consonant blend: Two or more consonants sequenced together within a syllable that flow together and are at the beginning or end of words, for example, bred, jump.

Consonant-vowel-consonant sequence (cvc): A pattern of three letters (e.g. c-a-t) or sounds (e.g. /s/-/a/-/ck/) that represent one of the most common sequences in English.

Content word: Any word with meaning such as a noun or verb.

Co-occurring conditions: A medical term used when a person has more than one condition e.g. Dyslexia and Dyspraxia, or ADHD and Asperger's Syndrome, or Speech and Language Impairment and Dyslexia. Co-morbidity is another term with similar meaning.

Decoding: Changing letters into phonemes/sounds and blending them together to form words.

Differentiation: The process by which curriculum objectives, teaching methods, resources and learning activities are planned to cater for the needs of all pupils, including those with dyslexia. Differentiation is necessary to identify and meet the needs of each individual pupil within the classroom, especially those with learning difficulties.

Digraph: There are two types of Digraph:

Consonant Digraph – a combination of two adjacent consonants that represent a single speech sound (e.g. *gn* as in gnat, *th* as in thumb, *sh* as in ship, *ph* as in phone)

Vowel Digraph – a combination of two adjacent vowels that represent a single long vowel sound (e.g. *ee* as in meet, *eu* as in euro, *oo* as in moon).

Diphthong: A vowel speech sound or phoneme made by gliding (through a change of tongue position) one vowel phoneme into another in a syllable as *o* glided into *i* in *oi* as in boil, or *o* glided into *u* in *ou* as in crouch. Note that each of the two consecutive vowels contributes to the diphthong's sound. The true diphthongs are: *au, aw, oi, oy, ou* and *ow*.

Dyslexia: A continuum of specific learning difficulties manifested by problems in acquiring one or more basic skills (reading, spelling, writing, number), such problems being unexpected in relation to other abilities.

Encoding: The techniques required to spell word parts and then whole words by breaking syllables into sounds and matching them to appropriate letters.

Function word: A word, which does not have lexical meaning but primarily serves to express a grammatical relationship (e.g. of, or, and, the).

General learning difficulties: The term usually describes intellectual functioning where the person finds all aspects of learning difficult. A person with general learning difficulties will have been assessed as being in the Exceptionally Low range of intellectual ability on an IQ test (scoring below 70 on such a test). General learning difficulties are categorized as mild, moderate and severe. The difficulties extend to general functioning and are not specific to any one area of learning. An IQ score between 70-79 is usually described as 'borderline mild general learning difficulty'.

Grapheme: The smallest, single unit of a written language (letter).

Inclusion: The process of providing services to students with disabilities in local mainstream schools in age-appropriate general education classes with the necessary support services and supplementary aids for pupil and teacher.

Individual education plan (IEP): A programme designed to address the individual educational needs of a student who is usually in receipt of supplementary teaching. An IEP should specify long-term and short-term learning targets and provide an indication of how those targets might be achieved.

Individual profile and learning programme (IPLP): An individual programme prepared for each pupil who has been selected for additional help in school. Like the IEP, it summarises the outcomes of diagnostic assessment and indicates medium term learning targets related to the pupil's needs, and learning activities for school and home that are designed to meet these needs. It involves the pupil's class teacher, special needs teacher and parents.

Information and communications technology (ICT): The hardware, software and infrastructure used for the creation, processing and communication of information, as well as applications of that technology such as email and the world wide web.

Kinaesthetic: Movement of the body involving large or small muscle groups.

Learned helplessness: This refers to the tendency of some pupils to be passive learners who depend on others for decisions and guidance. In individuals with dyslexia, continued struggle and failure can heighten this lack of self-confidence and lead to learned helplessness.

Learning support teacher: Learning support teaching is provided to children with low achievement. It was formerly called remedial teaching. Assessment for access to such help is done in school through the use of standardised testing. The Learning Support Guidelines state that when selecting pupils for such help, priority should be given to those who achieve scores that are at or below the 10th percentile on a standardised test of English reading or mathematics.

Letter combination: A group of letters which, when combined, make a sound that is different from the expected blend of their individual sounds e.g. *ing, ang, ung, ong, eng, ink, ank, unk, onk, tion, sion* and *ture.*

Lexical: Refers to the words or the vocabulary of a language.

Long-term memory: The final phase of memory in which information storage may last from hours to a lifetime.

Metacognitive learning: Instructional approaches emphasising self-awareness of how one learns such as memory and attention.

Mixed/crossed laterality (cerebral dominance): The tendency to perform some motor acts (eye, ear, hand, foot) with a right preference and others with a left.

Morpheme: The smallest, single unit of meaningful language. All words are morphemes.

Multisensory learning: An instructional approach which uses a combination of several learning channels or modalities, i.e. auditory, visual and tactile-kinaesthetic, in one learning-based activity. An example is tracing a sandpaper letter while saying the letter name aloud.

Non-phonetic words: Words that do not conform to the expected letter-sound correspondences of English. Examples include irregularly spelled words such as *laugh, yacht, Wednesday.*

Non-word: A phonetically-regular, pronounceable string of letters with no meaning or in other words a nonsense word such as *gud, somp, shup.* A pupil's decoding (phonic) skills may be assessed by asking them to pronounce a set of non-words.

Orthographic awareness: Sensitivity to the structure of the writing system such as spelling patterns.

Percentile: A value on a scale of 100 showing the percent of the distribution that is equal to or below it. Many test results are now given as percentile scores. A person's score at the 35th percentile indicates that 34% of his/her peers would receive a lower score and 64% of them would receive a higher score.

Perception: The extraction of information from sensory stimulation.

Performance test: A test composed of tasks that call for non-verbal responses. Seven of the thirteen sub-tests of the WISC-III are performance tests.

Phoneme: The single, smallest unit of spoken language. There are approximately 44 phonemes in English.

Phoneme awareness: The ability to segment oral words into their constituent phonemes. Phoneme awareness is an important prerequisite for reading and spelling.

Phonically regular word: A word whose pronunciation may be accurately predicted from its spelling

Phonics: An approach to the teaching of reading and spelling that stresses symbol-sound relationships, especially in beginning reading instruction

Phonology: The study of speech sounds (phonemes) and their function in language. In English, there are approximately 44 phonemes. Written English uses 26 visual symbols or graphemes, commonly called letters.

Phonological awareness: A language skill that is critically important in learning to read. It is defined as an explicit self-awareness of the phonological structure of the words in one's own spoken language. It involves the ability to notice, think about and manipulate the individual sounds or phonemes and syllables within words.

Resource teacher: Resource teaching is granted based on an individual application for a child with special educational needs to the SENO for the school. Such applications have to be accompanied by an assessment.

Short-term memory: That aspect of memory that only lasts briefly, has rapid input and output, is limited in capacity and depends directly on immediate information. Short term memory enables a reader to keep visual and auditory information in mind long enough (or until there is enough material) for processing. An example is analysing a word for blending.

Sound (auditory) blending: A sound-combining skill based on the ability to blend individual sounds into recognised words.

Spatial orientation: Awareness of one's own position and movement in space, primarily from visual and kinaesthetic clues. Directionality depends on spatial orientation.

Specific Language Impairment (SLI): This describes a delay in the development of expressive language and delays in both receptive and expressive language which are not the result of intellectual disability, autism, hearing loss or other condition. Difficulties can occur at the level of phonics, meaning, syntax, fluency and appropriate usage.

Specific learning difficulties: A student's learning difficulties, such as those arising from dyslexia, that are specific to a particular area (or areas) of the curriculum such as reading. Such difficulties are unexpected in relation to the student's other abilities.

Special needs teacher: Increasingly the term special needs teacher is being used instead of learning support or resource teacher

Speed of processing: The term usually refers to both psychomotor speed and mental speed. On the Wechsler Intelligence Scale two/three subtests measure processing speed and results are in the *Processing Speed Index*. Research has indicated that one of the features of dyslexia is a slower speed of processing both verbal and non-verbal information.

Stimulus: An environmental event capable of being detected by the senses. Examples include speech sounds and spoken and written words.

Syntax: The conventions and grammatical rules for assembling words into meaningful sentences.

Tactile: Having to do with the sense of touch as a learning channel. An example is finger tracing over a sandpaper letter.

Transposition: A type of reading or writing error involving a change in the sequence of two or more sounds or letters in a word or words in a sentence. Example would include writing *desrcibe* for *describe* or saying *pashgetti* for *spaghetti*. Some errors appear like anagrams such as *breaded* for *bearded*.

Visual discrimination in reading: The ability to see similarities and differences and process the visually distinctive features of letters, words and phrases. Difficulty can lead to errors of letter or word identification and interfere with reading.

Visual-motor co-ordination: The ability to co-ordinate what is visually perceived with finer body movement (eye-hand). Examples include tying laces and handwriting.

Visual Processing: In the reading and writing process, it entails receiving, examining, weighing, understanding, ordering and remembering the constituent letters or syllables of words. A basic deficiency may involve a difficulty in retaining accurately in memory the order in which letters are perceived, i.e. visual sequential memory.

Wechsler Intelligence Scales (WPPSI, WISC, WAIS, WASI): These are tests of intellectual ability most frequently used by psychologists. They were originally developed in the United States of America under the direction of David Wechsler. The tests used in this country have been adapted for use in Britain and Northern Ireland. They are revised periodically according to the most up-to-date research. The WISC, for example, is now in its fourth edition. They measure a range of abilities, verbal and non-verbal.

Wechsler Preschool and Primary Scale of Intelligence (WPPSI) tests at the earliest stage.

Wechsler Intelligence Scale for Children (WISC) tests children of ages 6 - 16.11 years.

Wechsler Adult Intelligence Scale (WAIS) tests adults.

Wechsler Abbreviated Scale of Intelligence (WASI) is an abbreviated scale.

Wechsler tests of literacy, numeracy and language are also used by many psychologists. Results on these can be compared with results one might expect from a child's level of cognitive functioning, assessed on the WPPSI and WISC

INDEX